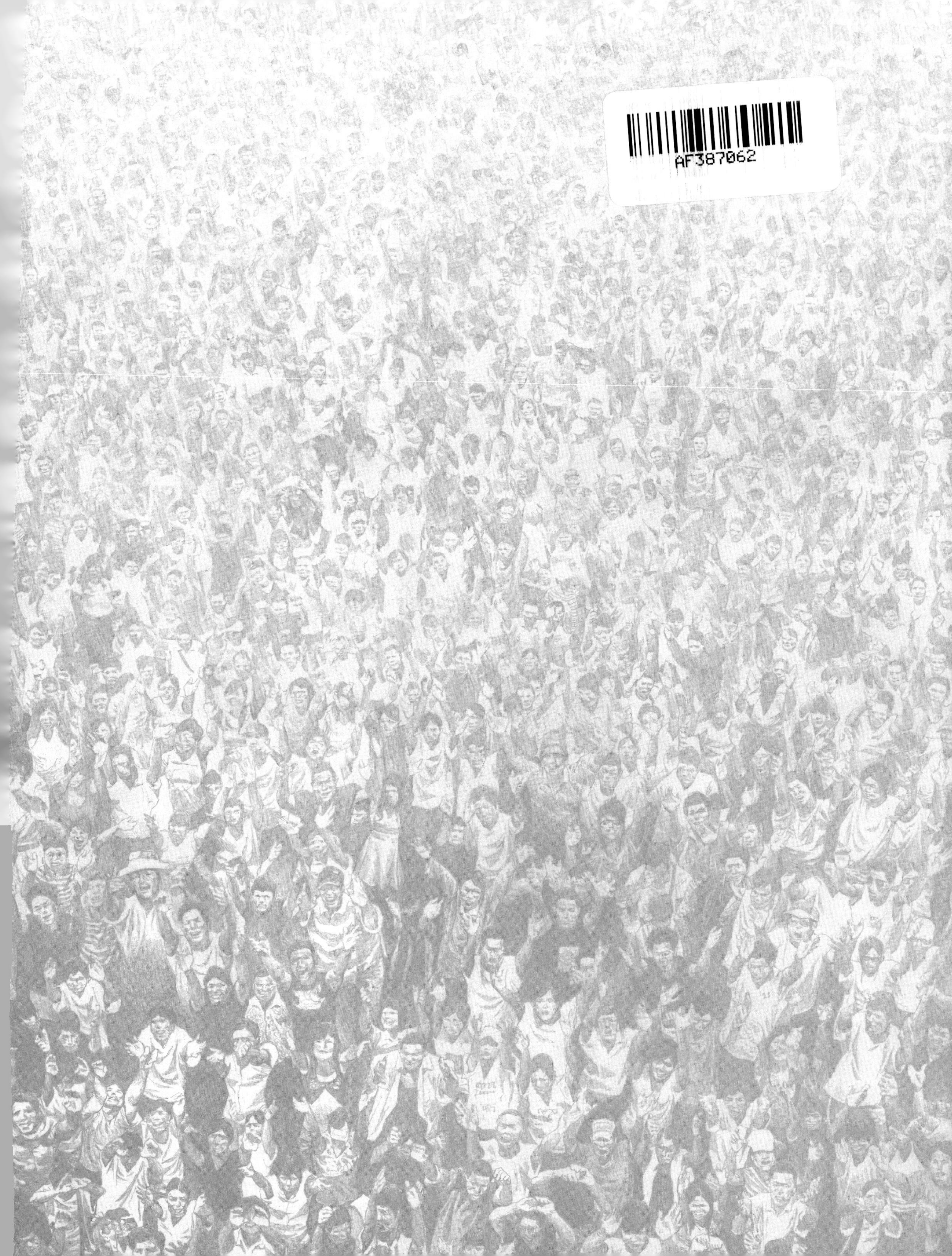

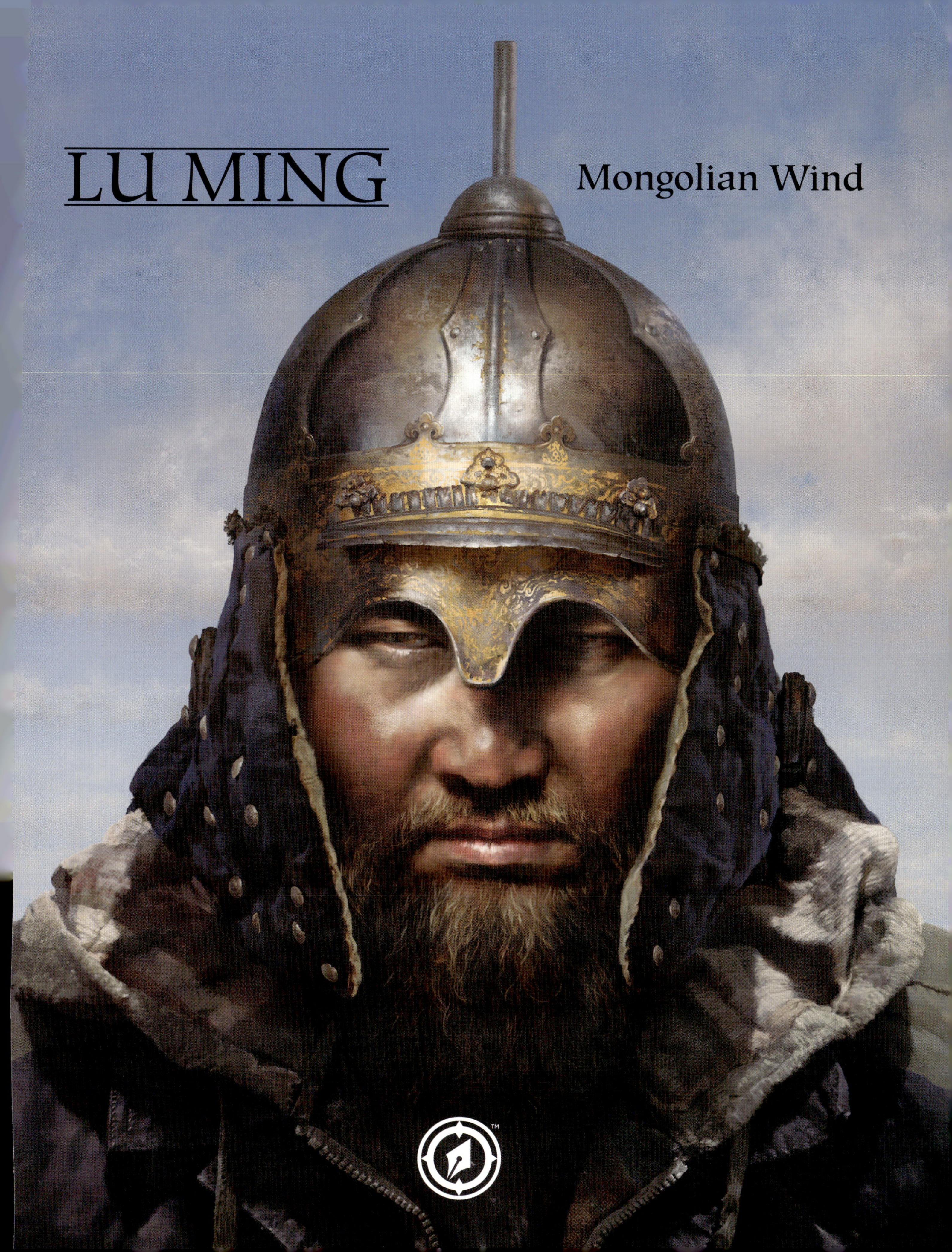

LU MING
Mongolian Wind

LU MING

Mongolian Wind

Translation, Layout, and Editing by Mike Kennedy

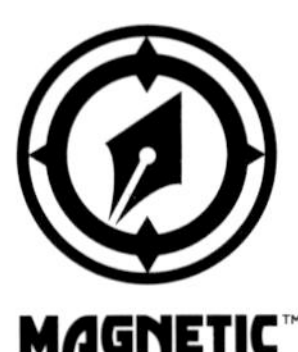

MAGNETIC™

ISBN: 978-1-951719-09-8
Library of Congress Control Number: 2021900687

Printed in China.

10 9 8 7 6 5 4 3 2 1

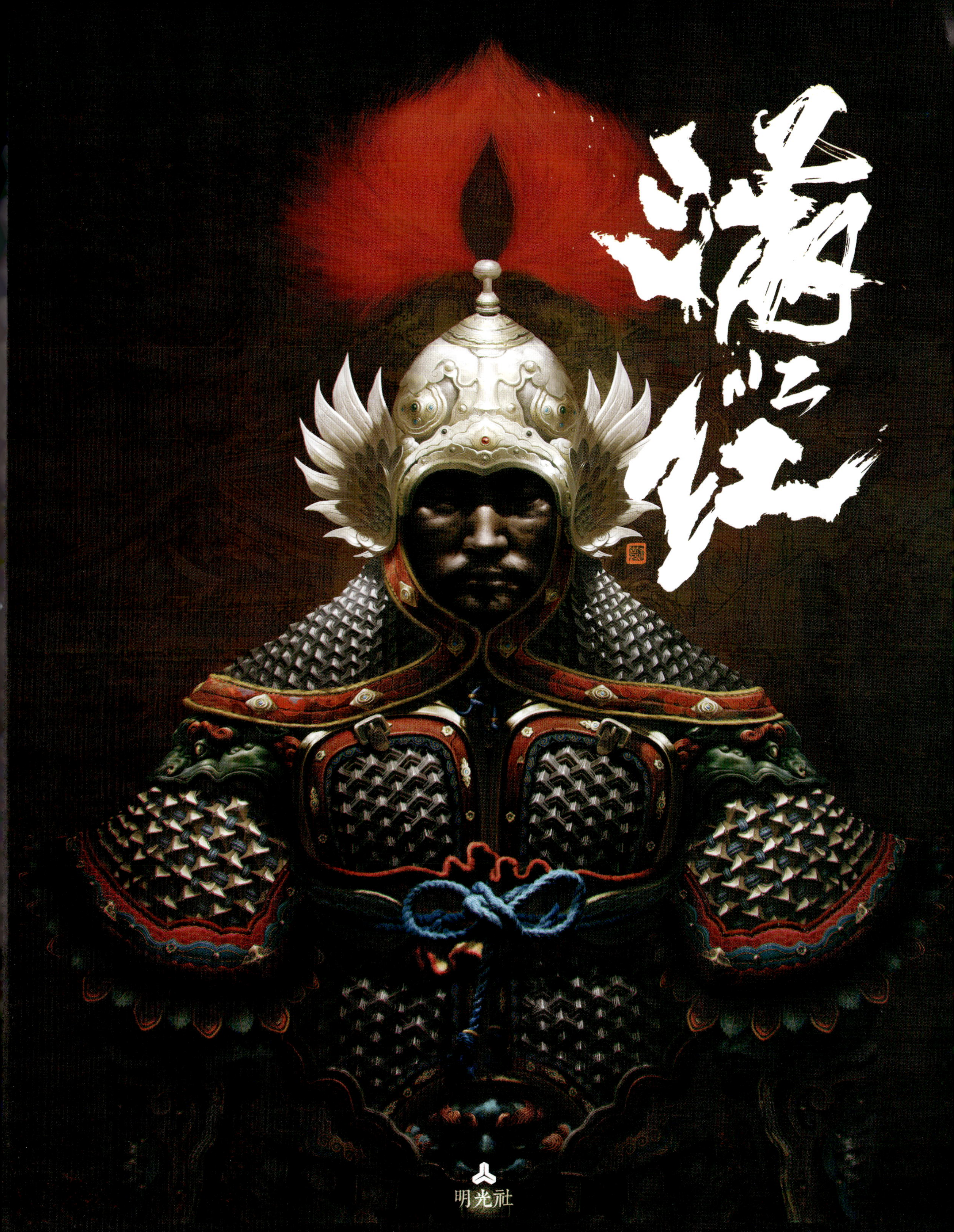

満江紅
明光社

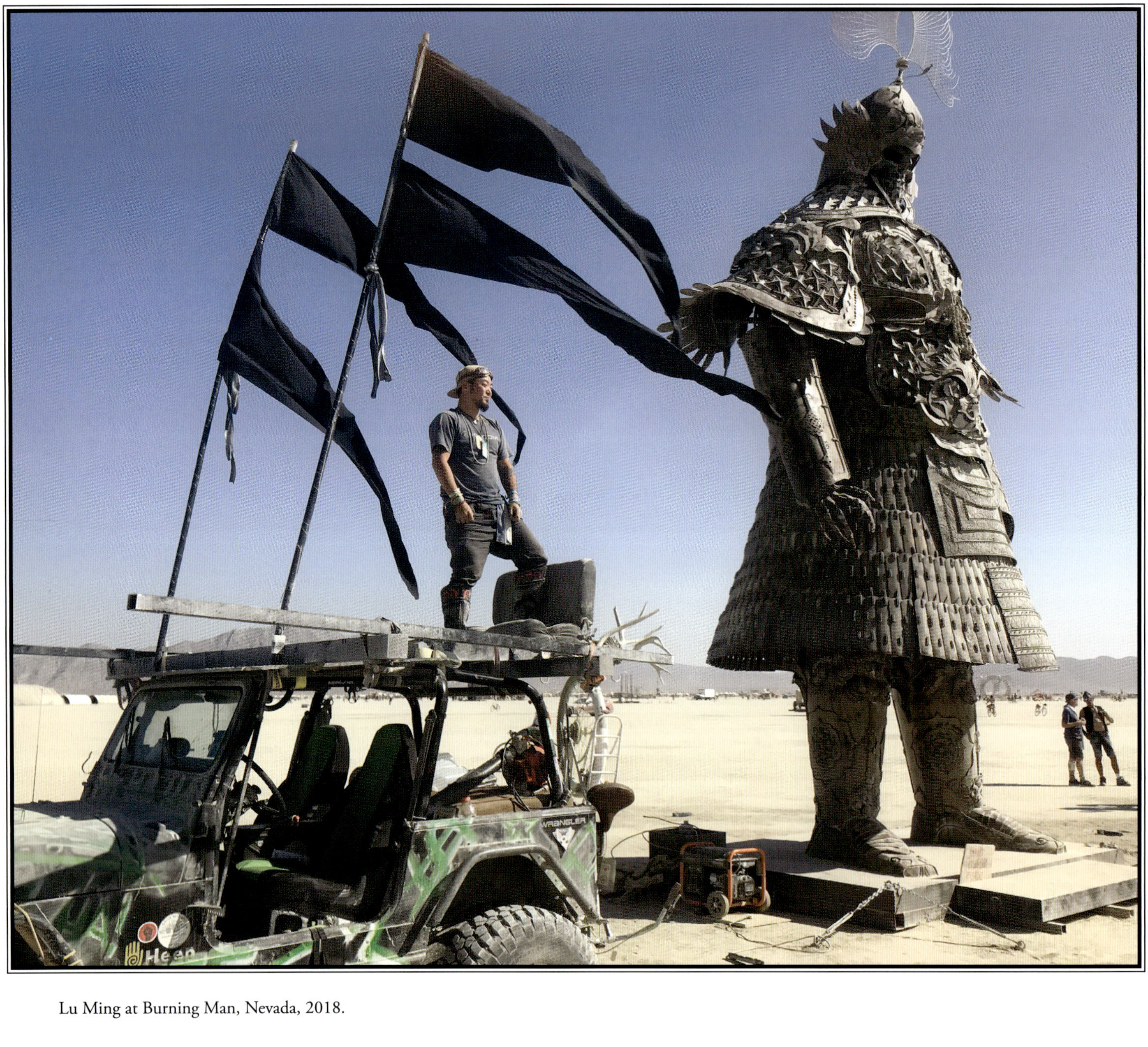

Lu Ming at Burning Man, Nevada, 2018.

Too much is not enough.

We call them "firefighters" — those French artists who, in the depths of the 19th century, depicted "with pomp," that is to say with great flair, historical scenes of proud orientalists and warriors. These supporters of academia were fatally flawed in the eyes of posterity: being foolishly opposed to the Impressionist movement. However, there is now a resolution, one more readily accepted that, despite their Rococo aesthetic and assumed "kitsch," firefighters were, after all, very talented. It is true that surrealism has evolved beyond the emphasis of academic art, and now pierces the unconscious. Let's look at the facts...

Lu Ming's work reminds me of those firefighters. There is no pejorative intention in that reference, quite the contrary. It is simply the observation of a similar taste for fantasized exoticism, the more or less fanciful re-examination of a past long gone, and the outrageous theatrical staging of those times: declamatory poses, shining costumes, and grandiose cardboard decorations. If we were at the movies, we would talk about them like ancient Greek drama.

For his antiquity, Lu Ming went to look for it in ancient China. He came to the steppes of Mongolia and the nomadic Xiongnu peoples through roundabout paths: those of the Goths, Visigoths, and Ostrogoths. He approached with the touching candor of a young hard-rocker who naively leaned on Gothic history in the hope of understanding the association to post-punk Gothic rock… and it is suffice to say that he was disappointed. But he at least gained a rich historical basis, although sufficiently incomplete, for his imagination to easily take root... and for him to let go of particularly vigorous iconography.

Excess is, for Lu Ming, the only measure of worth. Flamboyant aesthetics, twilight colors, heightened passion: such excess is still not enough when it comes to expressing in graphic brilliance and lyrical outbursts this perpetual war of the worlds which seems to obsess Lu Ming.

Apocalyptic battles pitting demonic colossi and winged angels against each other, duels of monstrous chimeras or caparisoned fighters, virile exhibitions of titanic muscles and disproportionate armaments: carrying the warlike mythology of China, the young artist plunges us into a dizzying deployment of conflicting forces. As if his paper figures were caught in a whirlwind of mad energy that overtakes them... and forces them to evolve or be crushed.

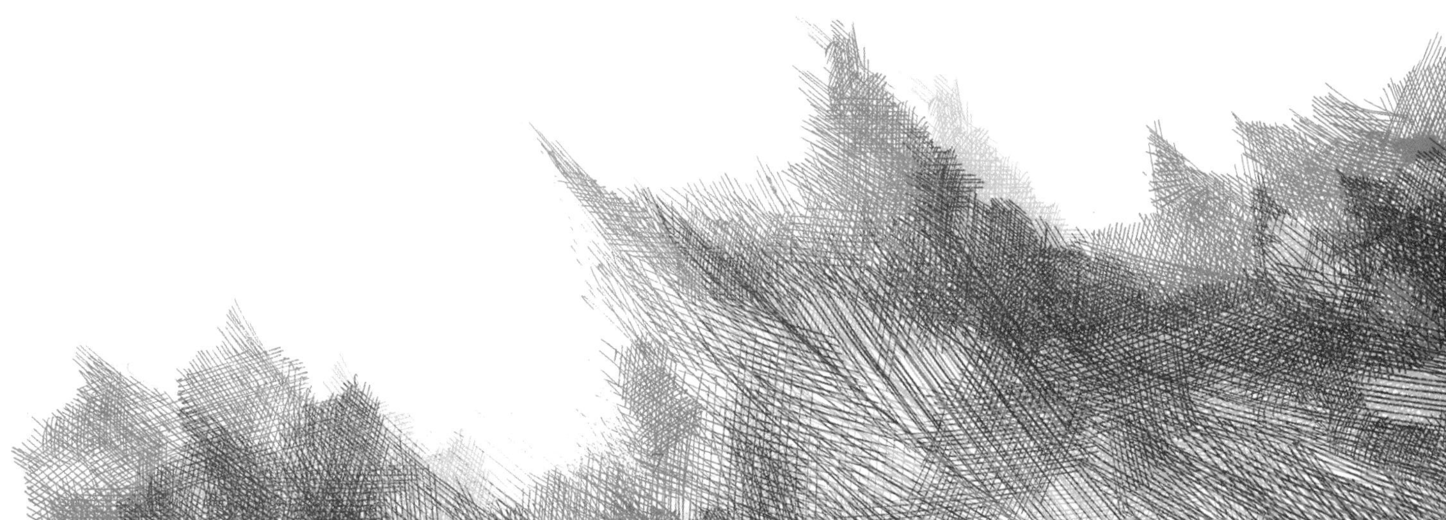

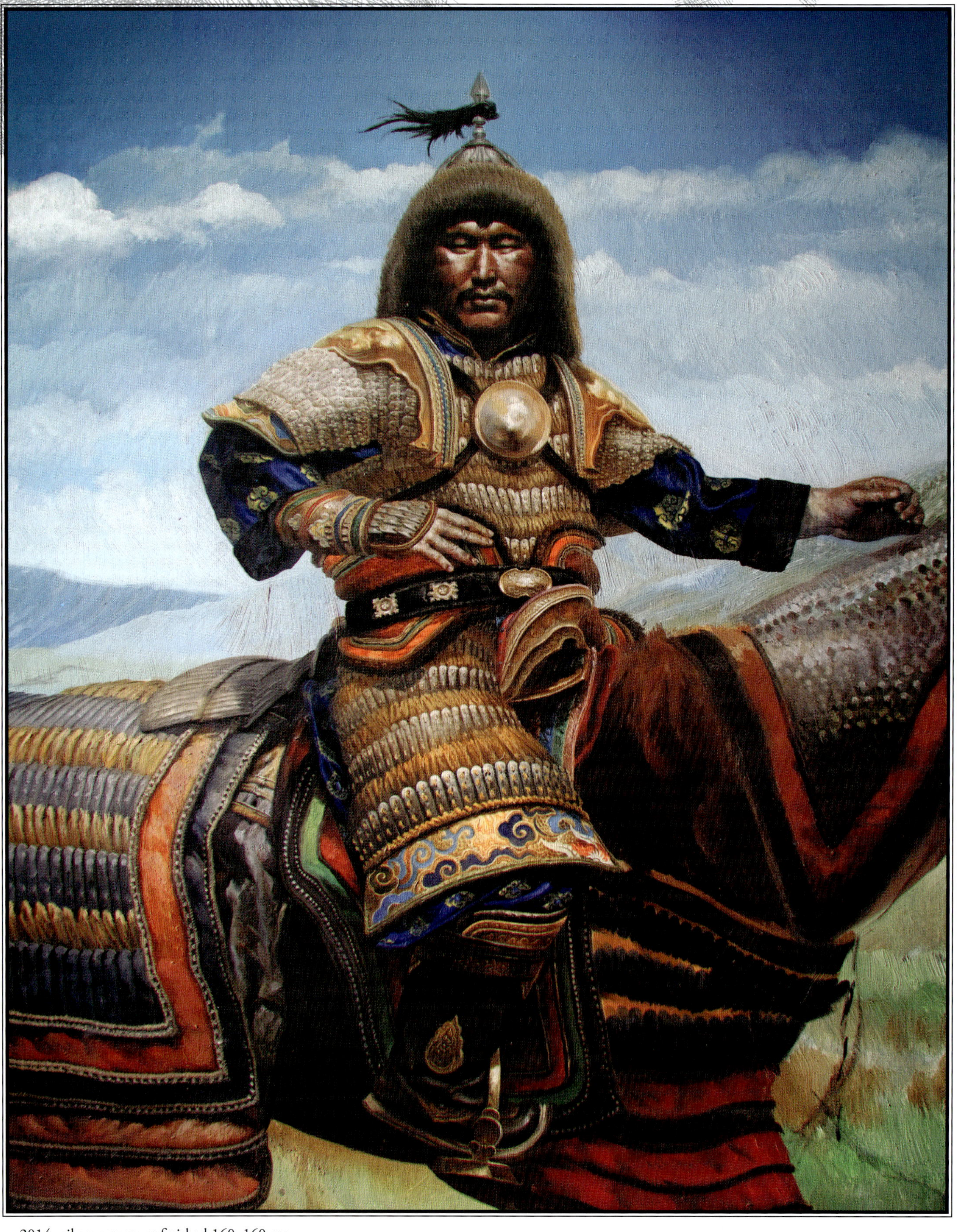

2014, oil on canvas, unfinished,160×160 cm

Lu Ming is steeped in nostalgia for the original myths in search of an epic grandeur that modern man has lost. "The brave warrior who lived inside us passed away a long time ago," he says with regret. This conflict between the desire for the Epic, drawn from an undoubtedly embellished past, and the disenchantment generated by a present plagued by banality and materialism, produces the powerful tension at work in Lu Ming's portfolio.

Between frozen and explosion, sacred and violent, lavish detail and furious anger, Lu Ming's artwork feeds on opposition. His first book, *Hard Melody* (first translated into French by Mosquito in 2014), already played on the alternating conflict between dreams and their brutal return to reality. *Mongolian Wind* continues in that vein, even as an art book collecting fragmentary and dissociated works which cannot be based on a linear or threaded story.

This sudden Mongolian wind juxtaposes "old-fashioned" paintings and drawings with digital graphic work, showcasing the range of Lu Ming's talent. The stylish, scribbled borders on a polished, finished composition, or the solitary storyboards where an expressive narrative is sketched out. *Hard Melody* had introduced us to his off balance tones. *Mongolian Wind* truly brings Lu Ming's graphic flexibility and dexterity to light, allowing him to juggle aesthetics while moving easily from one universe to another.

There is, in this book, as much adolescent frenzy as mature rebellion, the poetry of unexpected humor, tragicomedies of urban excesses, soaring church organs sounding like cheap clichés. Is Lu Ming a rocker romanticizing the mundane? It's well known that bad boys have a soft heart.

And so it is that, within these pages, fierce warriors in high-tech armor, before whom any common man wouldn't dare joke, let themselves be taken aback by an astronaut in a spacesuit smoking a cigarette on the moon. Or by this a dirty battle between popes and pigs brandishing huge forks-like halberds.

Let us then set sail and be amazed by these black and white pages with their tight hatching (it is for good reason that *Hard Melody* was dedicated "to the memory of the great master Sergio Toppi"), and this representation of military costumes in color, so accomplished that it is almost hypnotic, a fascinating and endless plunge into the shimmering golden tones and exorbitant luxury of details: feathers and strings, cut gems and chiseled gold, metal scales and top-stitched leather. Because Lu Ming never denies himself the pure enjoyment of creating a piece of graphic virtuosity. And he's right not to do so.

Jean-Louis Roux
Actor, playwright, and former Lieutenant Governor of Quebec

Lu Ming is undoubtedly one of the premier designers of our country, a testament to the evolution of present day China. We met at the Académie des Beaux-Arts where he demonstrated his qualities as a maverick in the field of popular arts, having already expressed himself through his comics full of originality and deep sincerity. Simultaneously a guitarist and professional drummer, he also showed his creativity in rock and roll as well as his thirst to taste all the pleasures of life, while continuing to draw and paint.

In the past ten years, Lu Ming has been bustling with activity, working in animation and advertising. His talents have been recognized and awarded internationally. He expanded his horizons by collaborating on major cinematic feature productions as Art Director. Growing graphically, he tackled many historical themes, adding a new dimension and depth to his work. We can bet that he will surprise us again!

Pang Bang Ben
Painter, cartoonist, and Director of
the Chinese Artists Association
November 2019, Beijing

Lu Ming was born in 1982 in Mongolia. He graduated from the Central Academy of Fine Arts of China. He began his career in comics in 1999, and pursued a career as an illustrator and a publicist, joining the team of long-time friend, film director Tsui Hark. As a professional, Lu Ming had established himself as a comic book author, illustrator, and professor of film making and advertising. As an amateur, however, he devoted himself to oil painting, his rock band, graffiti, directing animated films and shorts, and practicing Baji Quan (a variant of kung fu from the Hebei province).

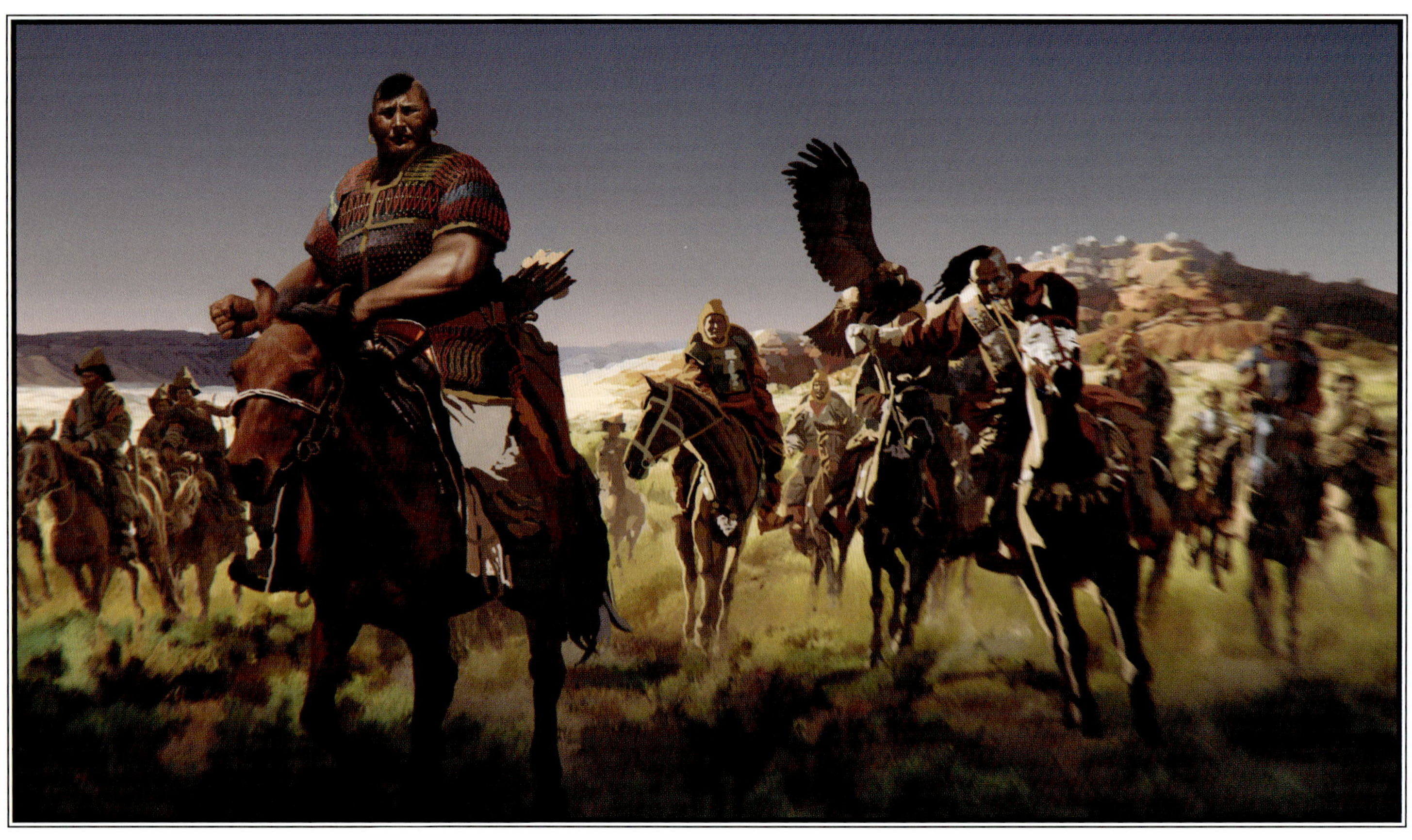

PROFESSIONAL MILESTONES

2000 He begins his career in comics, with the publication of a short story *The Doors* in a fanzine aimed at teenagers. He is first introduced to the mainstream Chinese-American style of contemporary Chinese comic books.

2001 He publishes a serialized version of *Hell's Melody* in a teenage fanzine.

2002 The one-shot *Hell's Melody* is published in mainland China by Beaux-Arts Populaires.

2003 He represents China at the top Asian comic festivals held in Yokohama, Japan.

2004 He participates in *Long Hun,* a collection of short comic stories about Bruce Lee, published in Hong Kong. He abandons the traditional "comic book" illustration style and begins to develop his own realistic style.

2005 He oversees the comic book adaptation of Tsui Hark's movie *Seven Swords.*

2006 *Hell's Melody* is published in Europe in French. The same year, he represents China at the Angoulême festival.

2007 He begins teaching animated film making and works on Wilson Yip's film *Dragon Tiger Gate.*

2007 Japanese publishing house Kodansha publishes short comic story *Save* in Mandala magazine.

2008 Kodansha publishes his project *Millennium* in Japan.

2008 His short story *Beijing* is published in Europe.

2008 He produces a series of large-format drawings intended for outdoor advertising for brands such as Adidas and the 2008 Olympic Games. This series earns China the Palme d'Or at the Cannes Lion Festival that same year, marking the first time a Chinese project has won this award, the highest distinction in international advertising.

2008 He signs a contract with the Beijing company Scream Records under the Wu Kong brand and MC Webber. They collaborate in the Spanish music festival *Mucho mas Mayo.*

2009 He becomes key concept designer and storyboard artist on the set of Tsui Hark's film *Detective Dee: The Mystery of the Phantom Flame.*

2010 He continues as a conceptual designer on Tsui Hark's film *Dragon Gate: The Legend of the Flying Sabers.*

2013 He self-publishes the one-shot *Hard Melody* in China.

2014 The French version of *Hard Melody* is published in Europe by Mosquito editions.

2014 He wins the award for Best Graphic Design at the Algiers International Comic Festival.

2014 He collaborates with Tsui Hark on the *Tie Yu Huo (Iron and Fire)* exhibition in Beijing promoting digital creation.

2015 He is reappointed as conceptual designer on the set of the film *Journey to the West: the Demons Strike Back* by Tsui Hark and Stephen Chow.

2016 He participates in the filming of the film *San Ben* as a conceptual designer.

2016 He creates the large-scale sculpture of a steel soldier, *"Desert Grade,"* inspired by ancient Chinese funeral statues.

2017 He joins the production of the film *Wu Kong* as a designer.

2017 Alongside Cui Jian, Jia Zhang Ke, and Wang Ya Bing, he becomes ambassador of the 13th edition of the Croisements festival organized by the Ministries of Foreign Affairs of France and China.

2017 He joins a handful of armor enthusiasts from ancient China to form the "Union of Armor" association in Beijing.

2018 He becomes the first Chinese artist to receive an invitation to participate in the Burning Man festival in Nevada where he presents his sculpture *"Desert Grade."*

2018 He participates in the first "Festival for the Cultivation of Armor" with other members of the Union of Armor in Hai Long Tun, Guizhou Province.

ADOLESCENCE

2001, Beijing, on the Fourth Ring Road where it branches off southwest. There, a shabby, grayish neighborhood tower stands at the edge of the freeway interchange. The metal bars on the windows and the paint on the outer facade are corroded by the north wind. It is in this sad and messy place, stinking of loneliness, that I lived on the ninth floor. This decrepit room suspended halfway up in the Hengfeng sky was already my third accommodation.

From a young age, I was the perfect example of a classic dunce: the only things I knew how to do were fight and draw pictures. Other than fine art and sports, I never got a single grade above a C and like any lazy slacker, I ended up getting kicked out of high school in my senior year. Subsequently, thanks to my brilliant artistic instincts, I was able to sneak into a private technical school for students who don't have a diploma. But I couldn't complete my high school education. As soon as I got there, I came to blows with a school principal who was even more of a pig than me, and I got expelled. In the end, I was discouraged and left home. From the beginning, I sought an independent lifestyle. My parents would have looked after me just fine at home, but I understood that, like in the Savannah, lions must know how to fend for themselves.

I became a cartoonist, and the 3700 yuan a month my parents sent me was more than enough to support a sixteen-year-old wanker like me, ensuring a comfortable life in New Millennium China. I never liked money, and money never liked me too much either. Not stopping to spend all the time, I gradually left too-familiar Beijing, with no other choice but to move far from the city center, in this shack, fasting to finish my first comic.

Immediately after publishing Hell's Melody, *I went to the movies for the first time with a girl. We went to see* The Lord of the Rings *which had just been released in theaters. When I left the movie theater, I had forgotten about the girl… All I wanted to do was write a story as strong as* The Lord of the Rings. *I called it* A Love Letter from the Death Squad.

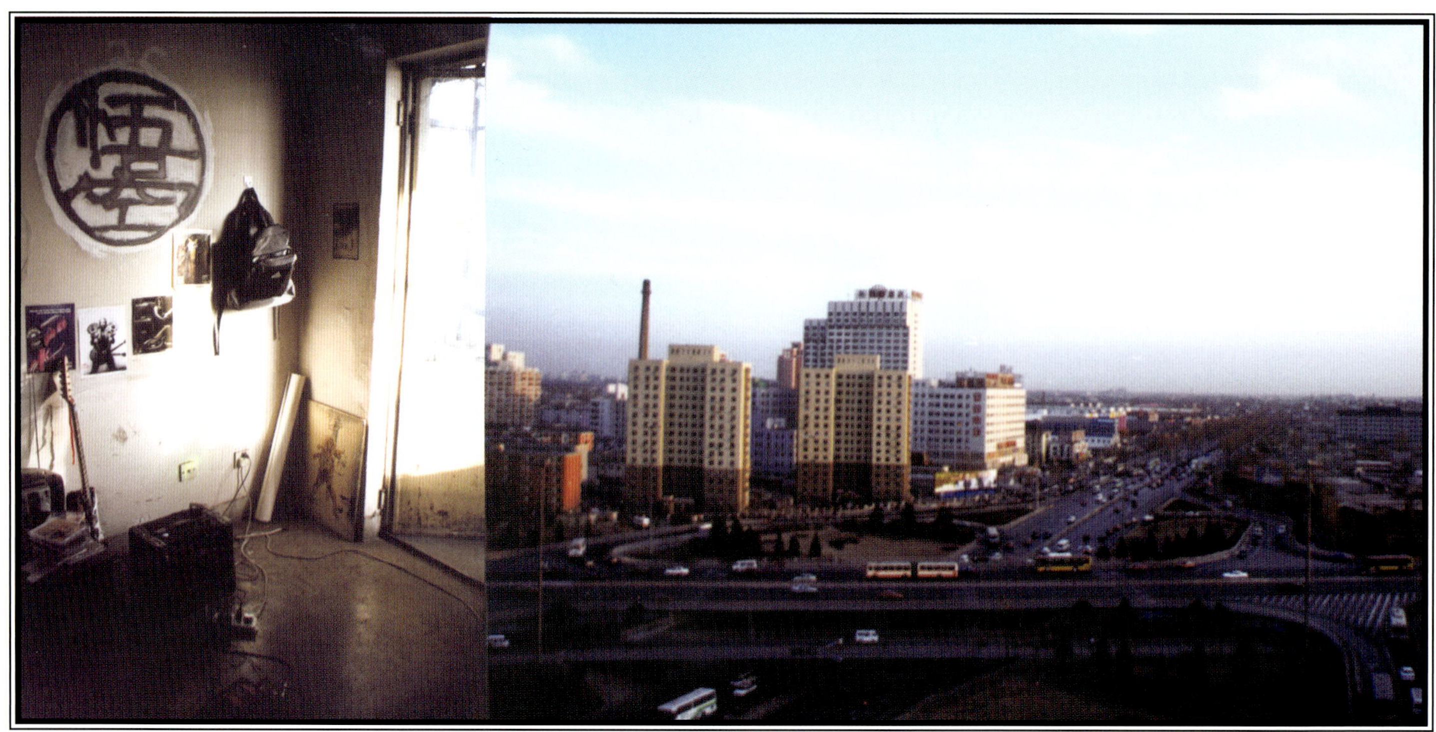

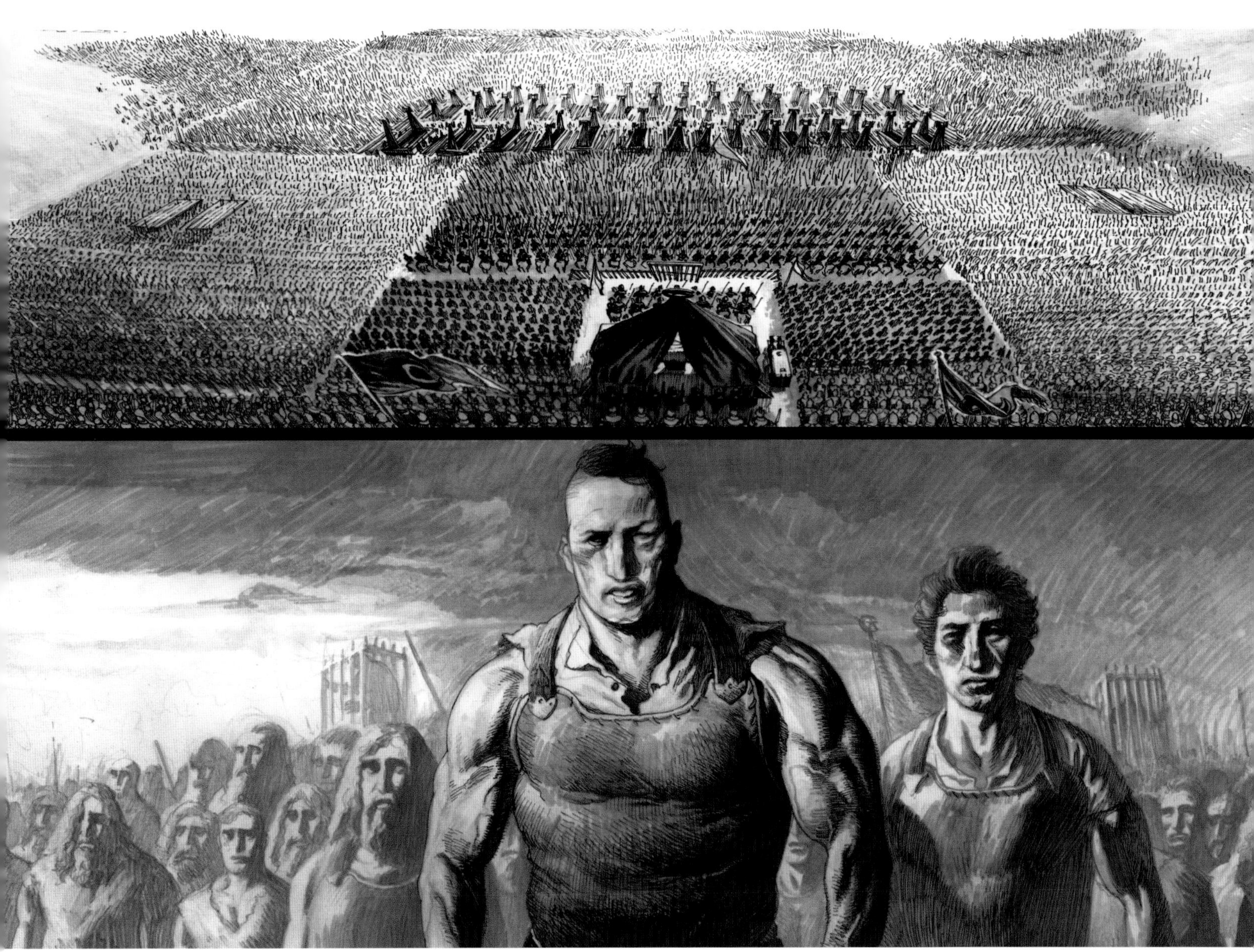

Panels from A Love Letter from the Death Squad.

A LOVE LETTER FROM THE DEATH SQUAD

In the year 410 AD, the Goths invaded the Roman Empire, their troops surrounded Rome. The Visigoth army is made up of Hun[3] and Alan[4] cavalrymen. They are commanded by a formidable Hun warrior named Vac. The Romans, realizing that they will not have the upper hand, negotiate with the invaders to spare the population. Princess Plasida, the Emperor's younger sister, meets Vac, who becomes deeply troubled by the beauty of this woman. Soon, after the sacking of Rome, he would try to find this princess who awakened feelings that he never knew. He met Plasida's mentor, who encouraged him to assassinate the leader of the Goths. Vac knew he wouldn't get out of this business alive. His best friend advised him to write a letter to the princess to declare his love. As he is illiterate, some of his soldiers write it for him on parchment, drawing inspiration from their feelings for their own brides back home. However, the princess would not receive this letter until much later when they are all dead. She would remember this proud warrior astride his steed with fondness.

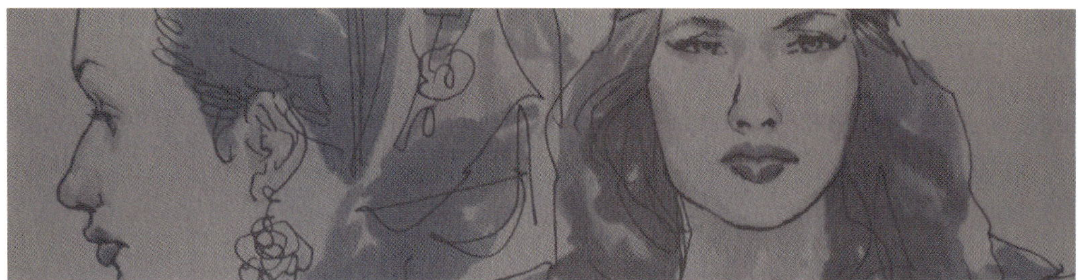

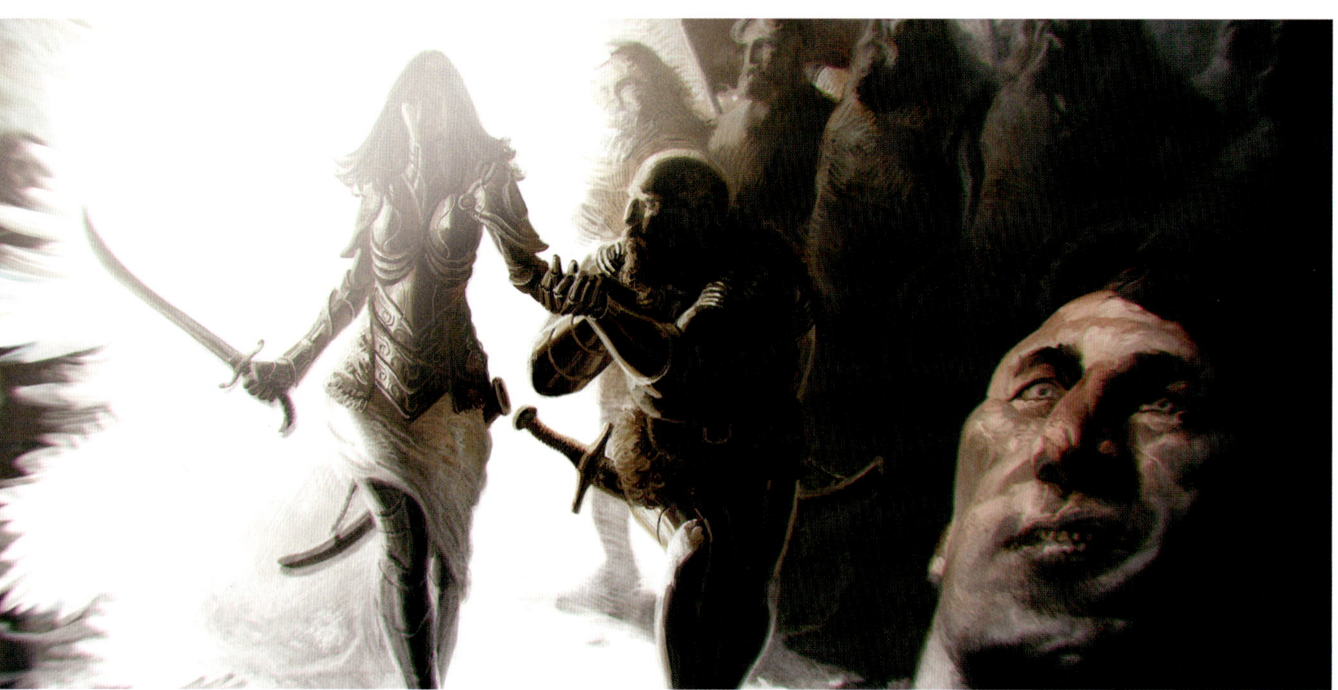

---

[3] The Huns were an ancient nomadic people originally from Central Asia, whose presence in Europe is documented from the fourth century.
[4] The Alans were an ancient tribe of Northern Iranian people dating back to the first century, from the plains to the north of the Caucasus region.

From the wealth of historical records, I chose the Goths as the basis for my story because they were a tribe during an era quite unknown to the Chinese. The word "Goth" appealed to me for everything it conjured up.

In 2002, I was living alone in my little room, and it had been a year since I learned the guitar. Ever since I discovered Van Halen in high school, I had been obsessed with the idea of becoming a drummer. Later, after seeing the DVD of the Metallica concert in San Diego, I bought my first guitar.

I wanted to become a virtuoso guitarist! That's how I plunged headfirst into the battlefield of heavy metal, watching the banners in the wind and hearing the mountains tremble. Towards the end of the 90s, the heavy metal scene had grown more and more popular with Chinese fans. A few metal bands with female singers emerged, and there were indeed phenomenal quantities of pirated CDs that came to us in the Far East. We have all been riding the same wave. In comparison to the Nu Metal and the screaming Rap Metal of the time, I had only listened to classical music with my uncle during my younger years. I loved Gothic metal and symphonic metal even more, because it added a solemn aspect to the raw power.

When you are in front of the immensity of the sound barrier, it is impossible to contain the bubbling of your emotions or the flow of your thoughts. It feels like centuries worth of accumulated energy. And, even only standing on the surface of this Earth, one can feel all of its underground vibrations! It's all like the sound of my own heart beating!

This is how I took on the concept of Gothic music — to spring out of the darkness with thunderous energy and make it my own, in my own way. And around that time, the summer of 2002, I would bicycle through town every afternoon only to find myself drenched in sweat, hopping from one foot to the other in front of the Tom Lee Music [5] window, staring at my dream guitar: a Gibson Explorer Gothic.

After laying out the finale of my story about a great, scarred warrior who launched an attack on a city for a princess he had only met once, only to die in a cruel way, I started doing a lot of research on the history of the Gothic kingdoms.

I had only read three books in my previous seventeen years (specifically the biography of George S. Patton, The Flowers of the Sun, and Jack London). But I used the next two years to hunt down information on the subject. Finally, I discovered that in fact, Gothic style had nothing to do with Gothic kingdoms, and the trendy Gothic culture in underground circles was a derivative of Gothic music. Apart from bearing the same name, it had no relation!

As for the Goths and the history of their Ostrogothic and Visigothic kingdoms, I don't think it's worth going into. But what really struck me were these tough and savage Goths who, feeling on the verge of extinction, went to attack the supposedly impregnable city of Rome at the beginning of the fourth century AD. This ethnic group from the east continued to live on for a few more centuries, sweeping across Europe with their battle horses, conquering the entire Caucasus mountain range by oppressing the peoples who lived there, then ending up on the banks of the Danube. After plunging the entire Black Forest into a bloodbath, the Ostrogoths were defeated, and the Visigoths had no choice but to flee. Where were the allies with whom they had swept all over Europe, this army of demons from the East Asian steppes called the Xiongnu?

Of all the names that have gone down in history, I chose to remember that part of my ancestry.

---

[5] A chain of musical instrument stores in Hong Kong.

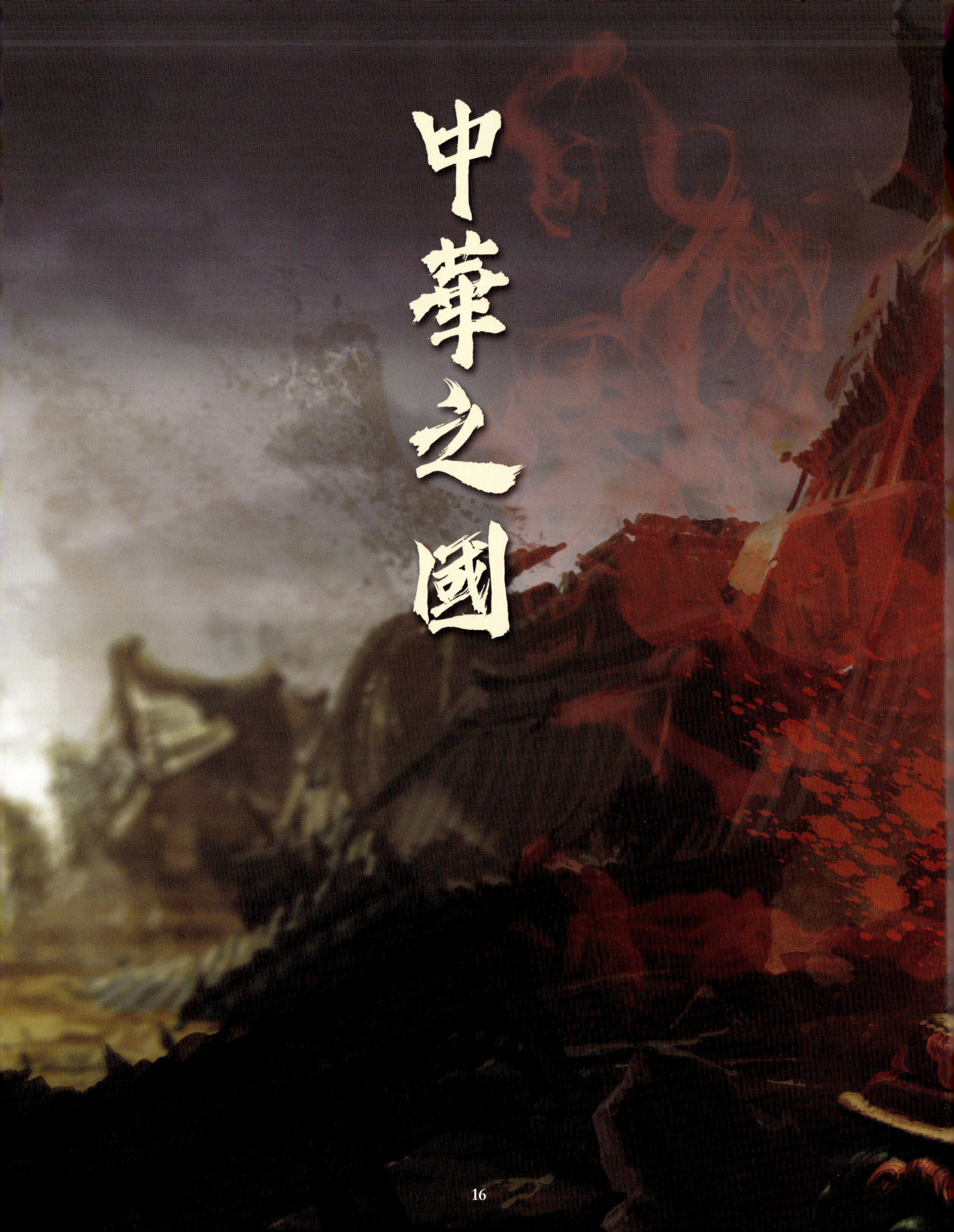

中華之國

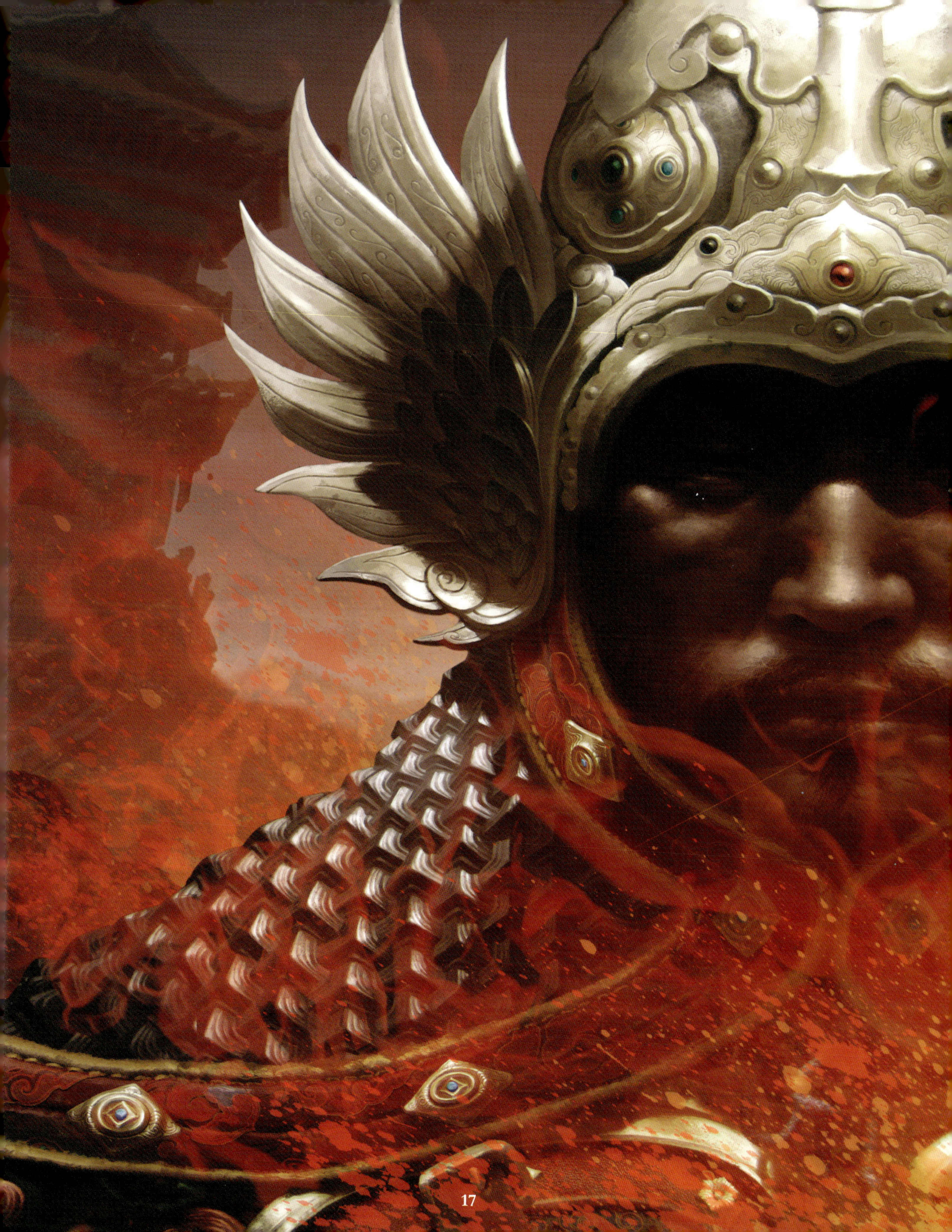

THE XIONGNU: ANCESTORS OF THE HUNS?

Towards the end of the second century and the beginning of the third century, the Xiongnu appeared along the southwestern edge of the Great Eurasian Plain. Weren't the Huns descendants of the nomadic herders and farmers who had built a kingdom in the plains of present-day Mongolia, in northeast Asia? The scientific world can't confirm anything at this time. Their language is lost and without a written system, could it be that these Xiongnu were the people who sowed terror throughout Europe two hundred years later? Could the famous "Scourge of God" and founder of the Hungarian Empire, Attila, have come from these people?

The Alans were the first to be conquered then assimilated by this group during their travels. Then, the smaller tribes of the Aral Sea, the Caspian Sea, the Sea of Azov, the Black Sea, as well as the regions around the Caucasus that had grown their ranks through conquest or alliances. They began to be mentioned in the archives of the Roman Empire following their conquests over the Alans on the shores of the Aral Sea.

One can legitimately wonder where these founding Huns of Hungary came from.

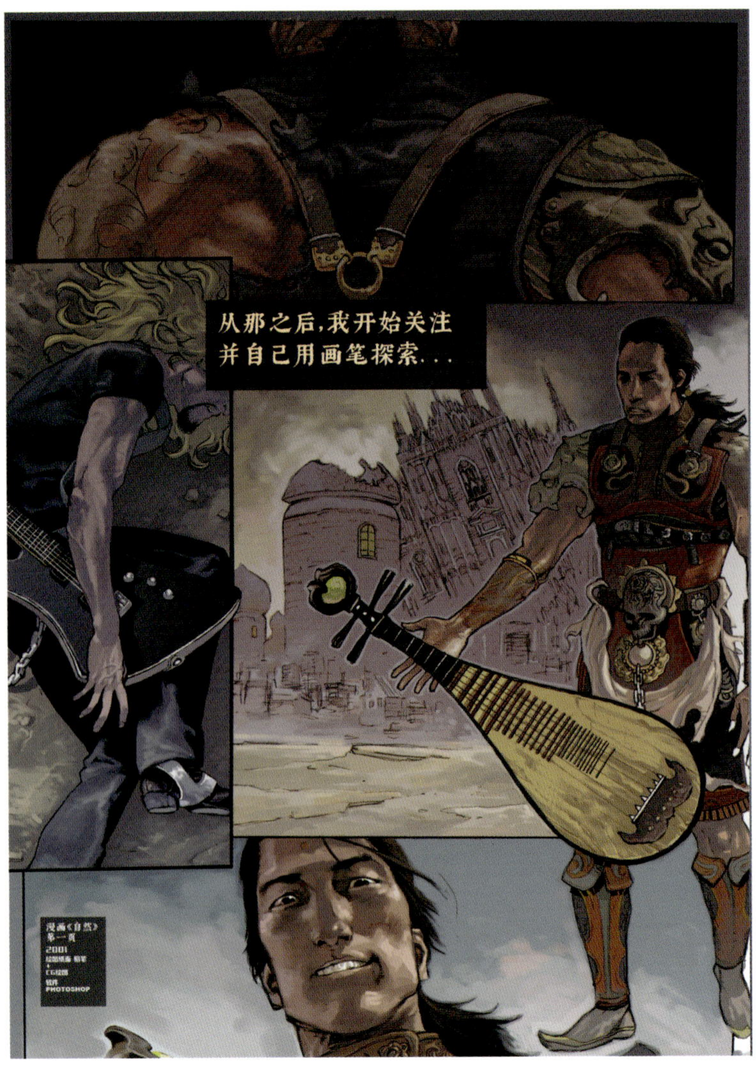

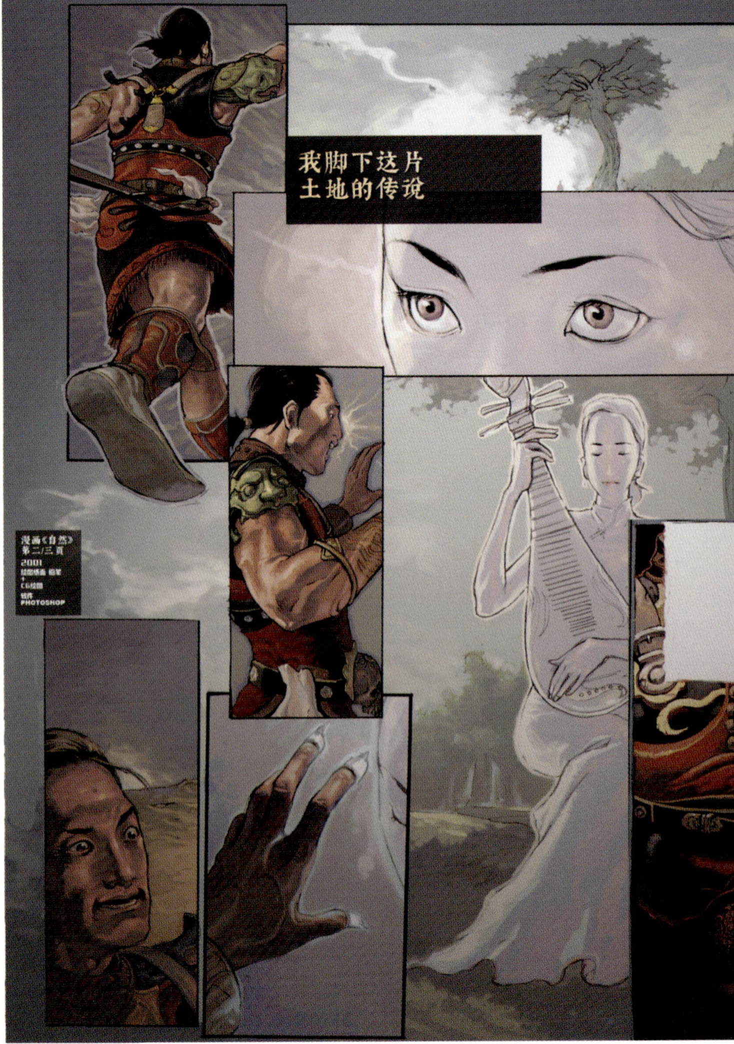

Brut, page 1 and page 2, 2001. Graphite on paper + graphic finalization in Photoshop.

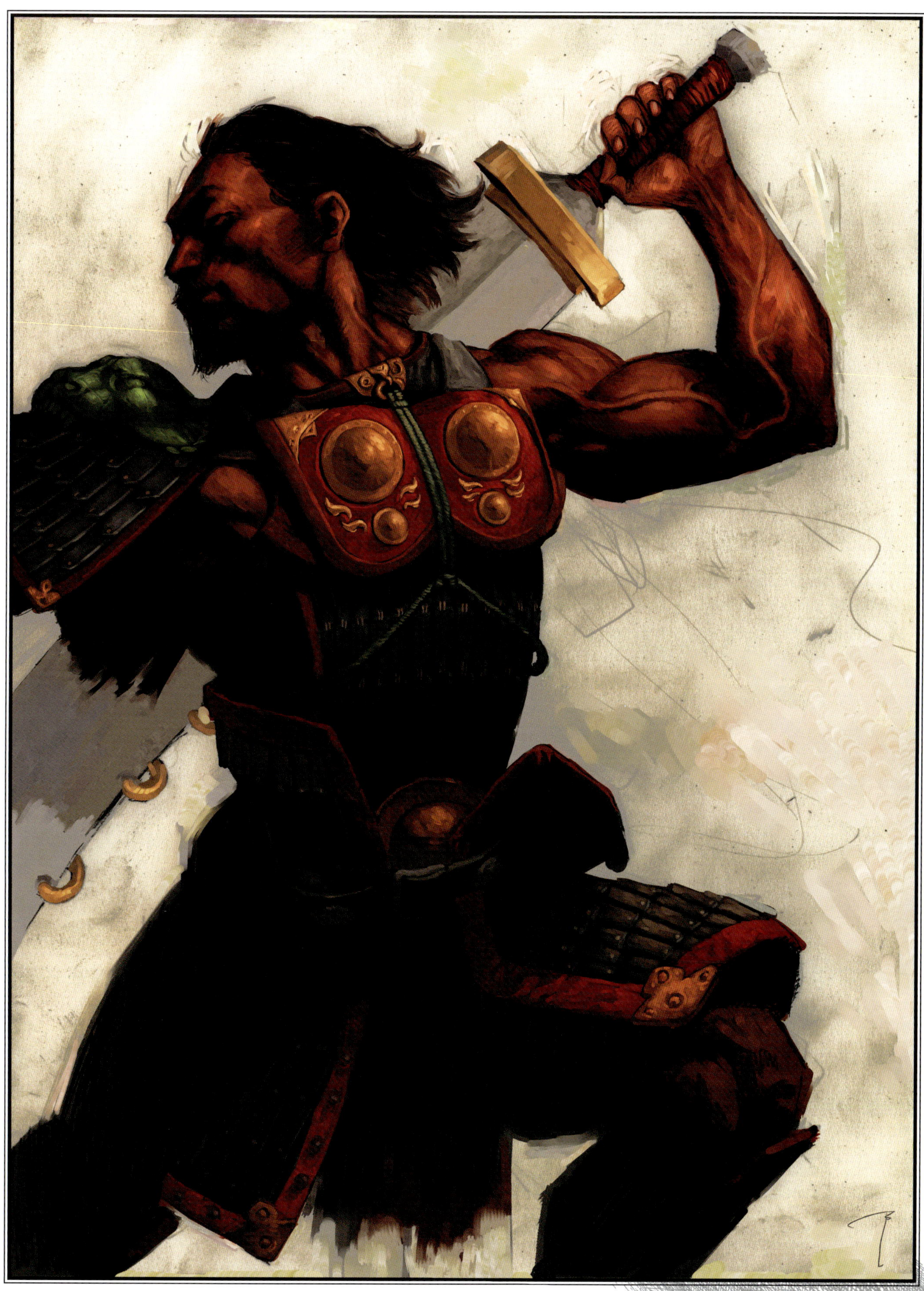

Cover made for *Fantasy* magazine, 2003. Graphite on paper + graphic finalization in Photoshop.

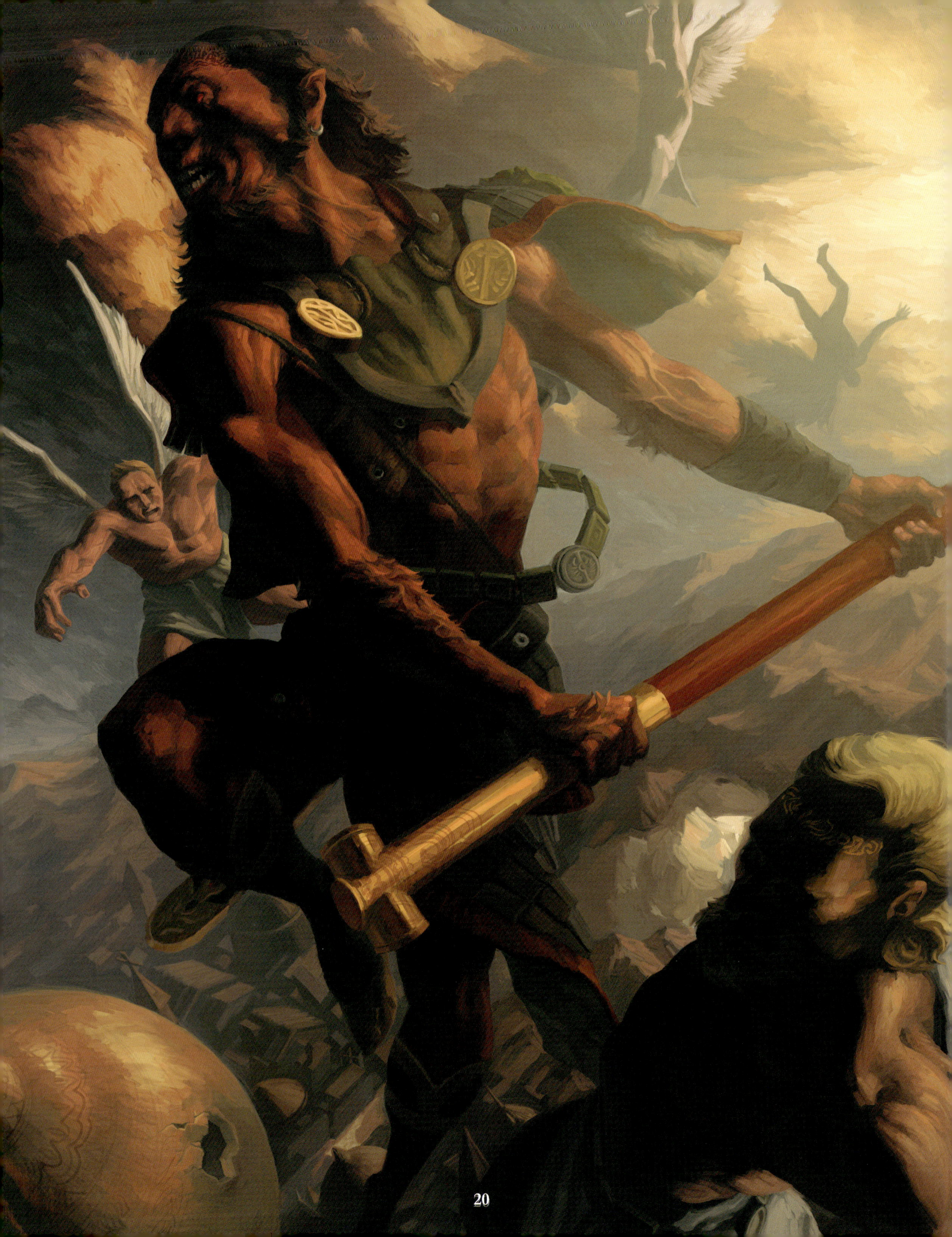

Due to my bad temper (I've always been a mule), I never accepted education during my mandatory period of schooling, nor paid much attention to a single textbook distributed during class. There were also history books in that bundle. But in the summer of 2002, in my little room in Beijing, I began to seriously read books about this historical period in order to write this comic book set on the distant banks of the Danube. So I ended my obscured period.

(The history of the Goths, the history of the Germanic Peoples, the history of the Roman Empire, general history of the world, Greek mythology, the expansion of the Turkish Ottoman Empire, the 303 dynasties of ancient Egypt, Memoirs of Mesopotamian and Sumerian Culture, the ancient books of Judaism, Catholicism, Christianity, the Orthodox Church, Islam, and Buddhism, the eastern countryside during the legend of Alexander the Great, the Venetian merchants, and the Renaissance.)

I think that among my circle of friends, there were many people who, like me, forgot about the existence of this distant legendary empire that continues in Asia and influenced part of the history of this planet.

This legend lives on in the ancestral blood running through my veins, existing in the collective memory of the various peoples of the world. It hasn't marked minds as deeply as the industrial revolution, the world wars, fast food restaurants, personal computers, or classical culture, but it reminds us of its existence all the time. Considered non-essential in our compulsory education system, it is hardly mentioned in history books, and from the moment we entered the current profit-based society, it no longer interested anyone. Because it does not bring a penny to white-collar workers or their corporate banquets. By the end of the century, it had been given so many other names by the different countries it encompassed that it gradually faded from its original form. When it is mentioned, it no longer inspires the respect of the past because even her own descendants have nearly forgotten her. In the legends, we used war chariots and gold halberds, or gigantic tripod cauldrons in which we shaped our bodies to the sound of ritual music while donning blood-stained armor.

This is how the idea spread that one can only understand the universe through the wisdom of one's own heart, as it had been recorded in collections of parchments, or carved on stone tablets.

During that summer, looking into the history of the civilizations that were influenced by this legend, I who had grown up with it while ignoring it, suddenly had a flash of lightning and I finally remembered its name: "The Middle Kingdom."

LEFT: *Qi Tian*, 2004, graphic tablet and graphic finalization in Painter. ("Qi Tian Da Sheng" was the self-appointed name for the Monkey King in the legendary epic *Journey to the West*.)

I ended the Spring and Autumn period [6]: these heroic borders shaped by the Qin [7] and the Han[8] bathed the imagination of the Tang until their peak, and the memory of the quest for the Nine Tripod Cauldrons [9] floats in the clouds over the fires of the border fortresses in the Dunhuang frescoes. They are still present in temples like Luoyang, outside the city walls.

We still find these Confucian classics. Clothing and written language endure, these mountains and rivers still exist, the Great Wall did not collapse. The Shining Moon from the Qin[10] era, Jiayuguan Fort from the Han[11] era are still present …

This Middle Kingdom I pursue, looking at these Buddhist statues[12] and these buildings that I represent drawing after drawing recedes a little more each time, like the blur of a mirage.

We still use chopsticks; we still sometimes wear the clothes of yesteryear, but the body no longer remembers the reverent protocols; our children still continue to write with the order of the lines[13], but they don't wait until they are adults to learn greed, tyranny, and unbridled desires on their own.

These temples and these divinities, these palaces and these literary works, these utensils and adornments, this language and these customs, are none other than the elegant vestiges of the vigorous titans of old. They are remnants eroded by a thousand and one years of winds crossing through this world. They were buried alive alongside these declining giants, and all of these talented and awe-inspiring beings have become legendary figures. When their souls went up in smoke, there was no more talk of Huaxi or the Middle Kingdom.

Of their six hundred and fifty-plus years, only an elegant and fragile shell remains.

---

[6] Chun Qiu period: early part of the reign of the Eastern Zhou Dynasty, 770–476 BC.

[7] Qin Dynasty, 221-206 BC

[8] Han Dynasty, 206 BC. AD - 220 AD

[9] Chinese mythology: the Nine Ding (tripod cauldrons) were melted down under the Xia dynasty (-2070 / -1076), and therefore considered symbols of the authority conferred to them by heaven. They were moved from the royal palace at the end of the Zhou dynasty (-1046 / -256), but were never found despite numerous searches to locate them, in particular by Qin Shi Huang (-221 / -206)

[10] The Shining Moon refers to a legendary pearl that shines in the dark.

[11] Jiayuguan Fort is located in Gansu province, in the northwest, near the Gobi Desert. It is a strategic point along the Great Wall to prevent attacks from nomadic plains tribes, including Xiongnu and Mongol invasions which were frequent at this time.

[12] Reference to the statues of the Mogao caves near the town of DunHuang, near the Gobi desert.

[13] Literally "A vertical line, a horizontal line." Chinese characters are written line by line, respecting a precise order and direction to draw each line (e.g. from top to bottom, left to right, the left or top part first, etc.). This comes from the fact that the texts were originally written in calligraphy. If these rules are not respected with the brush, the ink smears the paper with stains and the characters become illegible. The teaching of characters is still carried out in this order and direction of the stroke, and calligraphy is still frequently used.

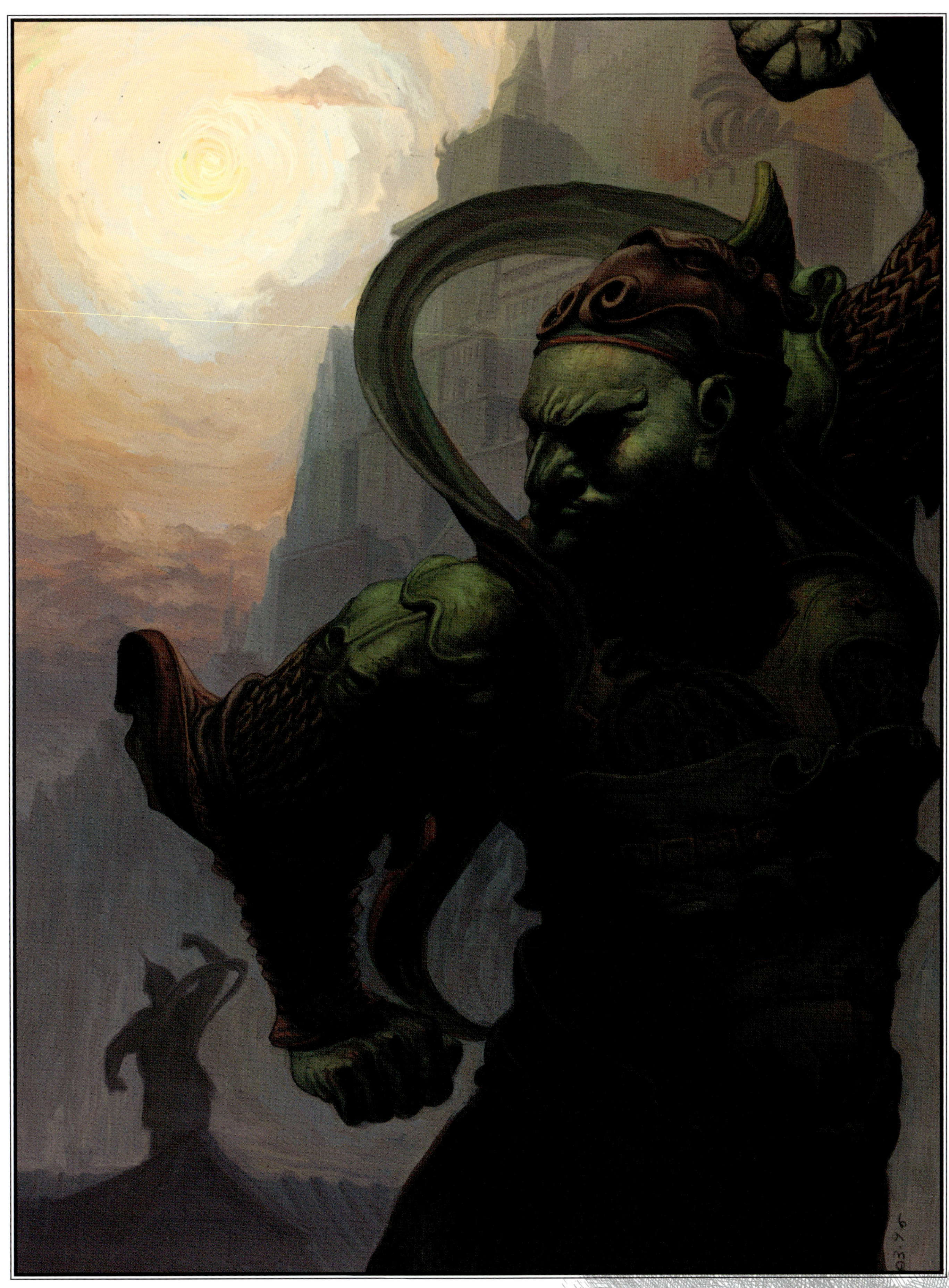

Tian Luo Han, 2004. Graphite on paper + graphic finalization in Painter.

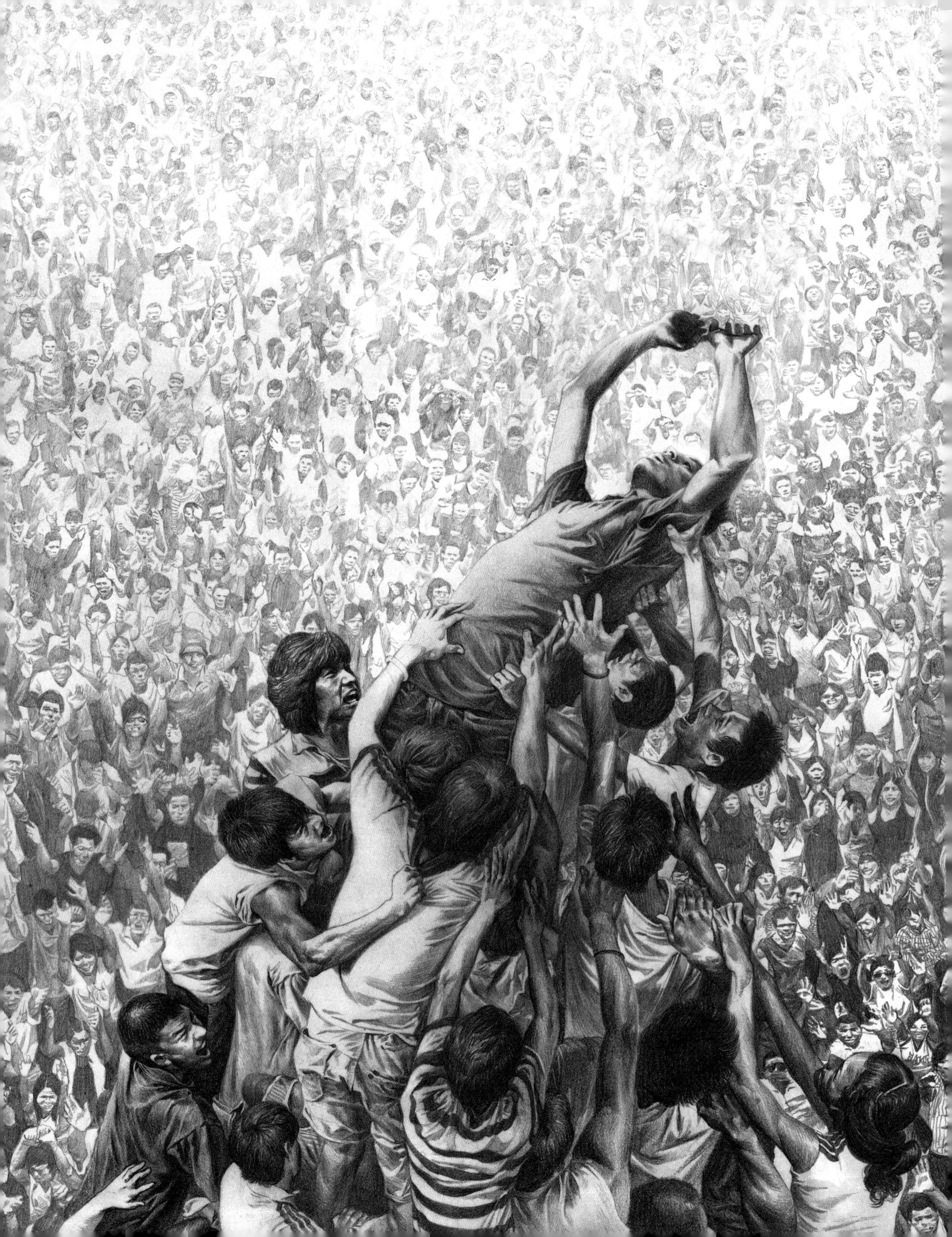

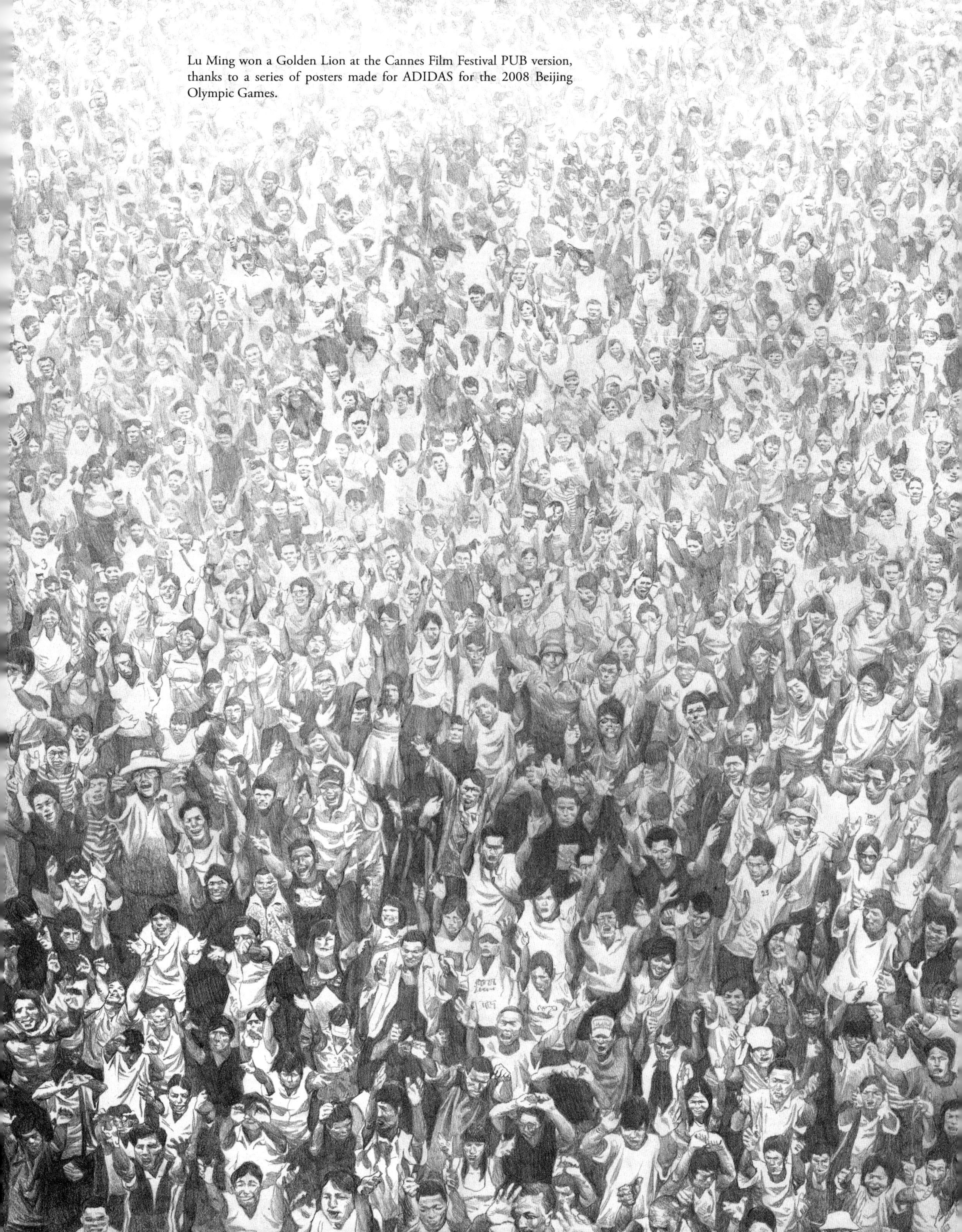

Lu Ming won a Golden Lion at the Cannes Film Festival PUB version, thanks to a series of posters made for ADIDAS for the 2008 Beijing Olympic Games.

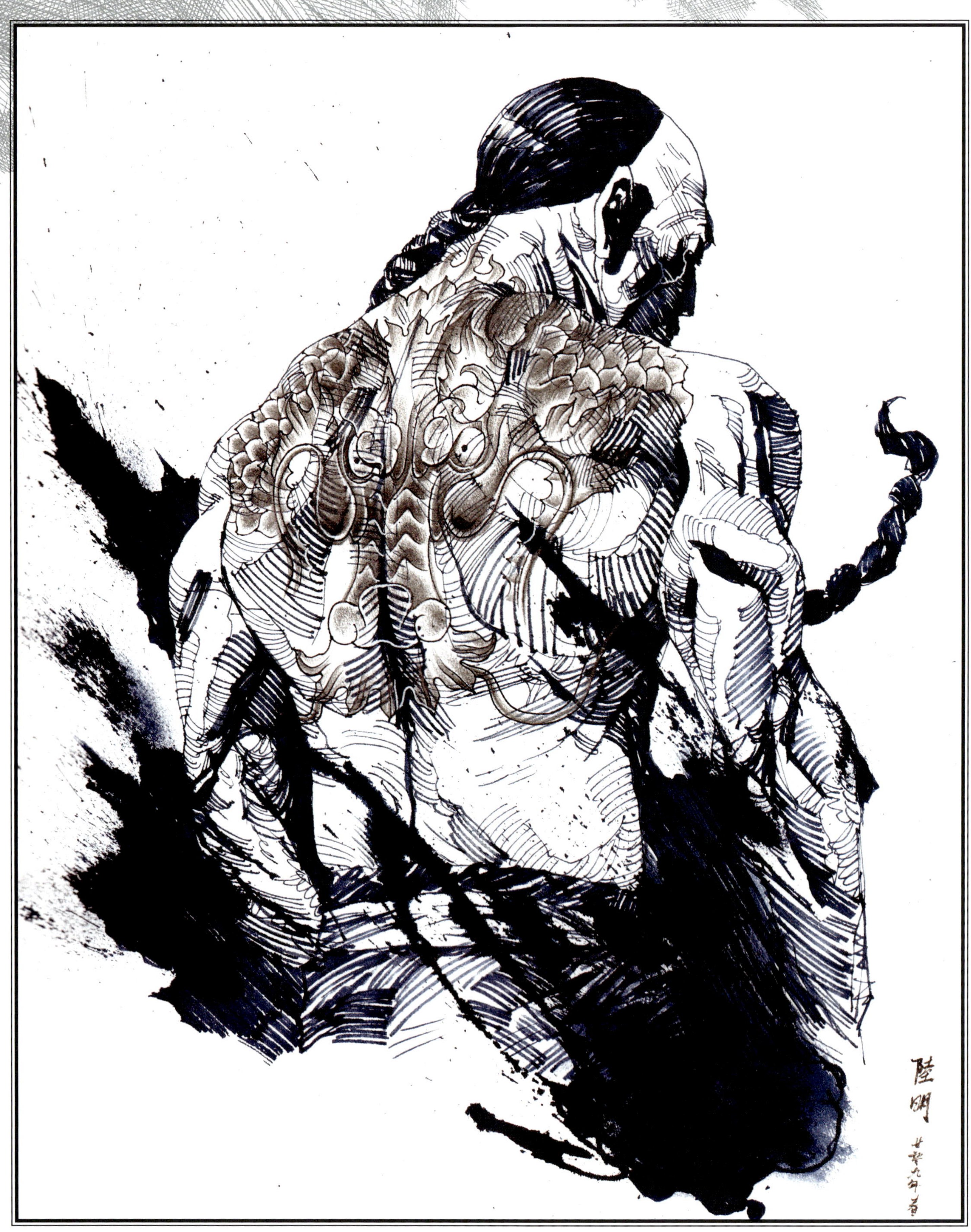

Illustration for the novel *Dou Hai,* 2009. Ink pen and graphite on A3 sheet.

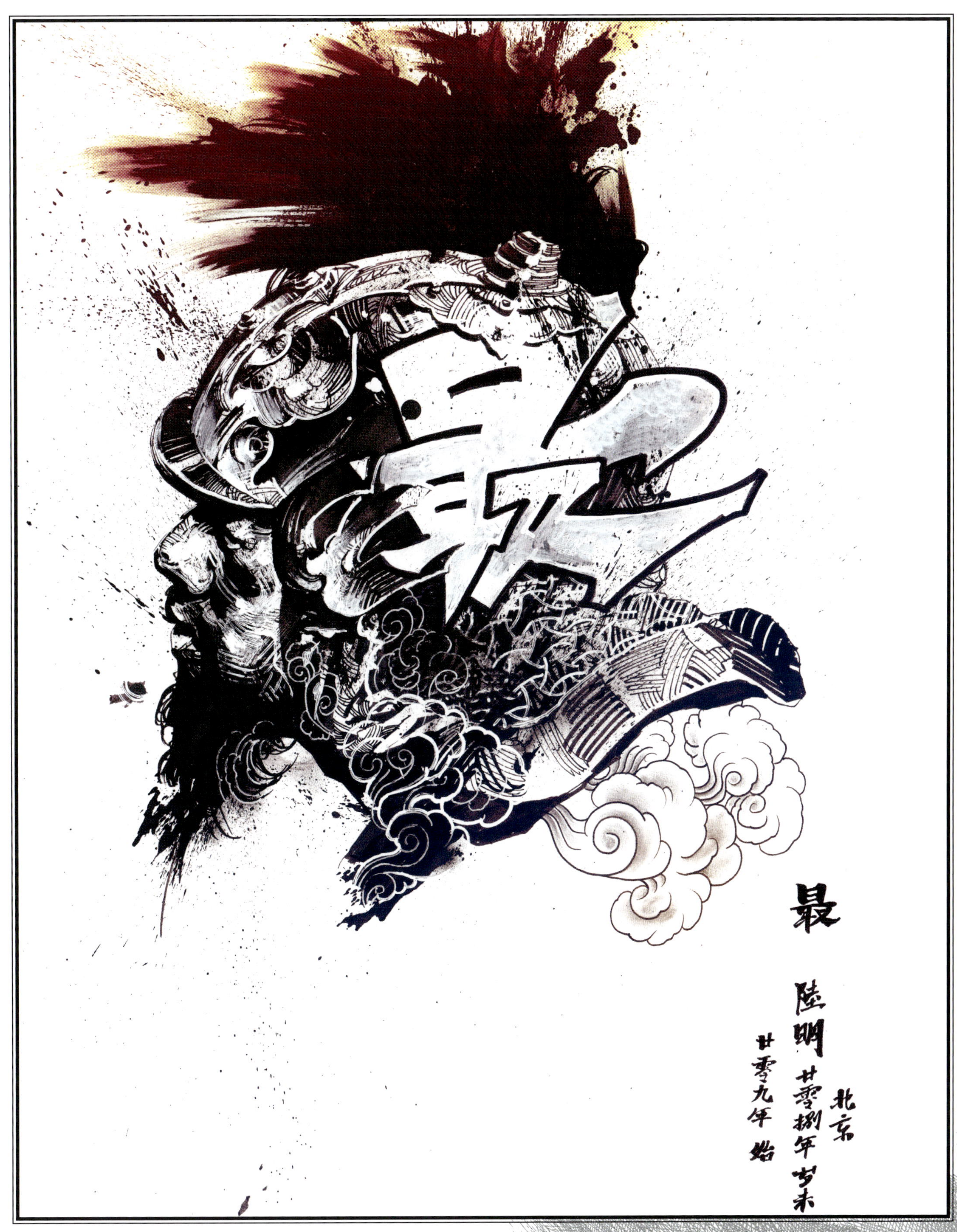

Zui, 2008. Ink pen and graphite on A3 sheet.

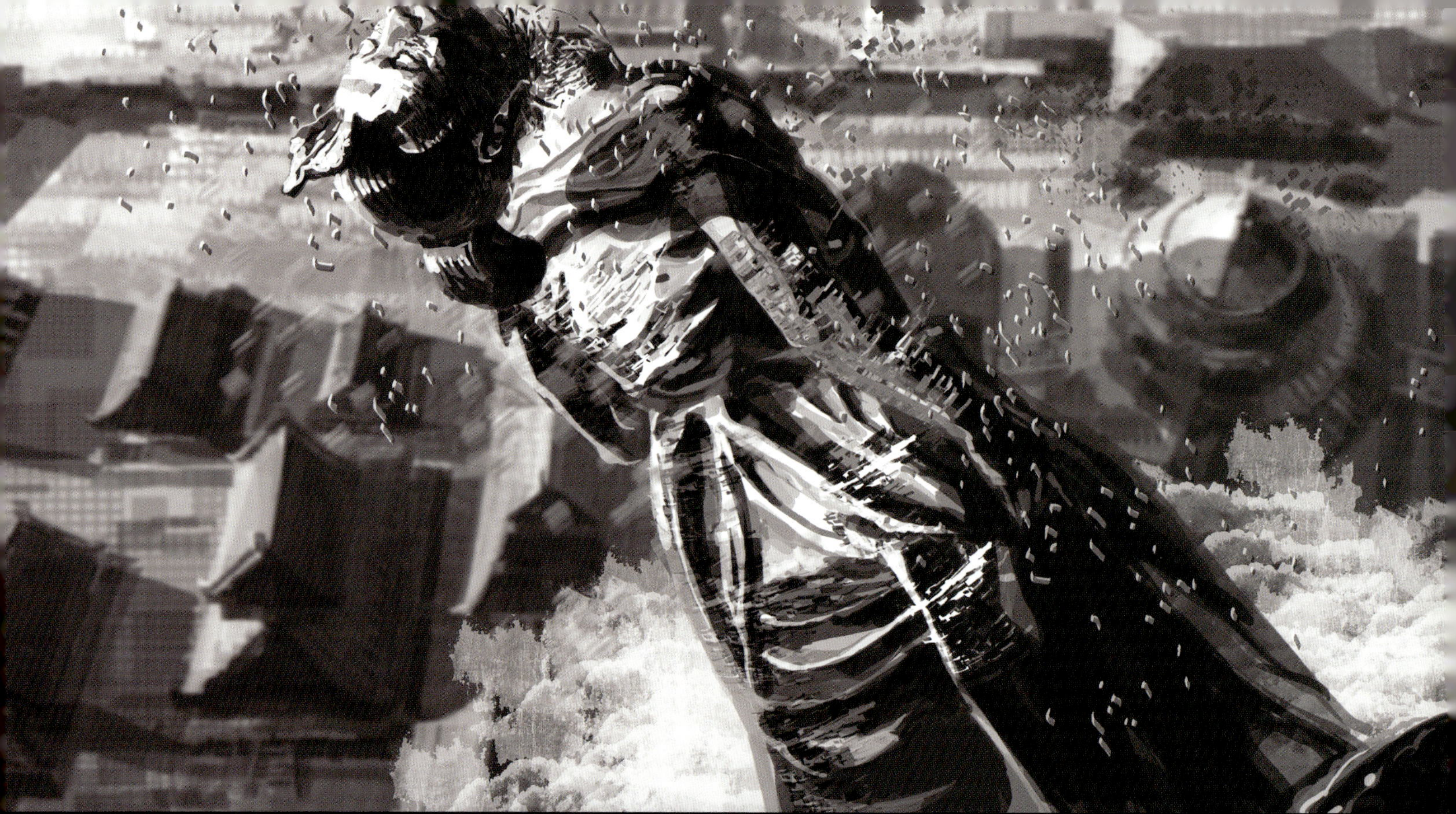

The Empress, concept diagram for *Detective Dee: The Mystery of the Phantom Flame*, 2009. Digital composition and graphic + finalization in Photoshop.

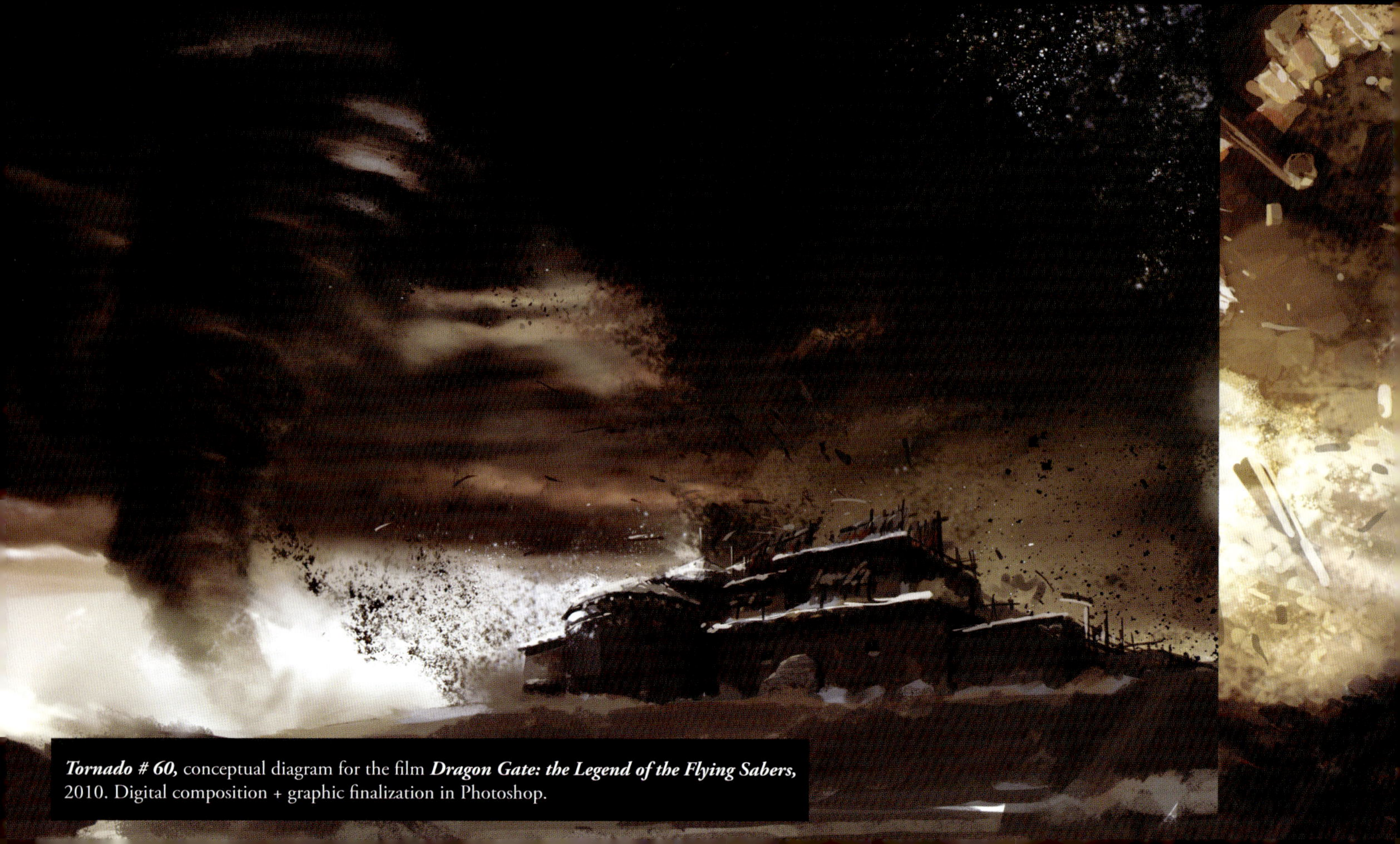

Tornado # 60, conceptual diagram for the film ***Dragon Gate: the Legend of the Flying Sabers,*** 2010. Digital composition + graphic finalization in Photoshop.

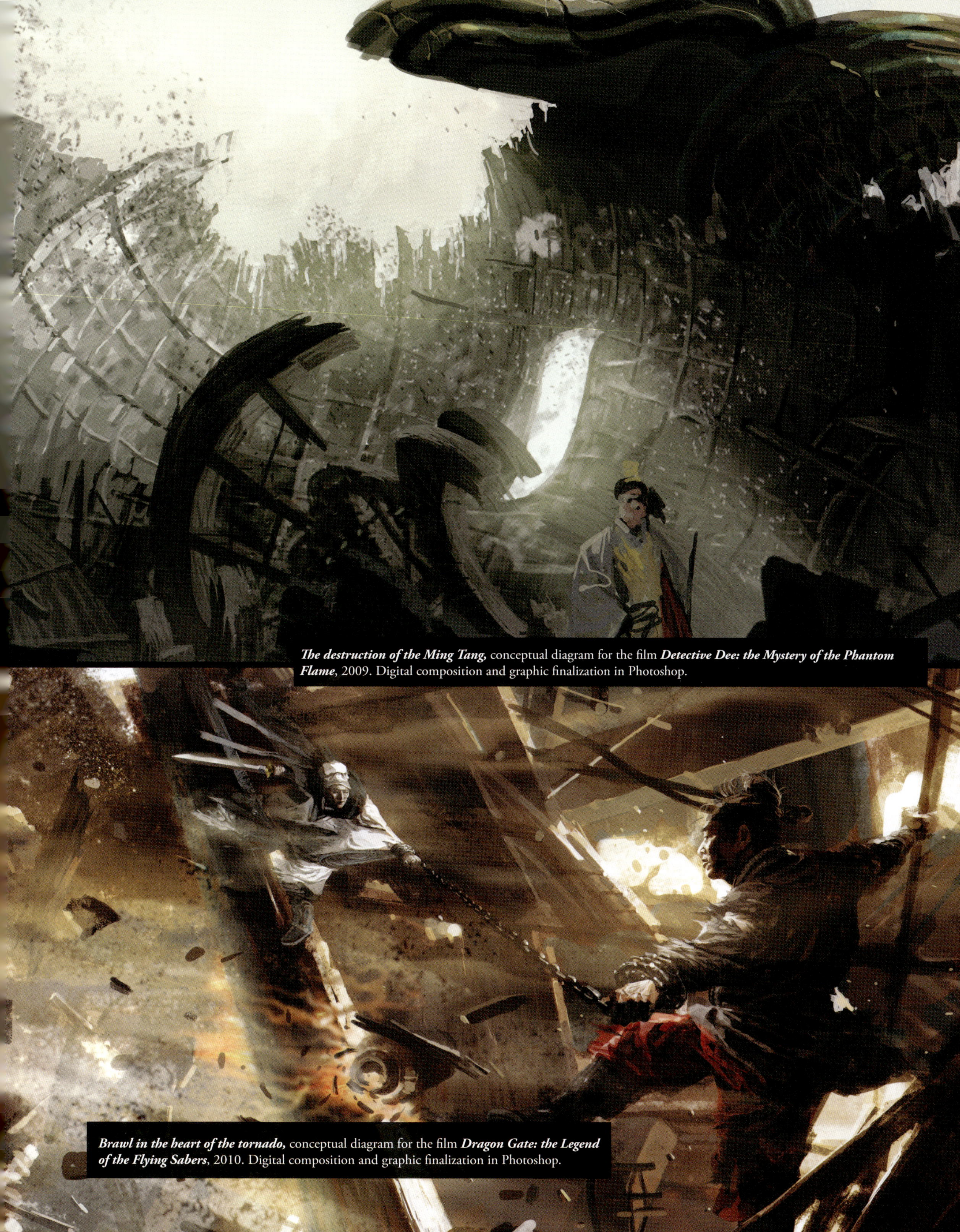

The destruction of the Ming Tang, conceptual diagram for the film *Detective Dee: the Mystery of the Phantom Flame*, 2009. Digital composition and graphic finalization in Photoshop.

Brawl in the heart of the tornado, conceptual diagram for the film *Dragon Gate: the Legend of the Flying Sabers*, 2010. Digital composition and graphic finalization in Photoshop.

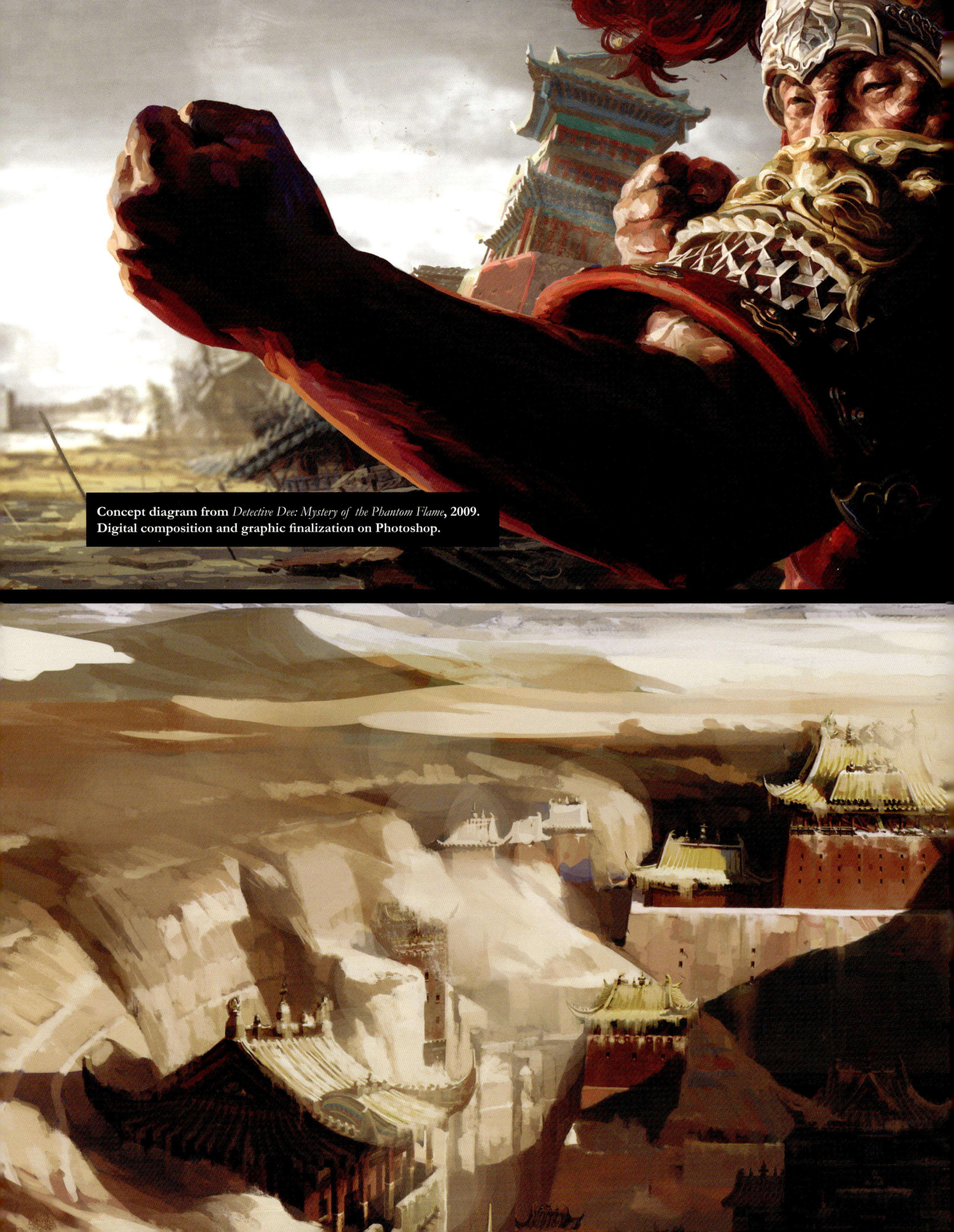

Concept diagram from *Detective Dee: Mystery of the Phantom Flame***, 2009.**
Digital composition and graphic finalization on Photoshop.

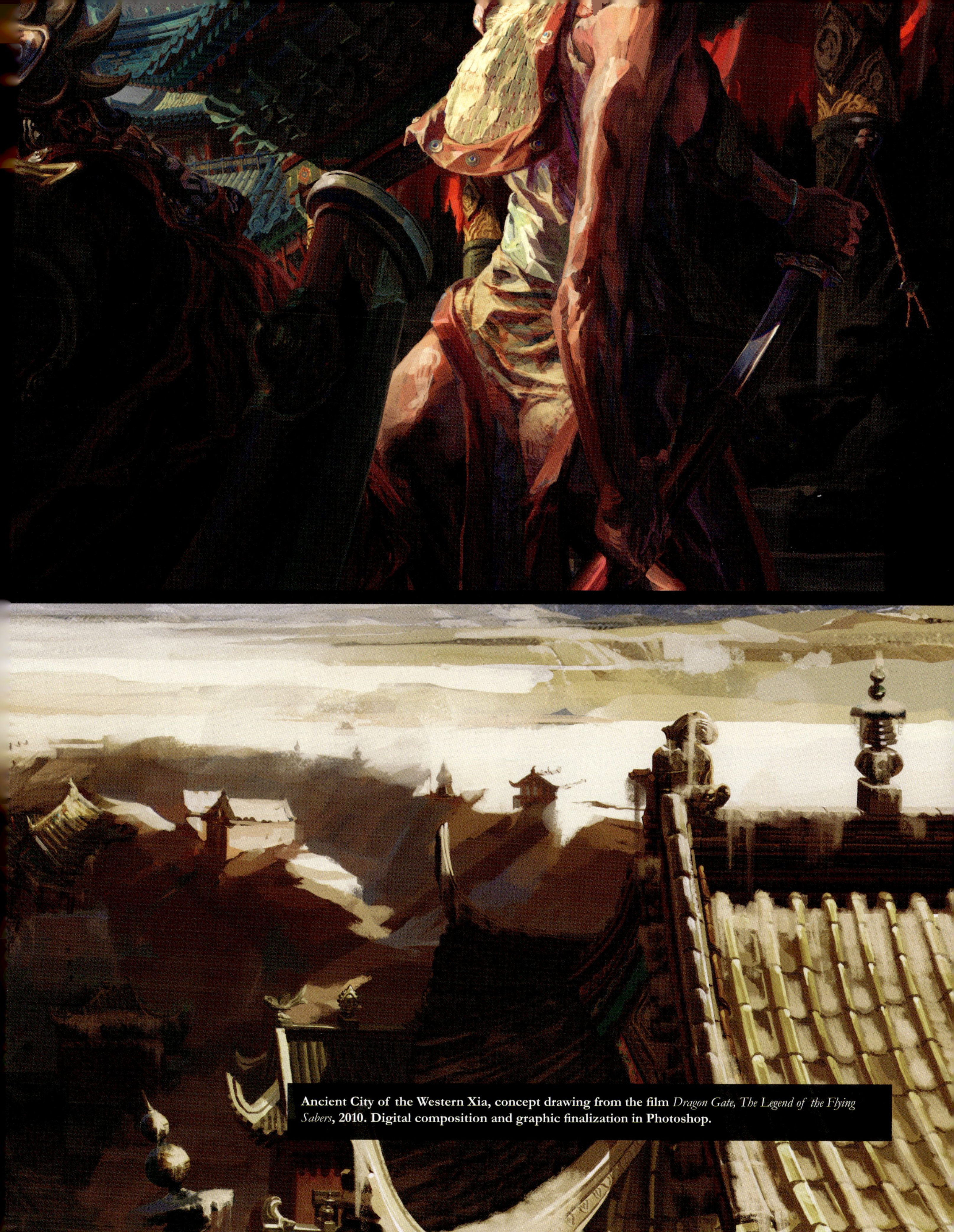

Ancient City of the Western Xia, concept drawing from the film *Dragon Gate, The Legend of the Flying Sabers*, 2010. Digital composition and graphic finalization in Photoshop.

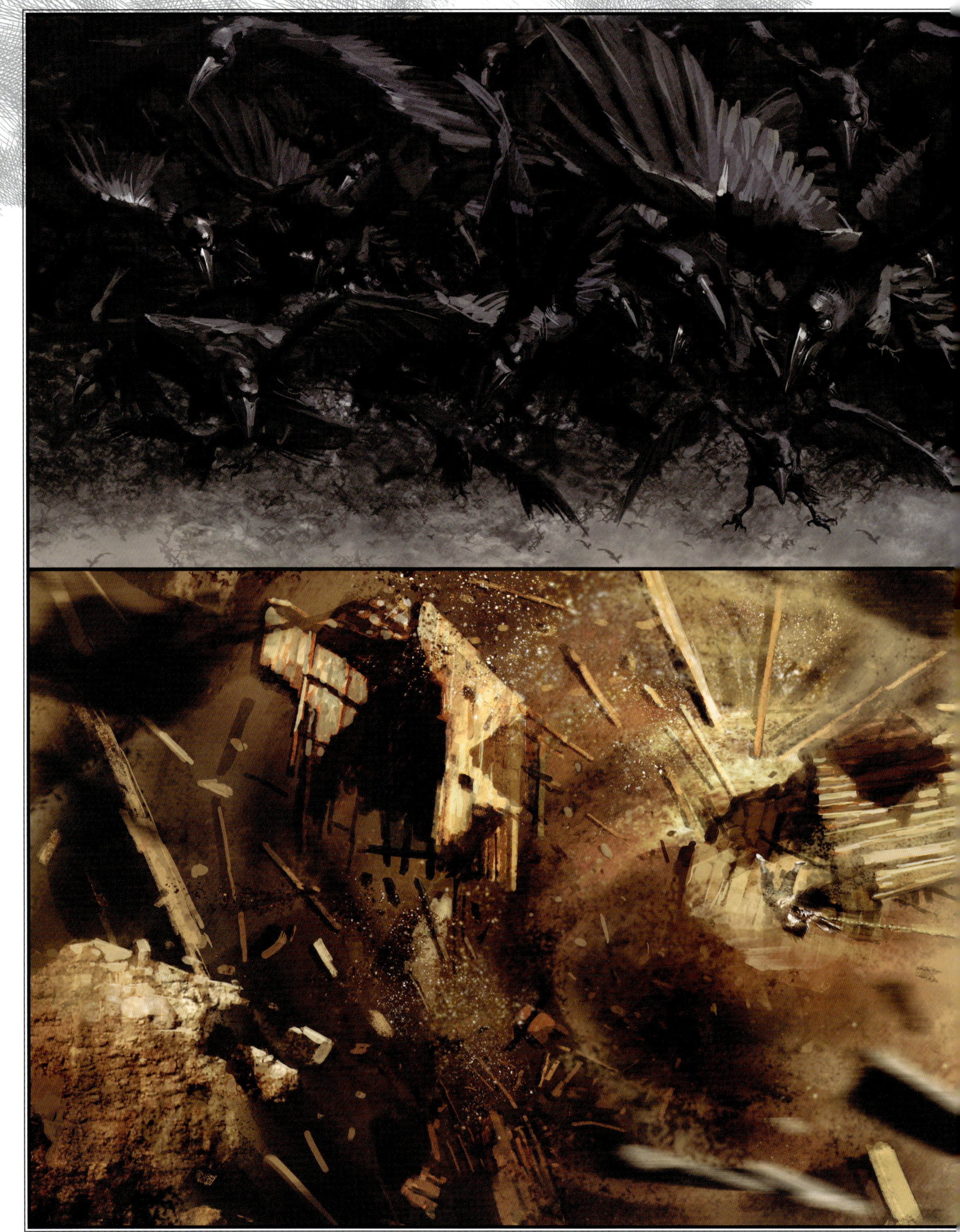

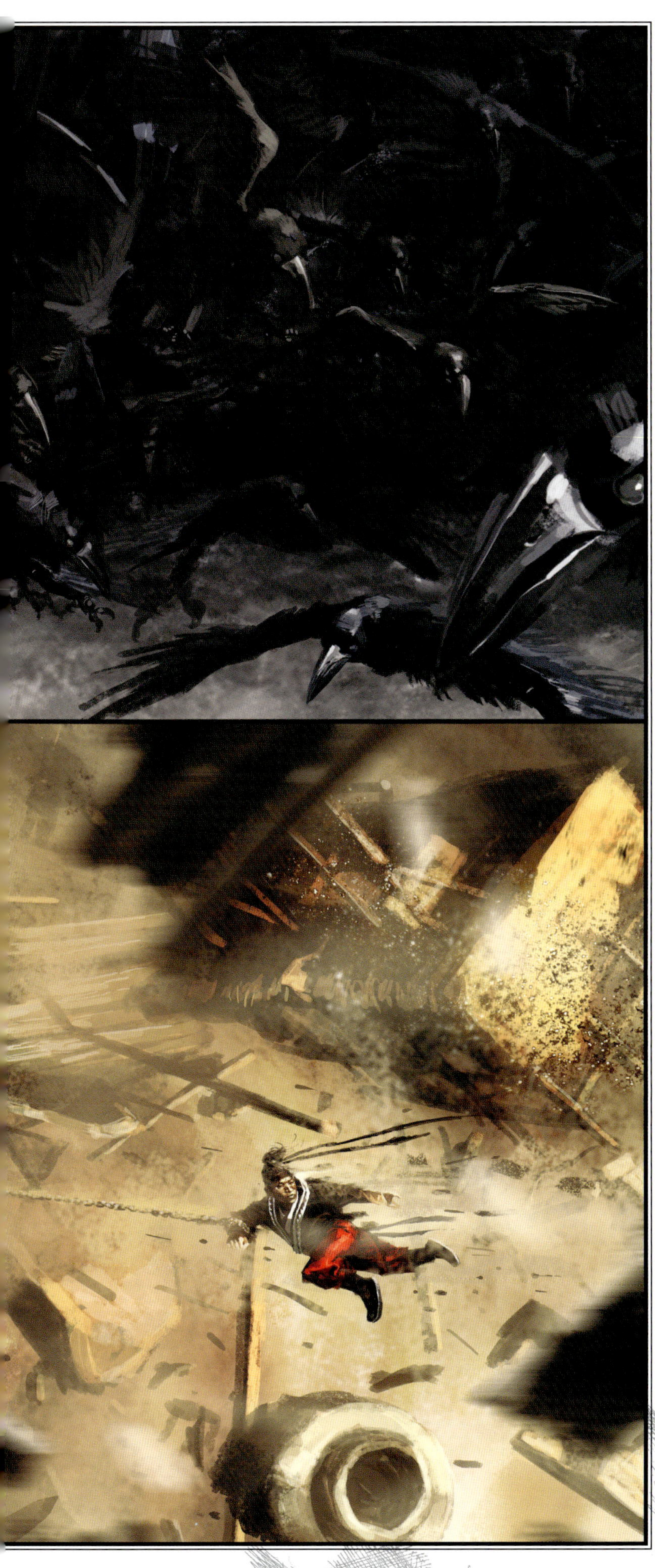

2010, Photoshop.

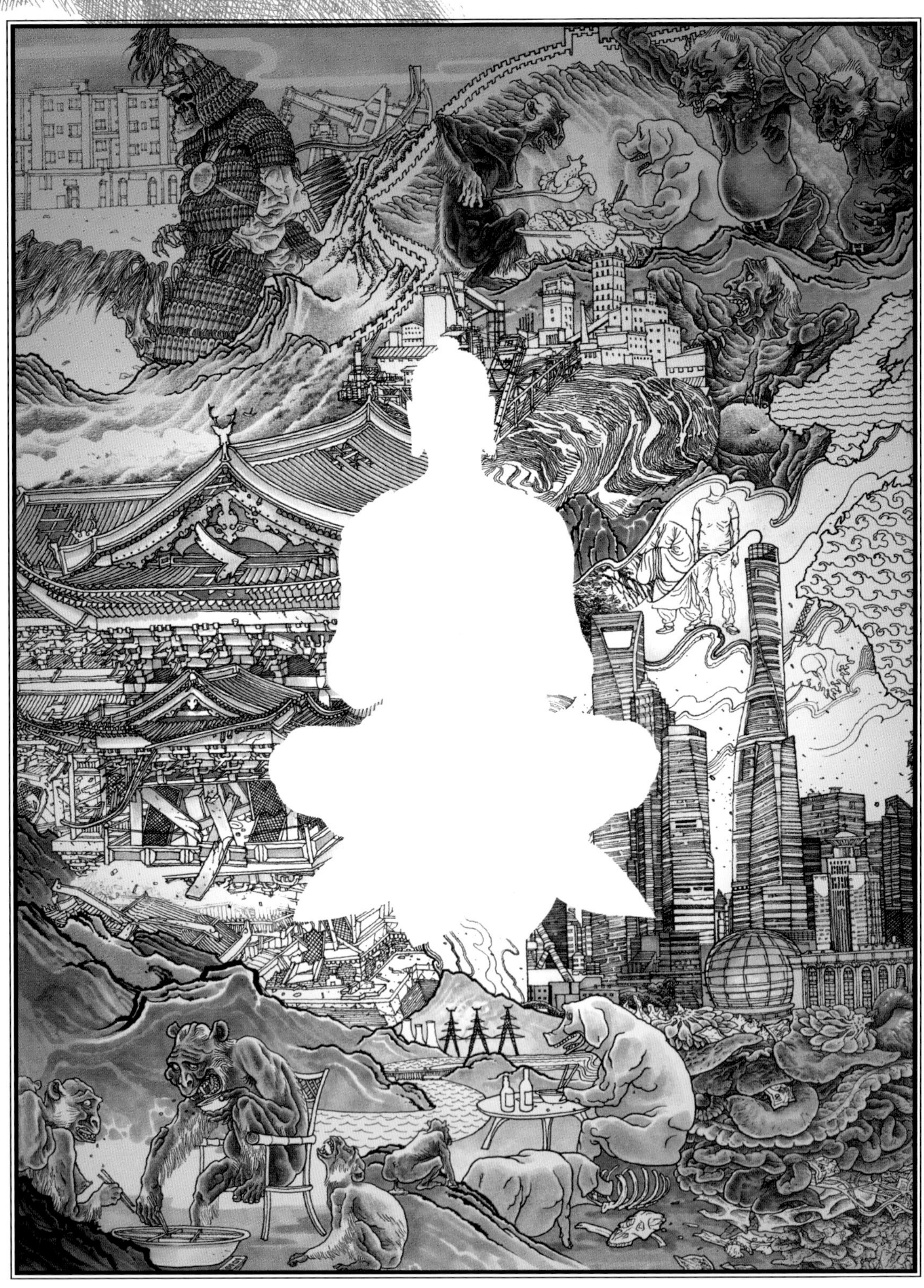

Hell, 2017. Illustration on A3 sheet, ink pen, felt tip pen and calibrated marker.

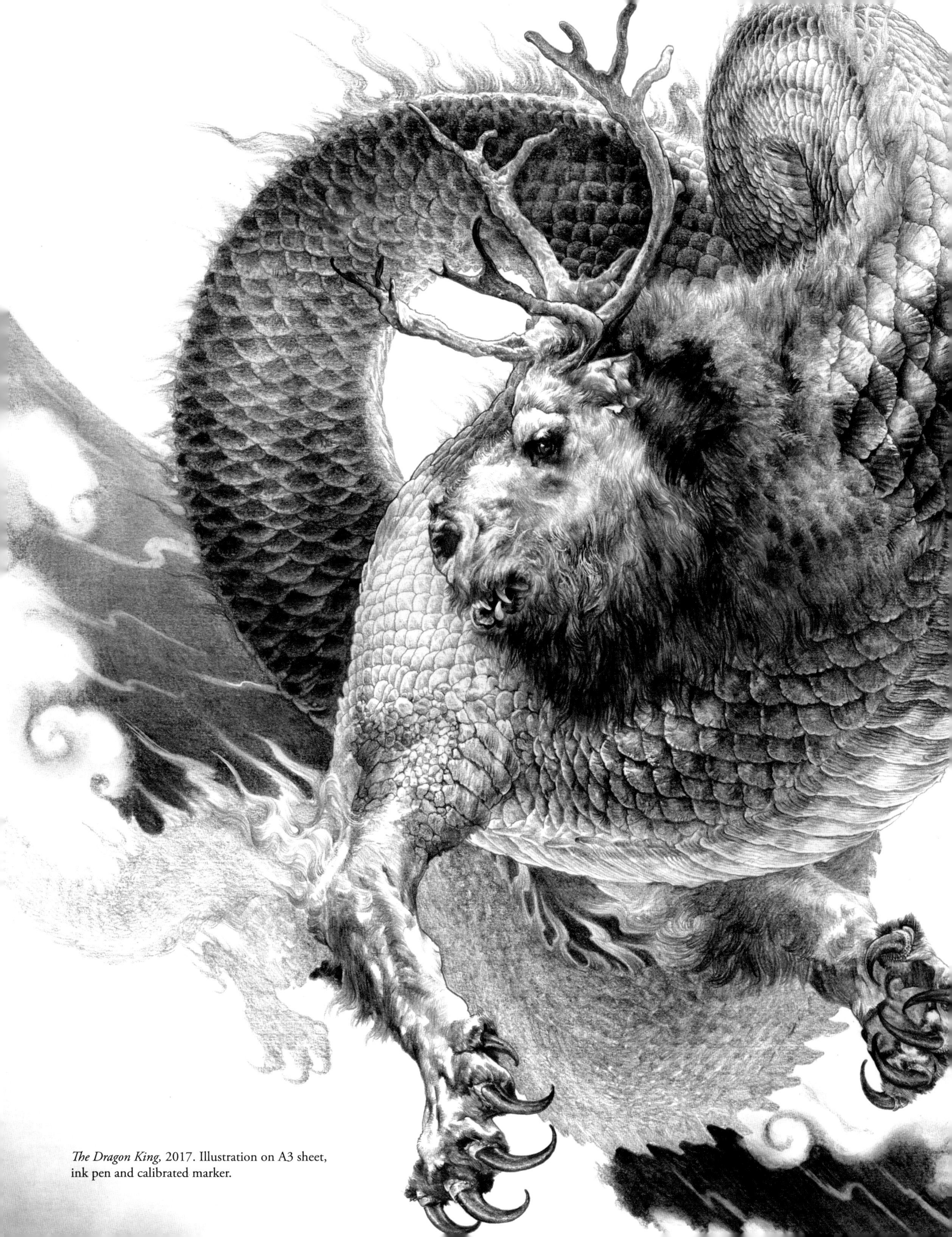

The Dragon King, 2017. Illustration on A3 sheet,
ink pen and calibrated marker.

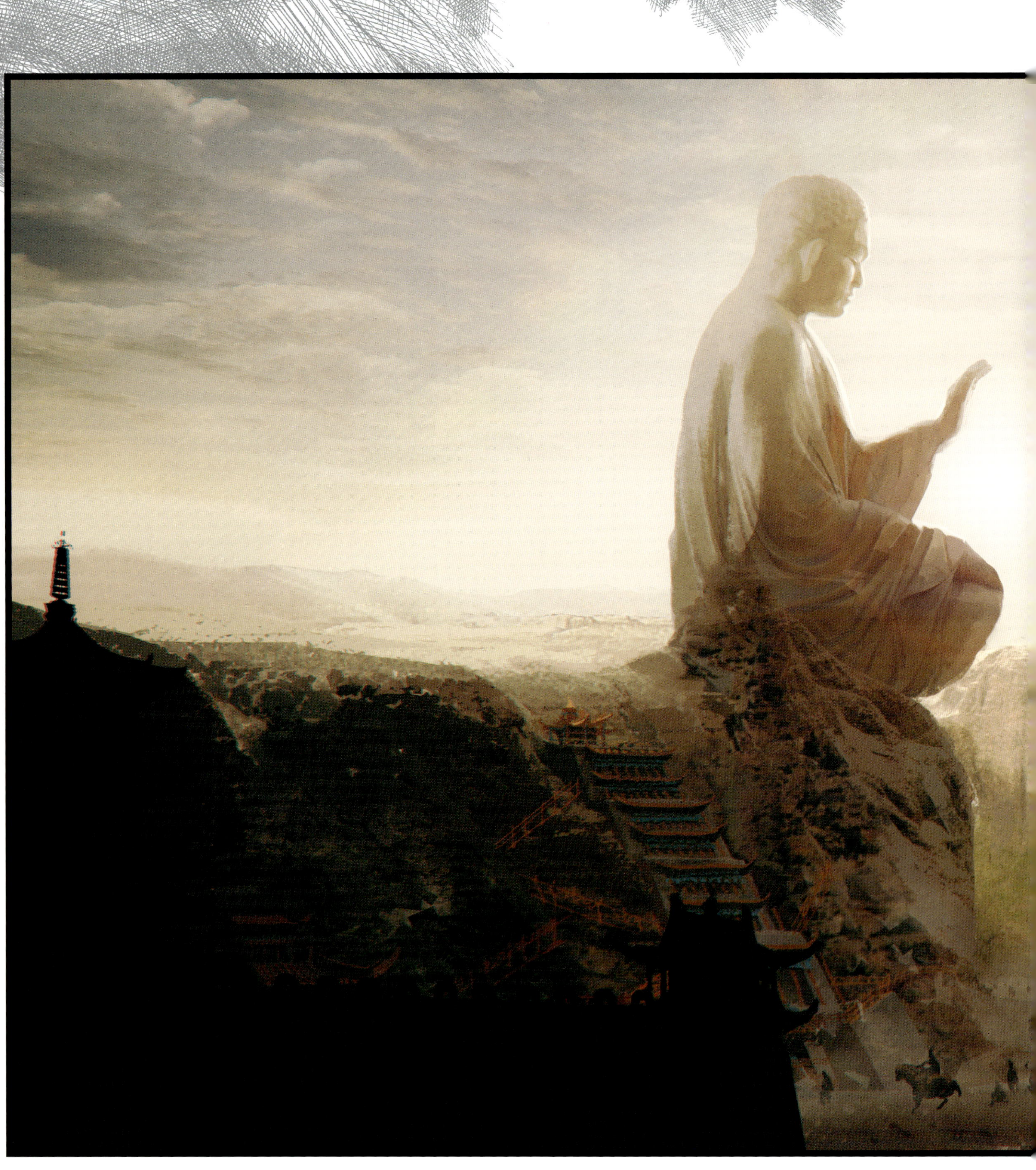

Dun Huang, 2016, conceptual image for the film. Digital composition and graphic finalization in Photoshop.

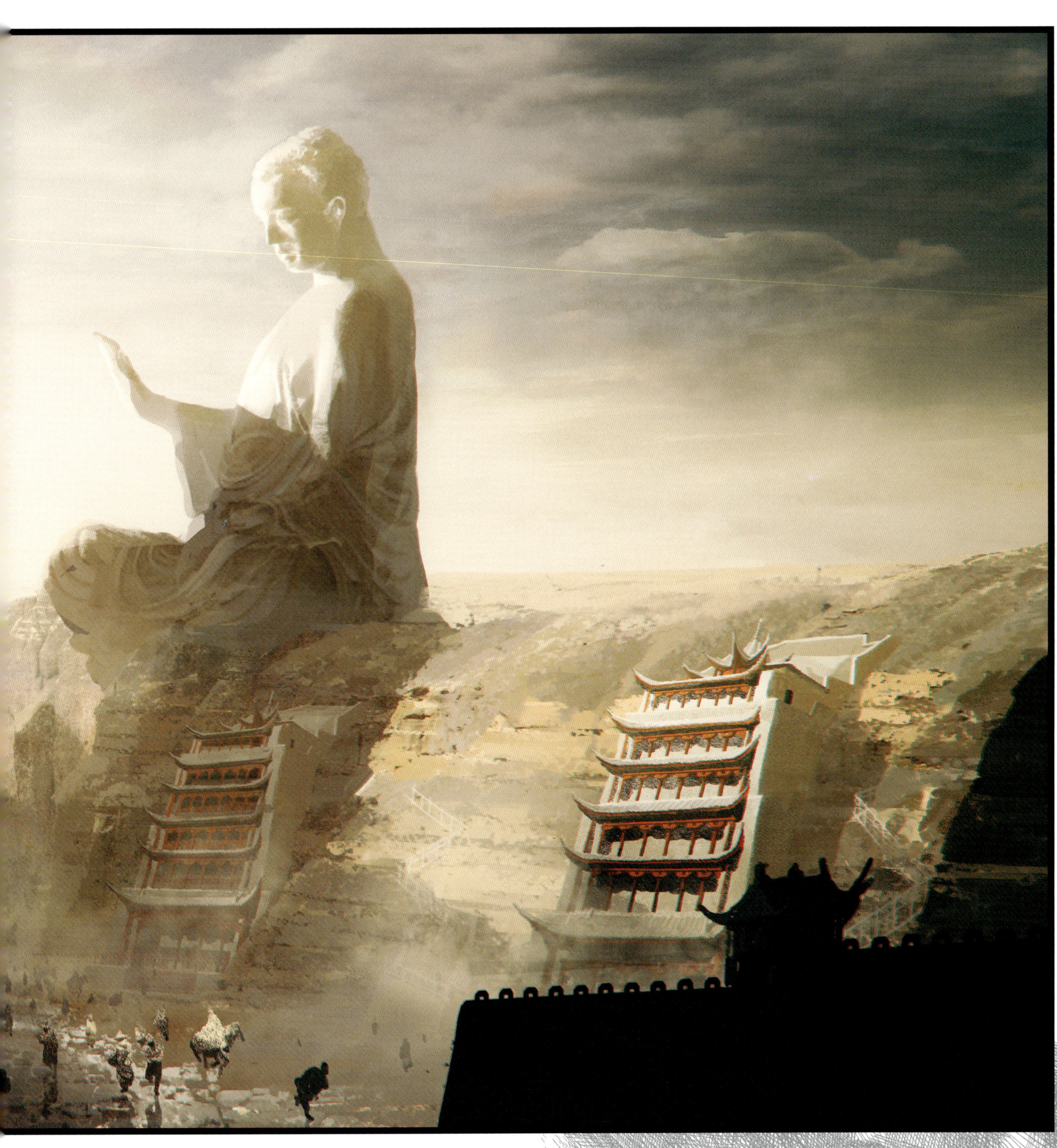

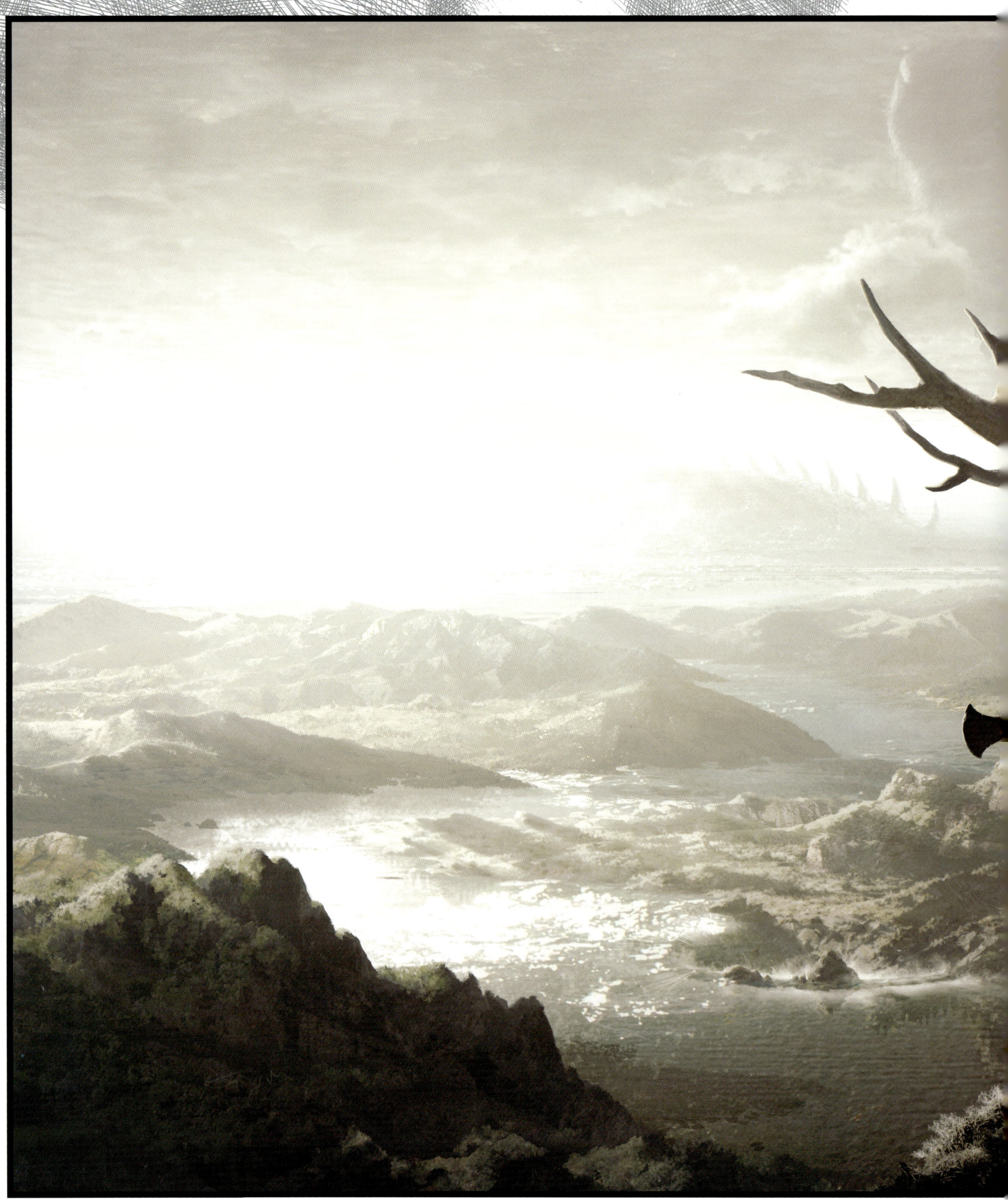

Shan Hai, digital composition and graphic finalization in Photoshop. The ShanHai Jing is a collection of mythological fables written in the 6th century.

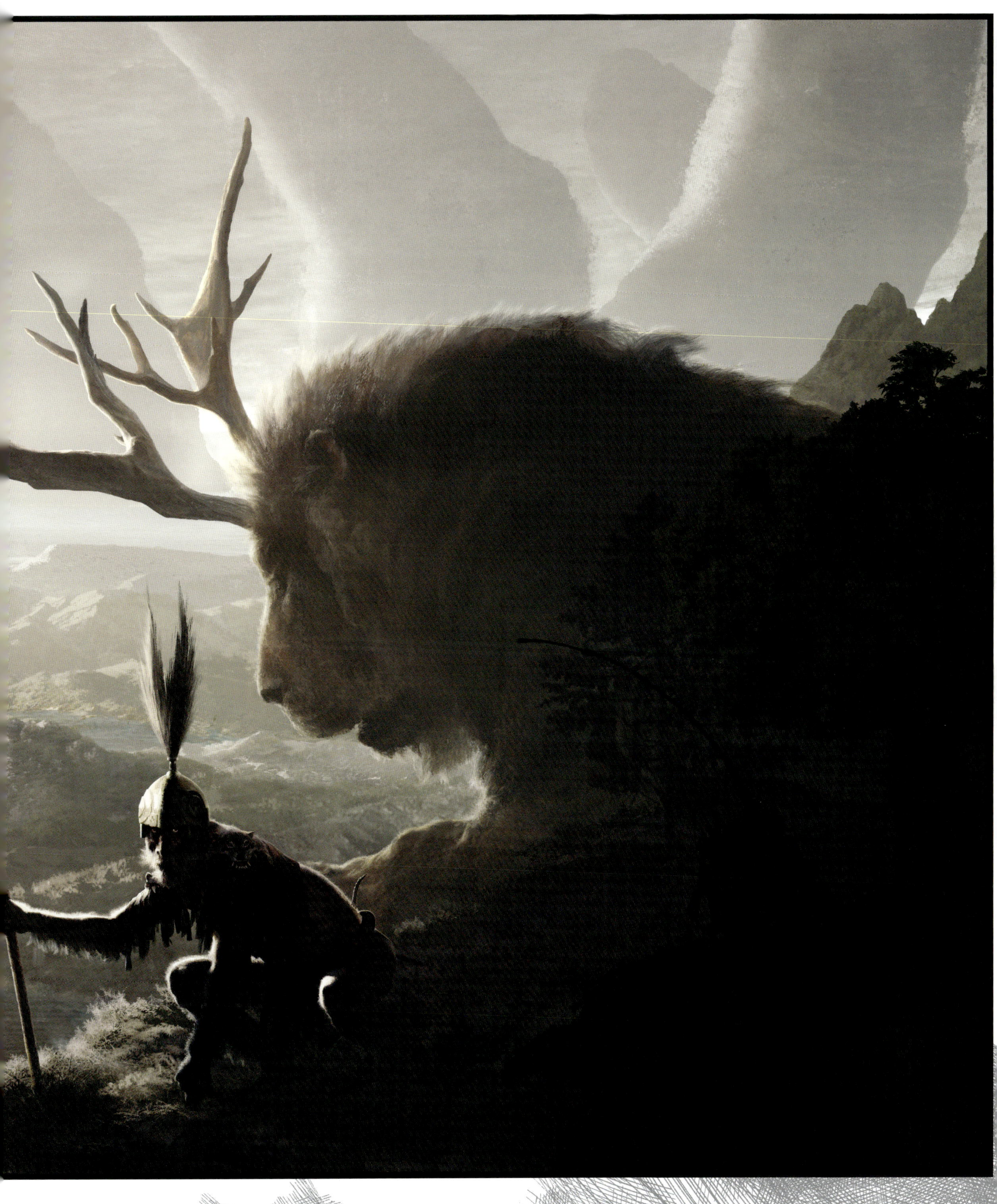

DESERT GRADE

Every civilization takes a similar journey. Like any living being, when it is born, it struggles to impose itself on a hostile universe. In its early youth, it makes mistakes, more mistakes, then in adulthood, it strives to expand its conquests, violently entering a fight to expand its territory.

When old age arrives, all of its movements grow more painful. It lacks energy, its fate is slipping hopelessly through its fingers. All it can do is wait for the end.

Even if one can still see whole sections of the Great Wall, ancient temples in Japan, traditional costumes of the Ming dynasty in Korea, even if one still finds books relating a glorious past, all of that is over now. The power of a civilization lies in the way its people carry on their way of life so that its cultural flame lasts through space and time.

Today we wear t-shirts and Nike, we use industrial products to send messages, we only give our emotions a secondary priority. We grow up on hamburgers and fries. We are far from those individuals who picked bamboo and sought Damascus steel. We don't care if we seek the true essence of the universe in our limited lives; we only seek to consume more and more.

All of these walls, temples, costumes, and foods are inherent in the design of the Desert Grade steel warrior armor I built. They are elements still present in the world, but they are mere relics of a bygone era, the brave warrior who had once been within passed away long ago.

This warrior of steel is like a ray of light that pushes me forward. He has become the torchlight before the tomb of heroes, the fire that shines like the Damascus steel of their armor.

RIGHT: Black Rock Desert, Nevada, United States, 2018.

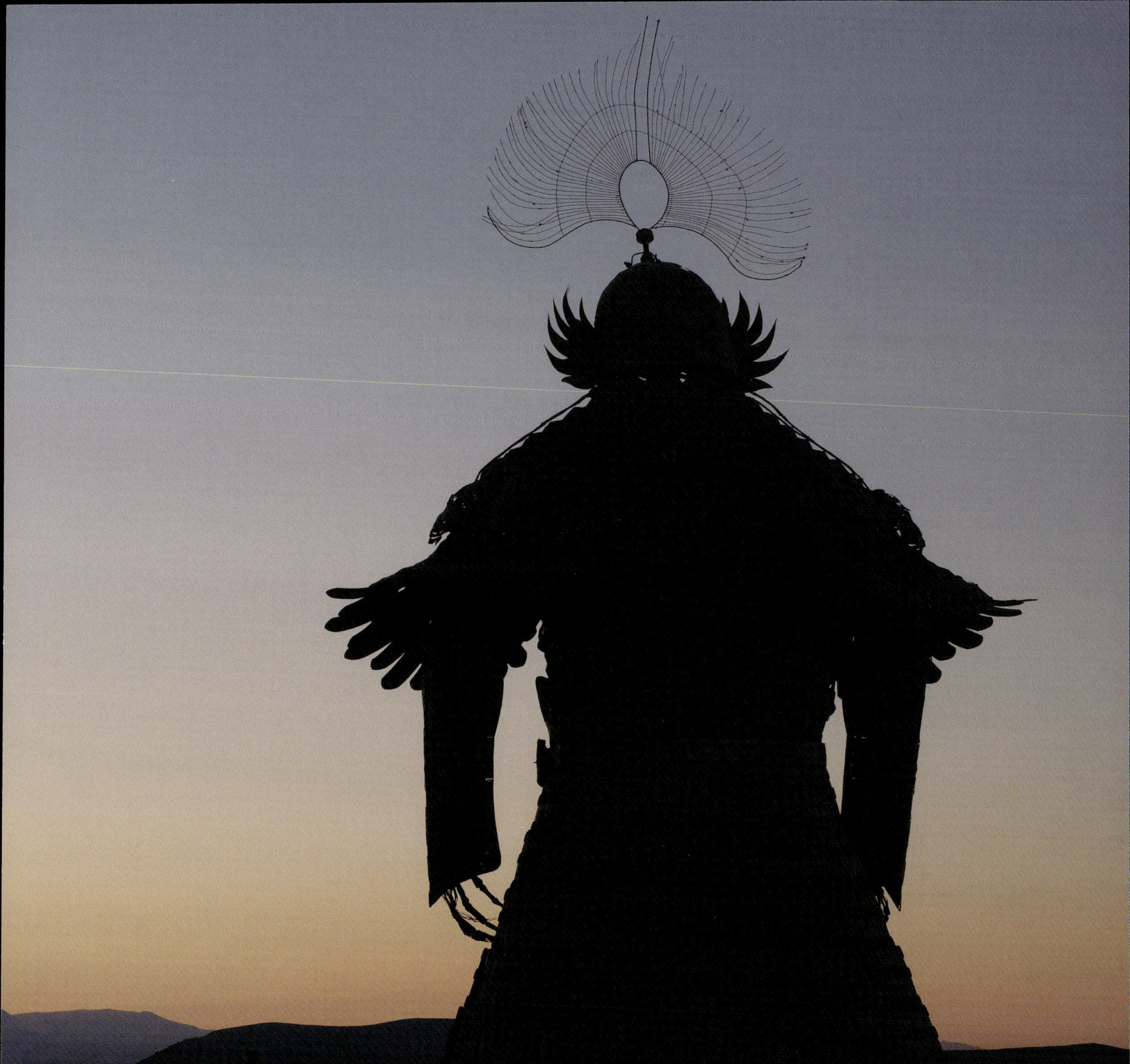

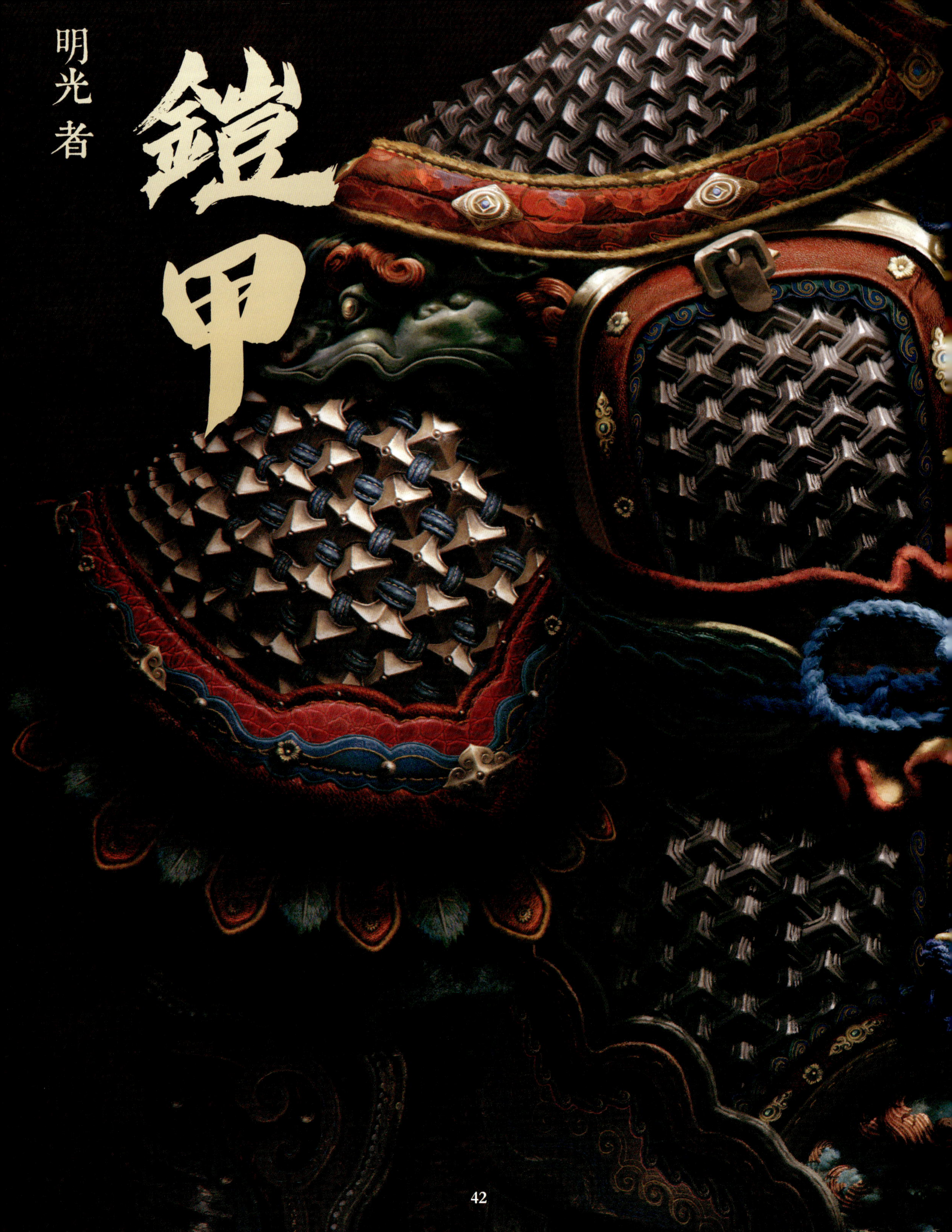
明光者
鎧甲
42

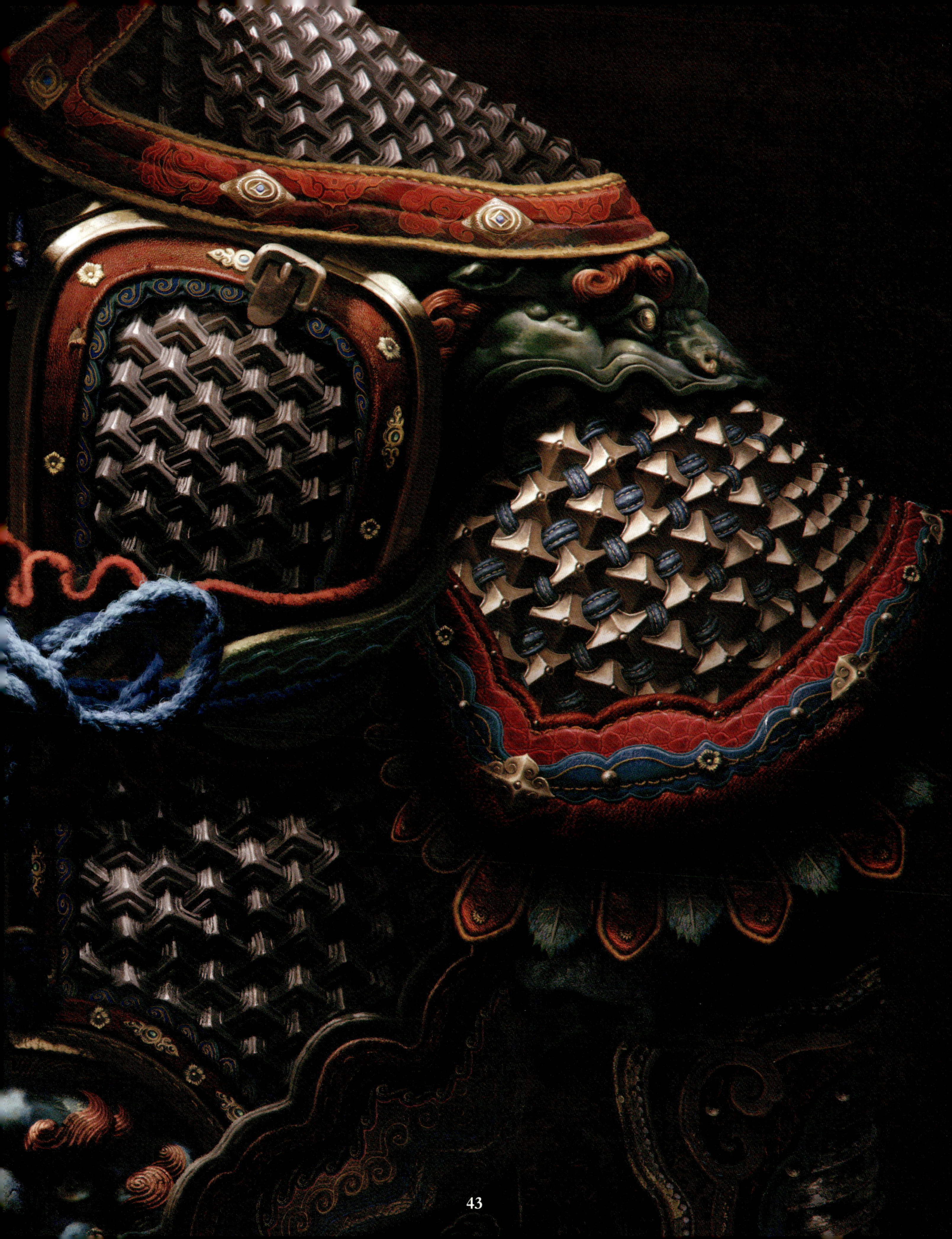

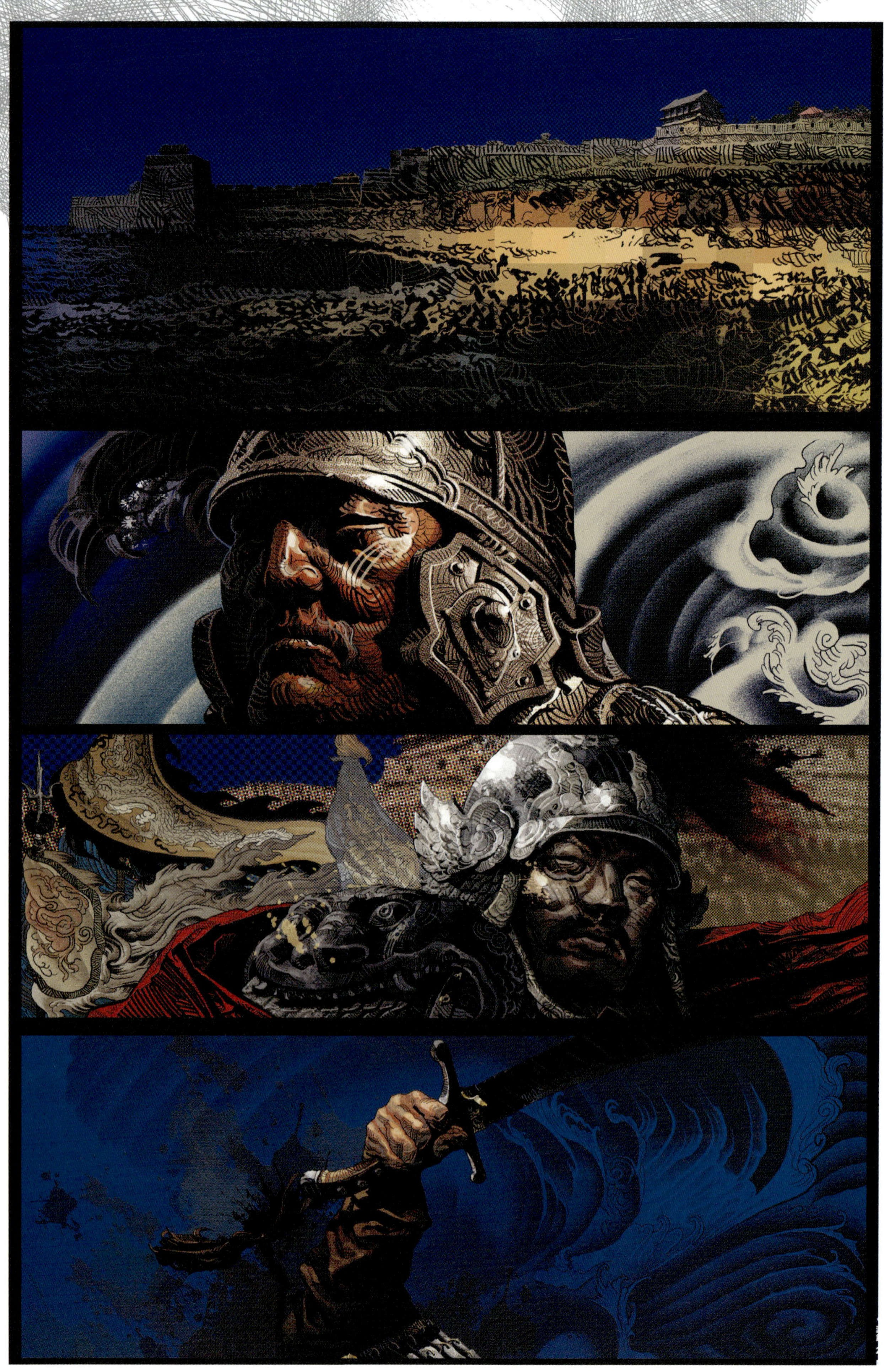

Millennium, page 1 and 2 of the comic, 2008.
Graphic design in Photoshop.

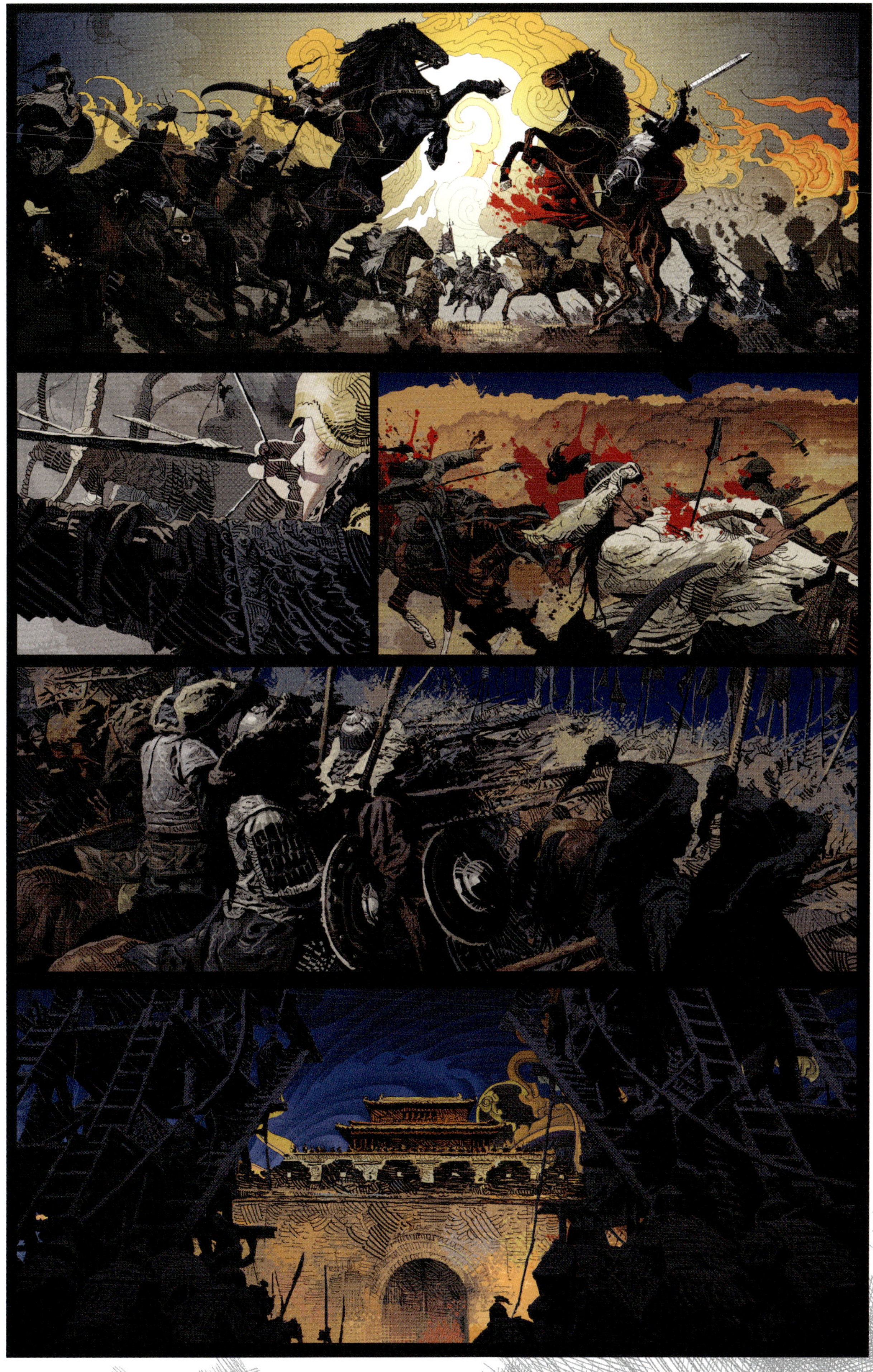

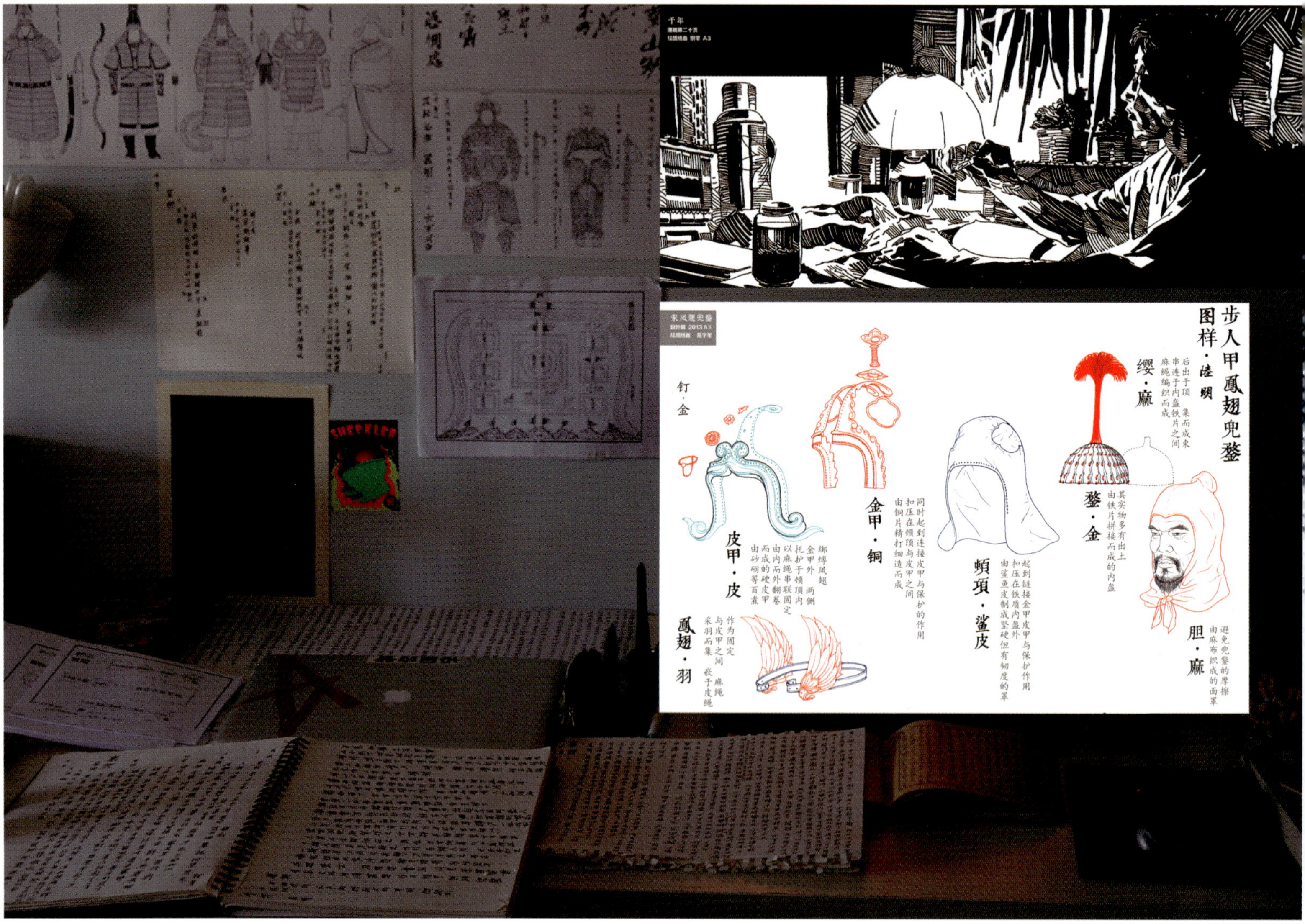

Armor and costume studies for the book *Millennium*. Small scale drawings, pen on paper.

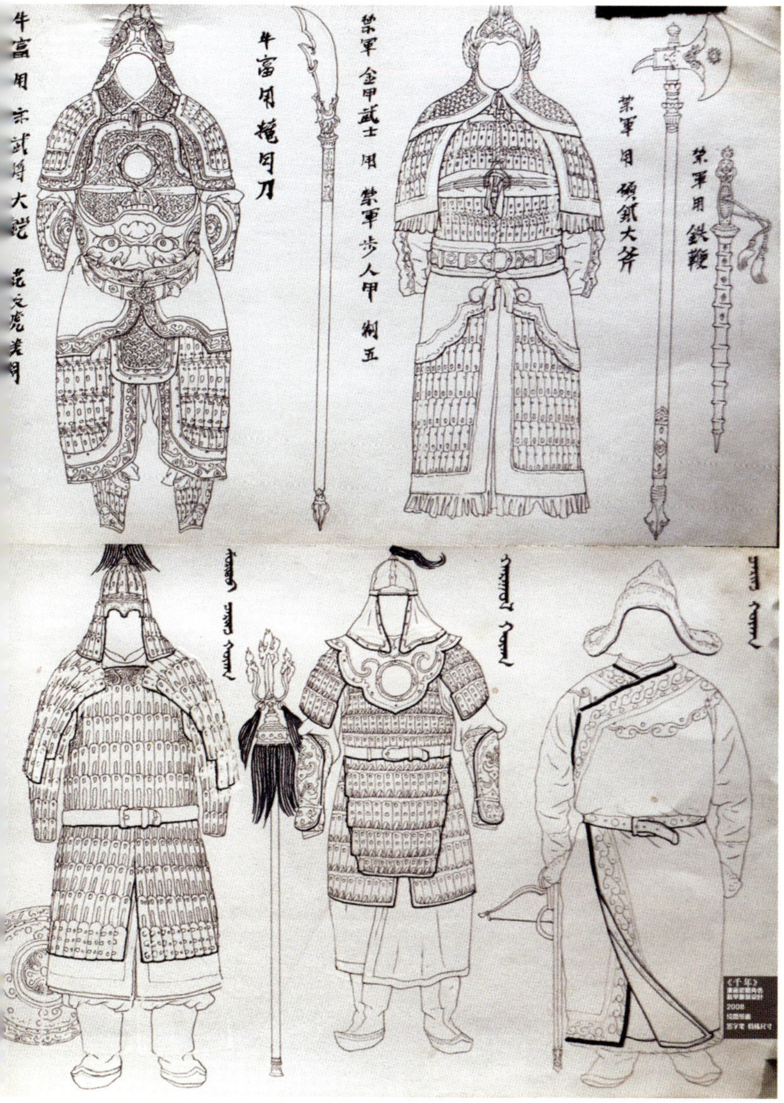

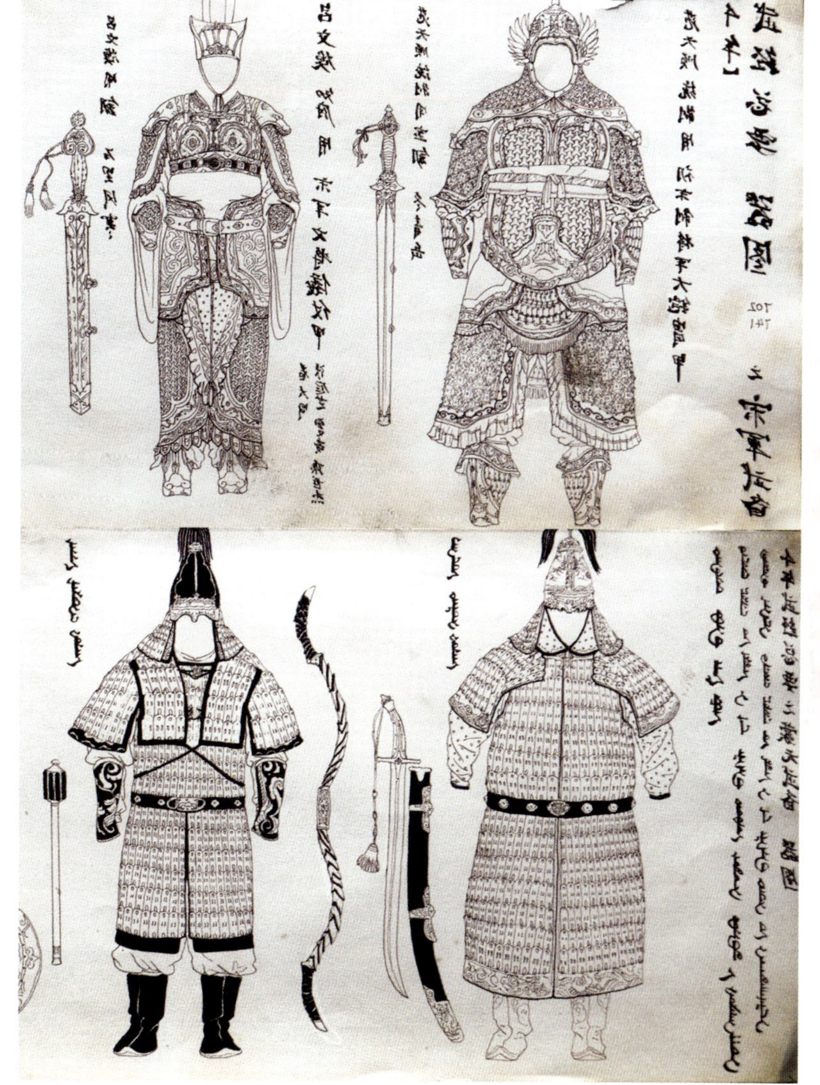

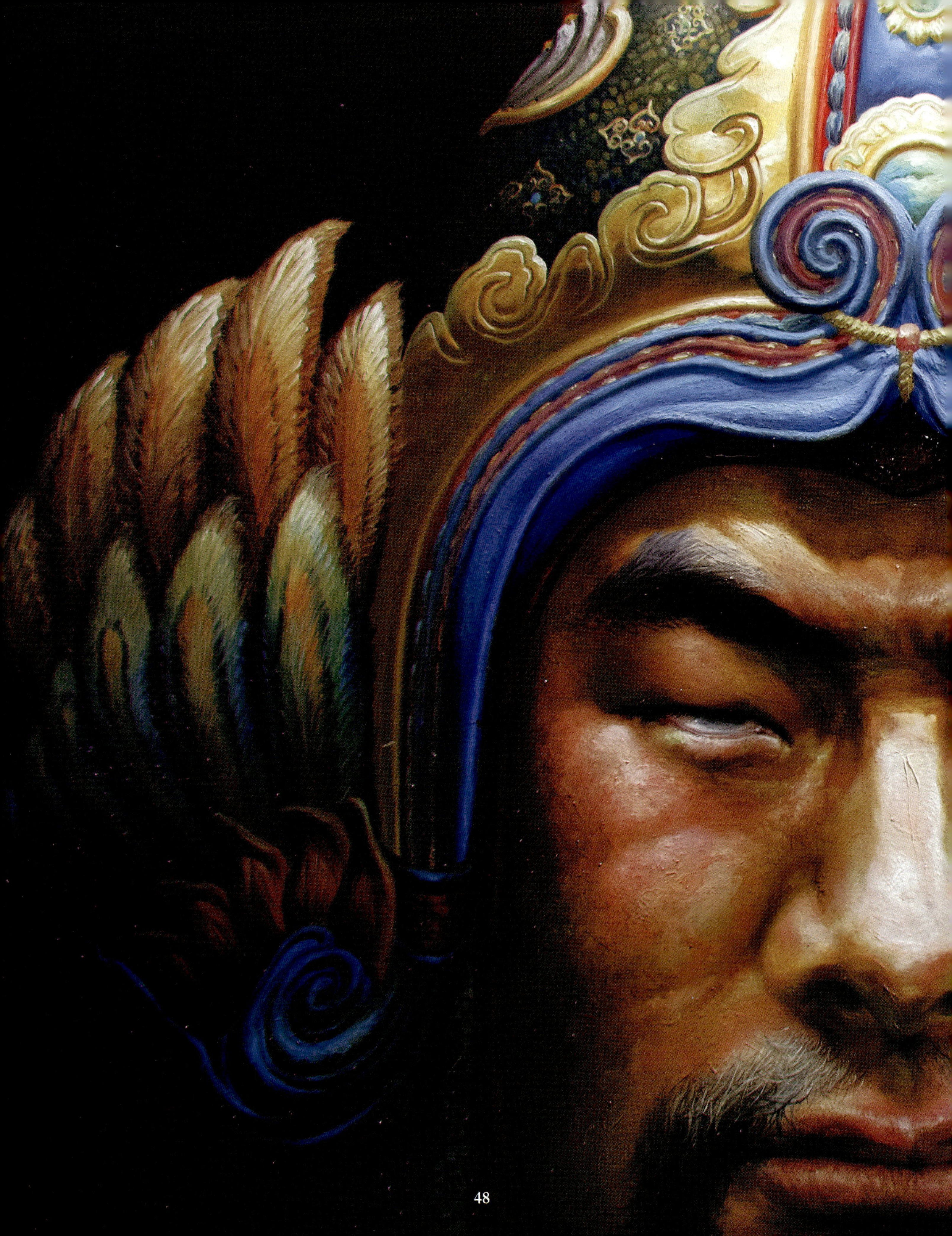

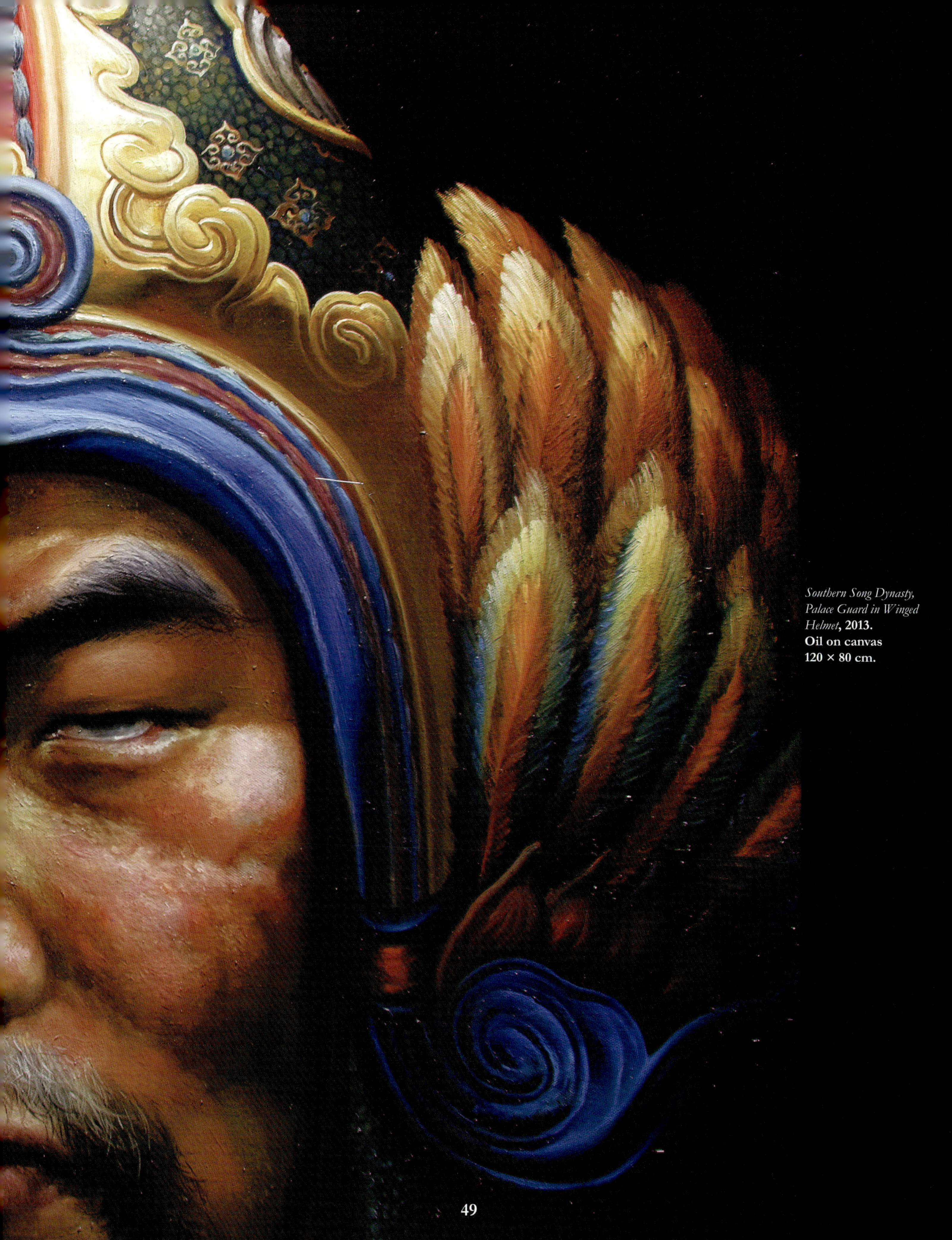

*Southern Song Dynasty,
Palace Guard in Winged
Helmet*, **2013.
Oil on canvas
120 × 80 cm.**

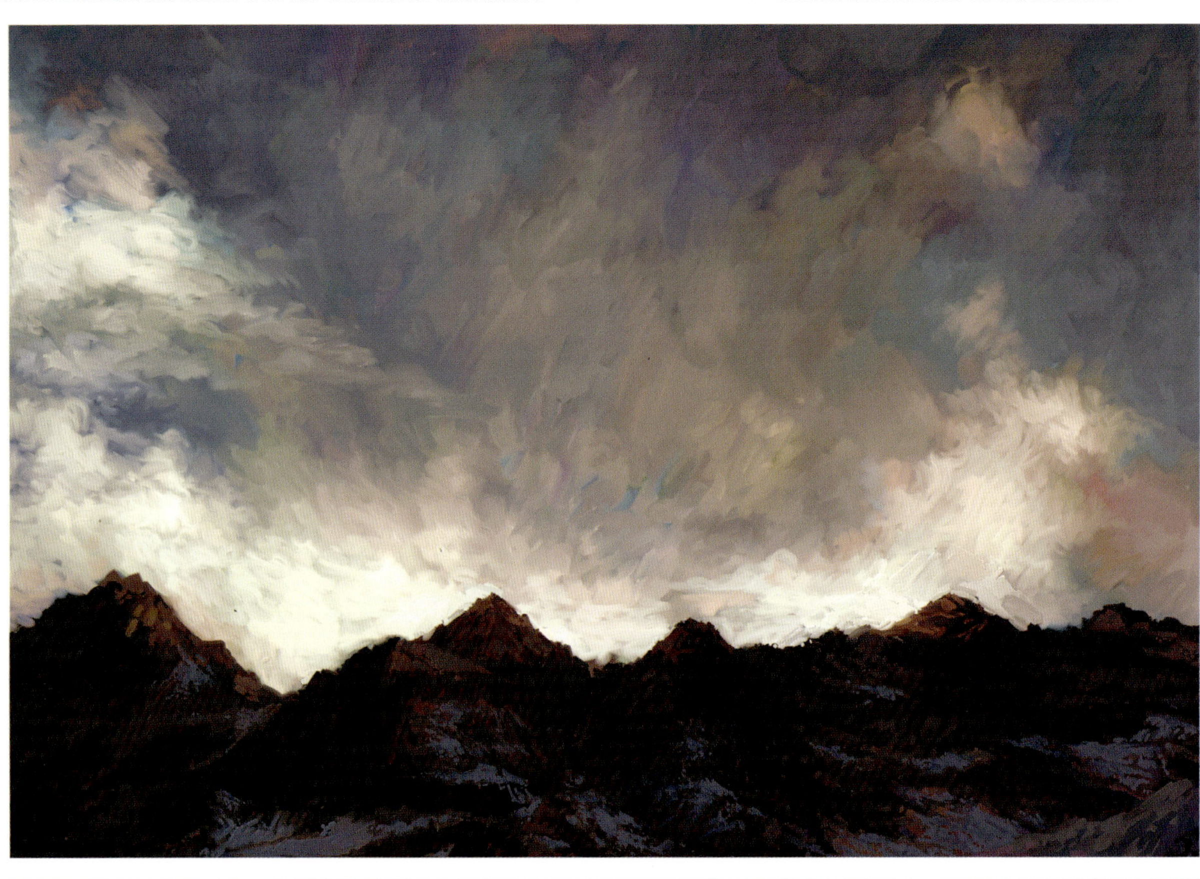

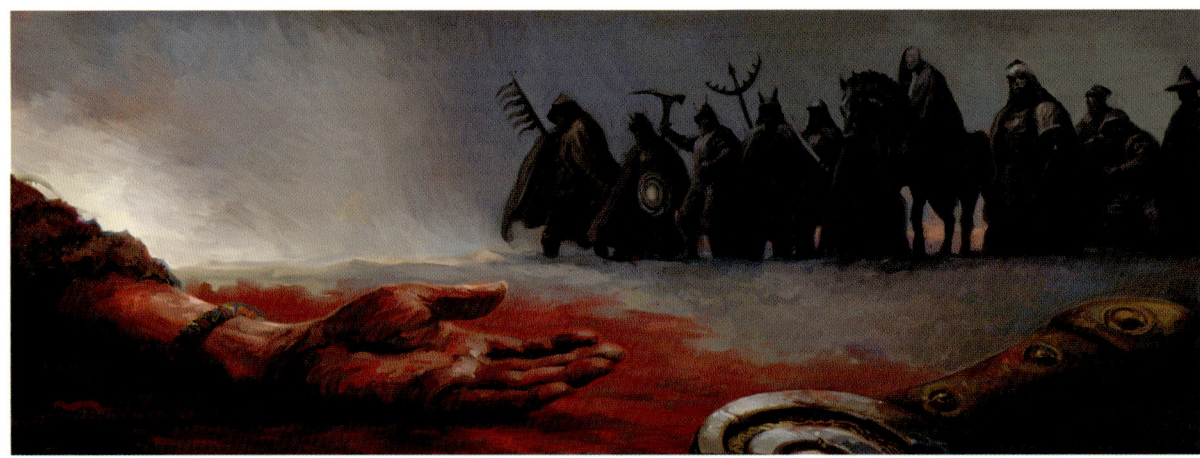

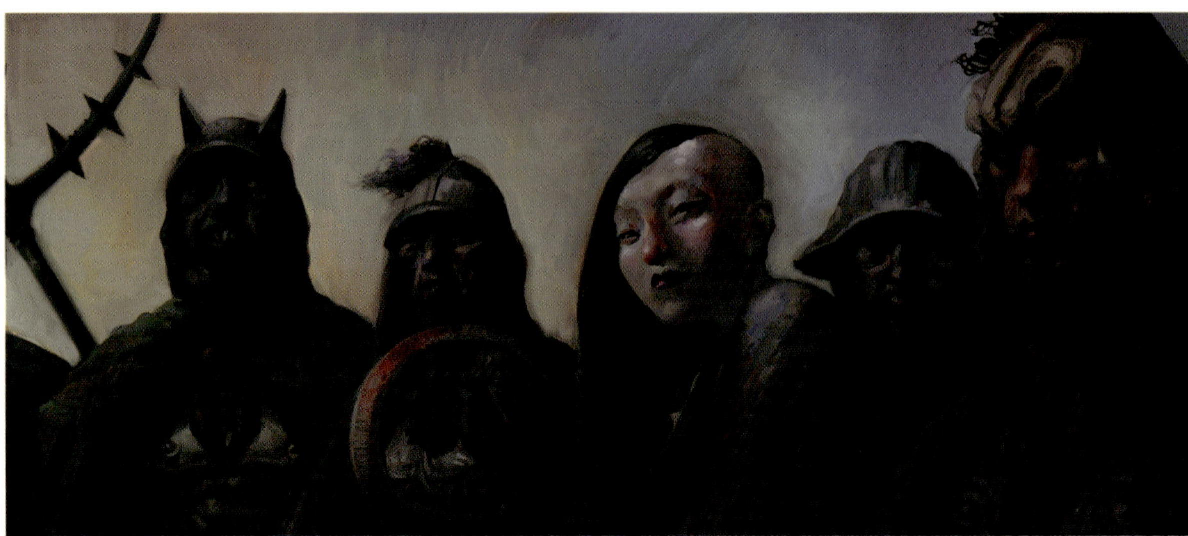

Comic adaptation of the film *Seven Swords*, pages 1 and 2, 2005. Composition and finalization in Painter.

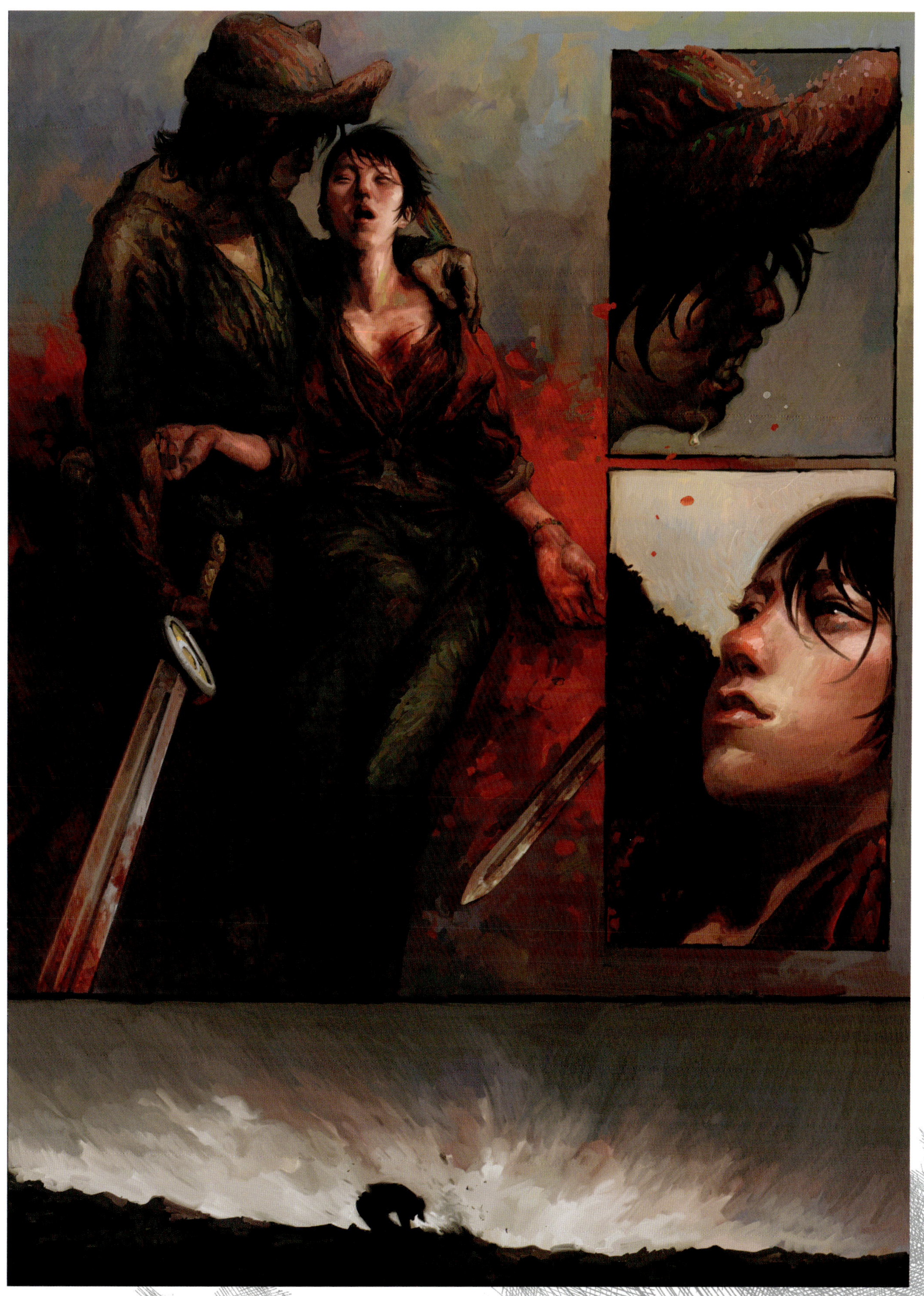

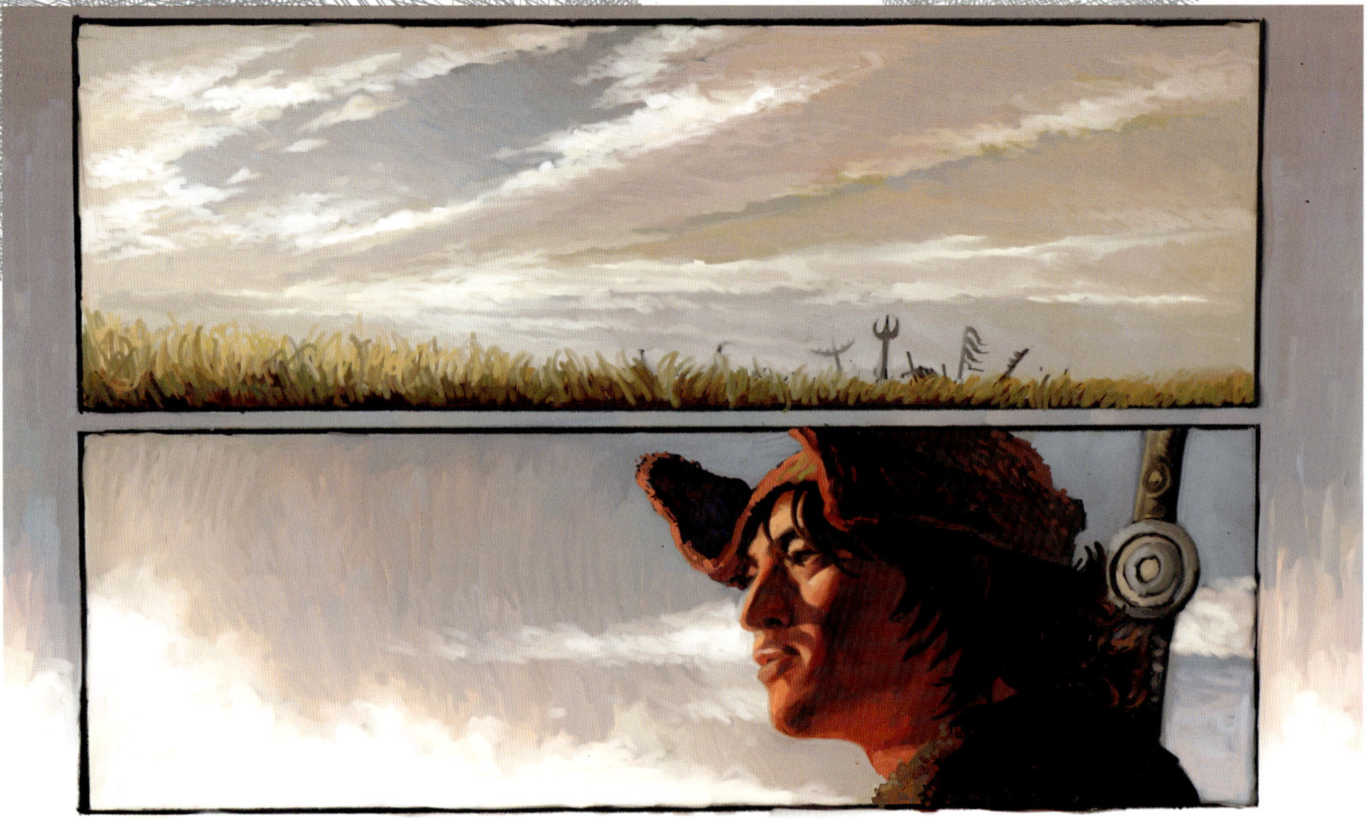

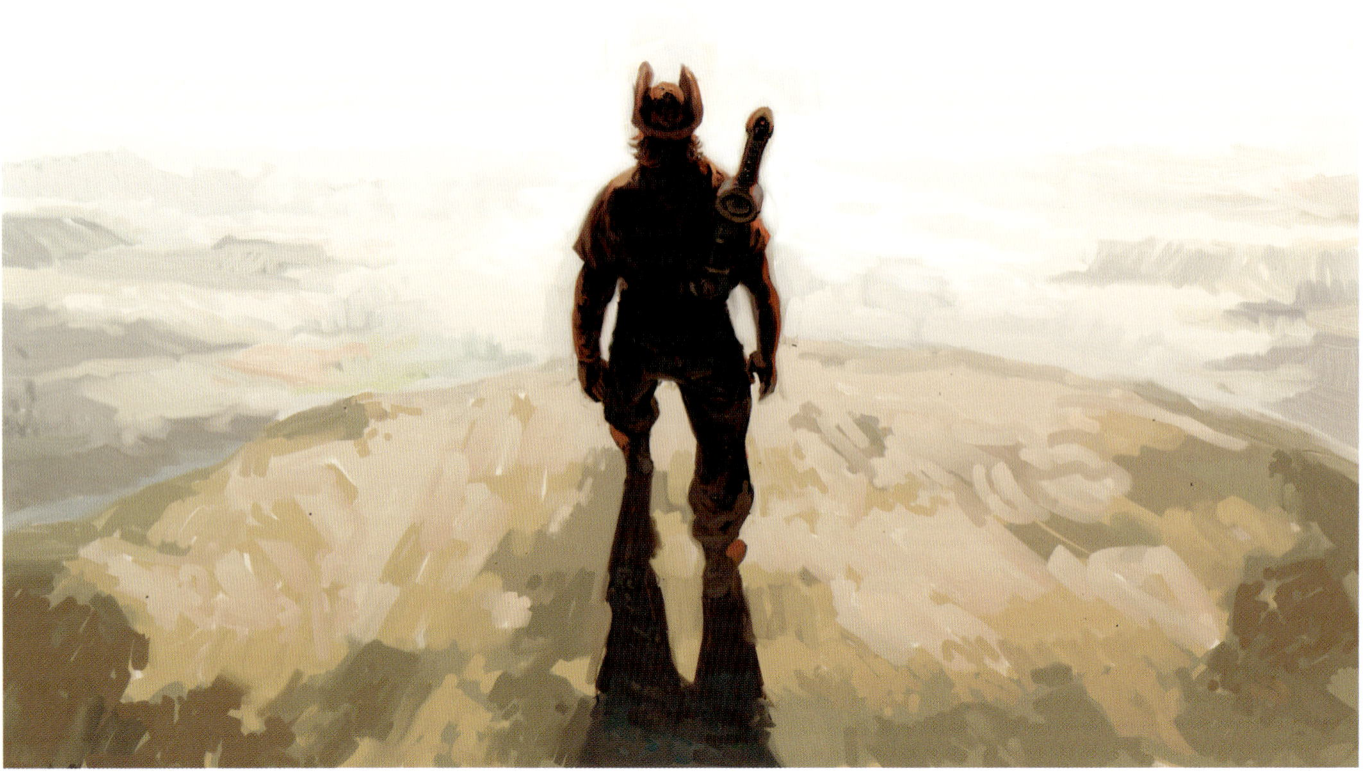

Comic adaptation of the film *Seven Swords*, pages 5 and 6, 2005. Composition and finalization in Painter.

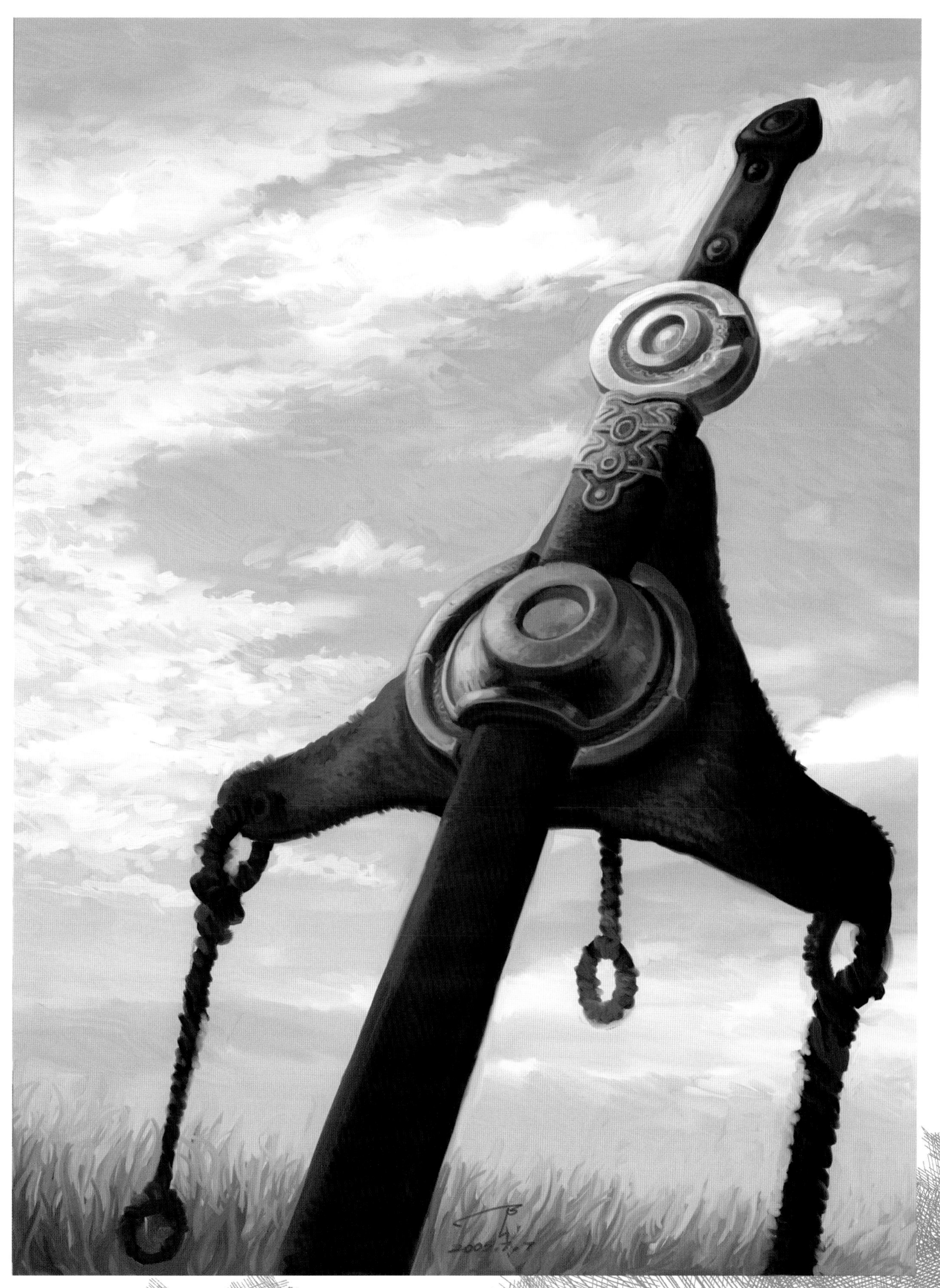

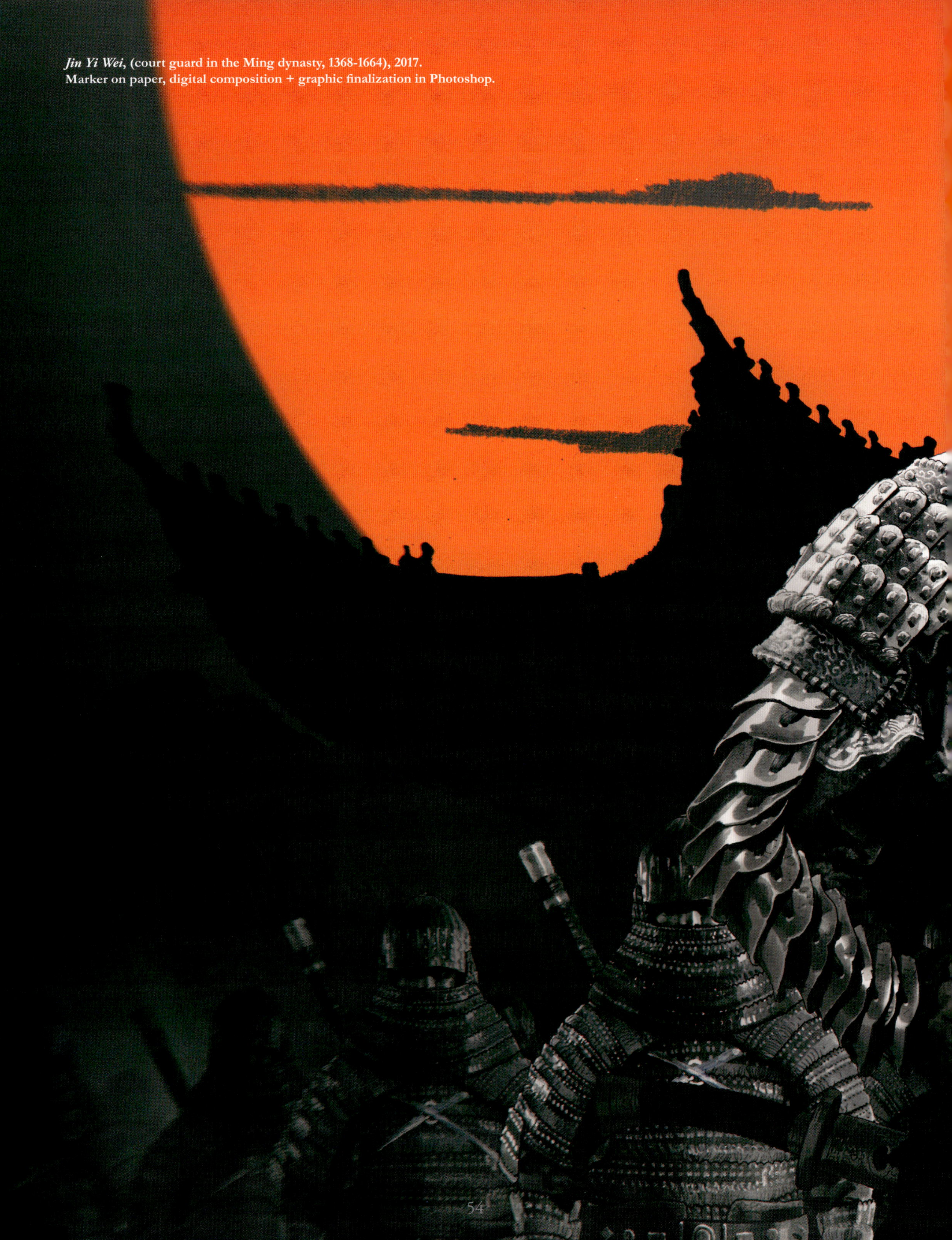

Jin Yi Wei, (court guard in the Ming dynasty, 1368-1664), 2017.
Marker on paper, digital composition + graphic finalization in Photoshop.

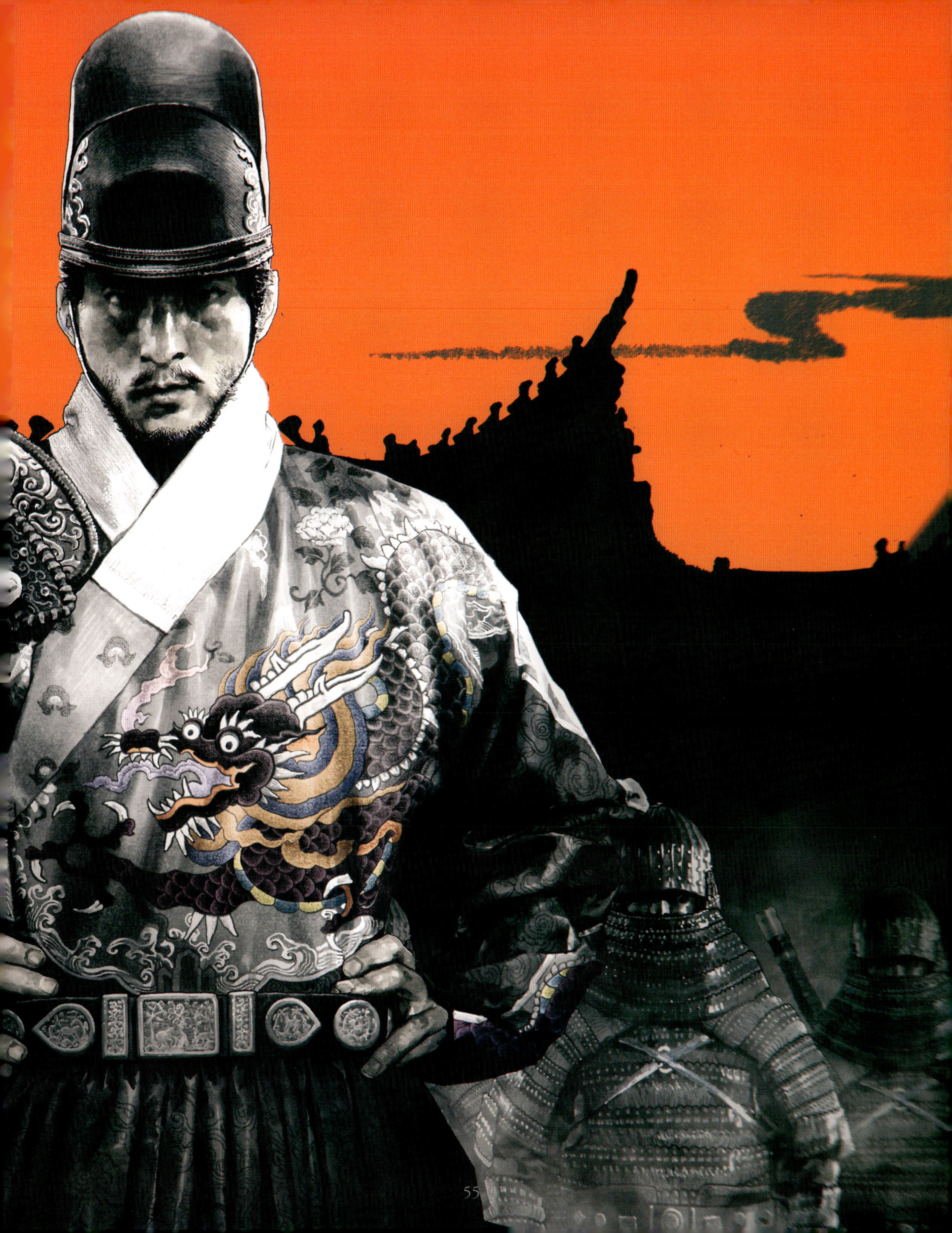

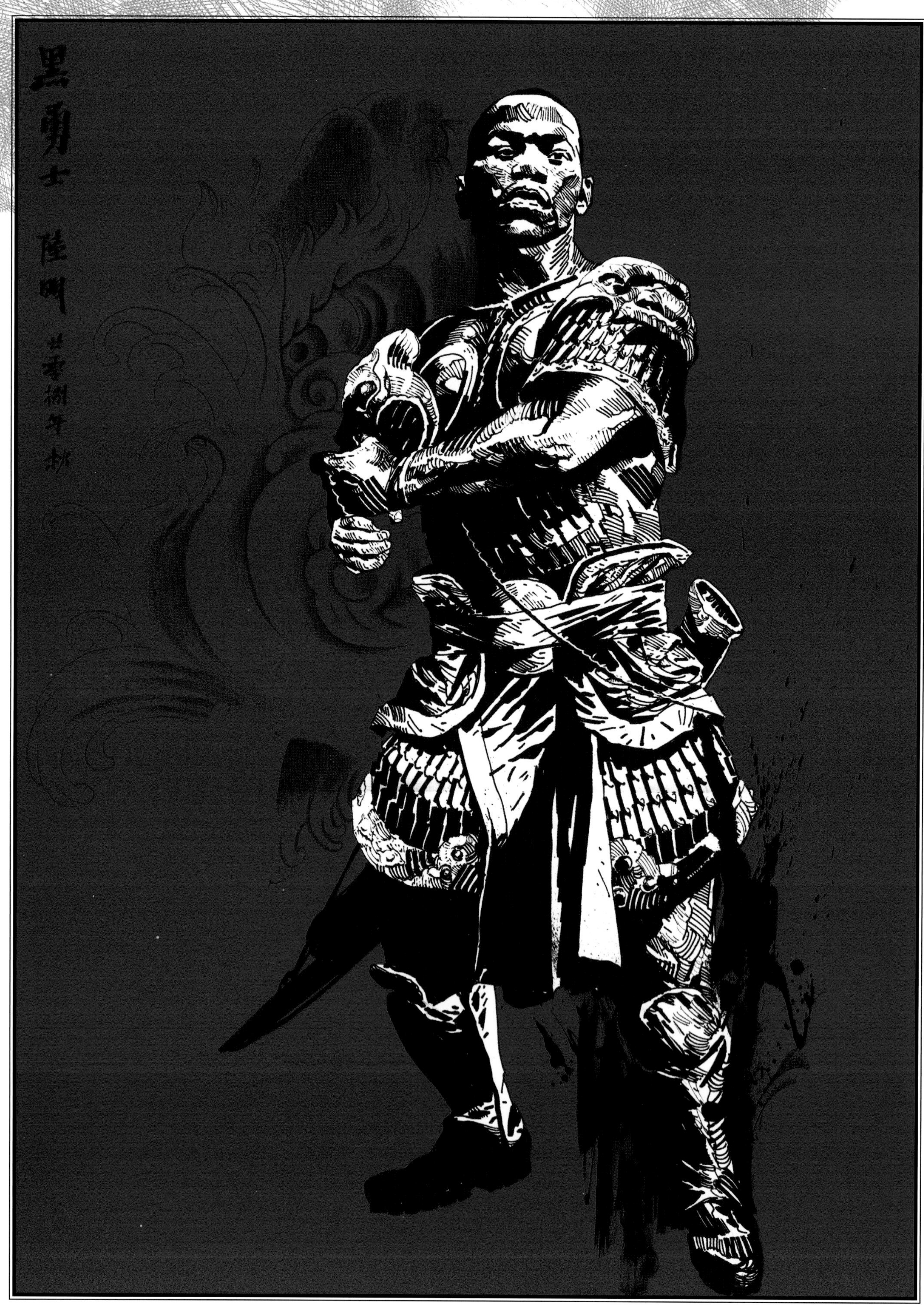

Black Warrior, 2008. Ink pen on paper,
digital composition + graphic finalization in Photoshop.

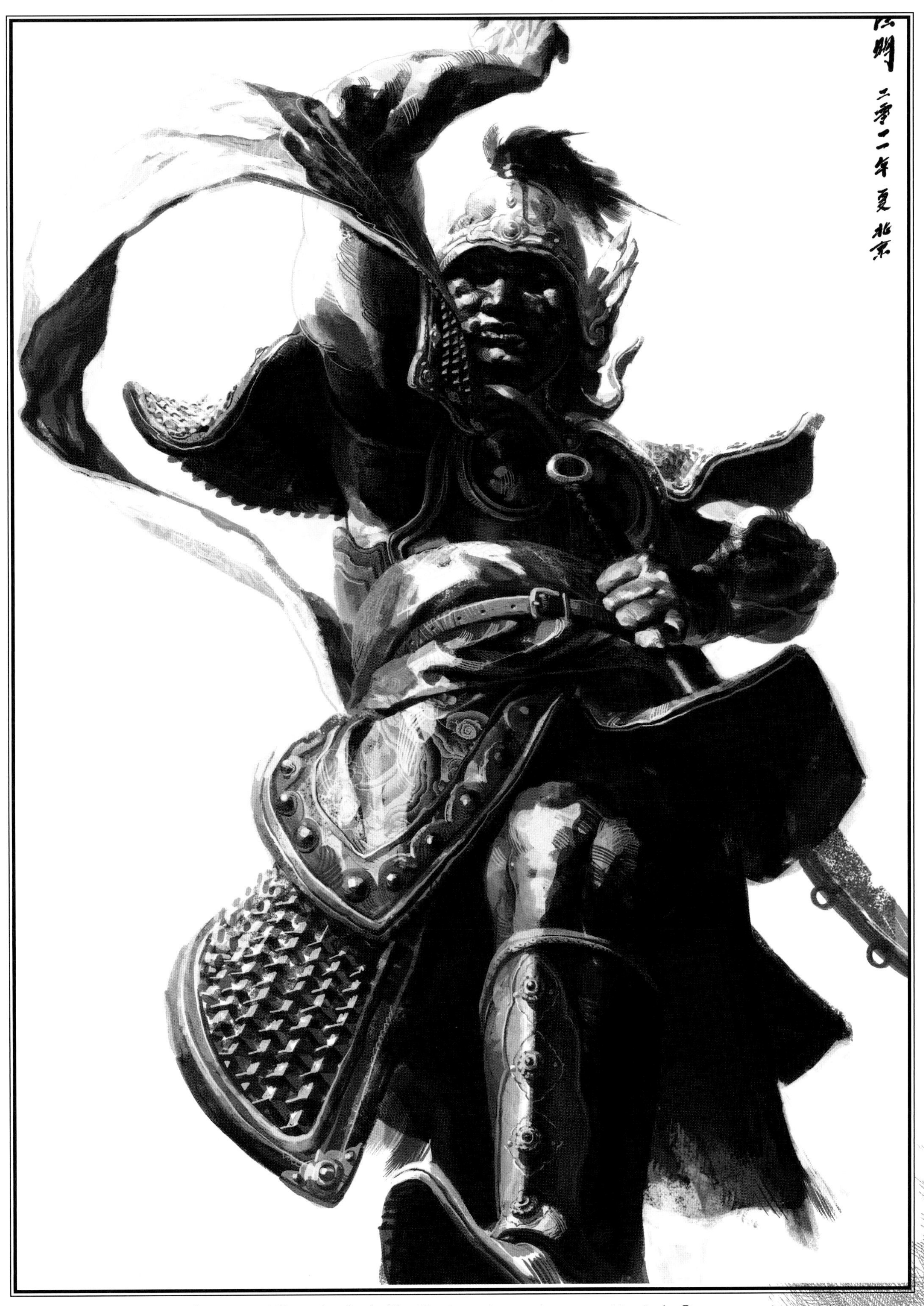

Tang Dynasty Warrior, 2011. Greeting card illustration for the TangComic comic magazine, composition in Art Rage.

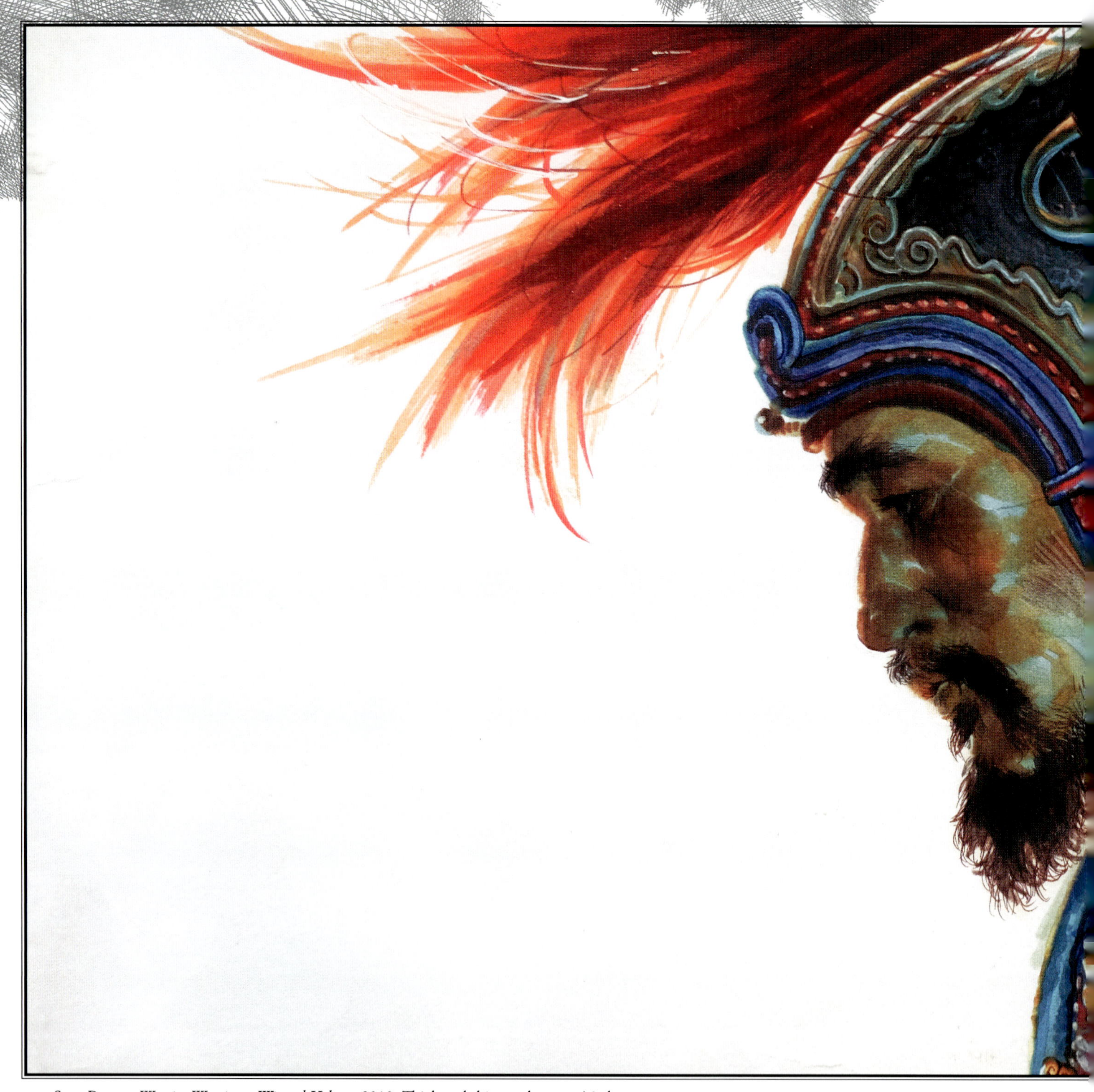

Song Dynasty Warrior Wearing a Winged Helmet, 2010. Thick and thin markers on A3 sheet.

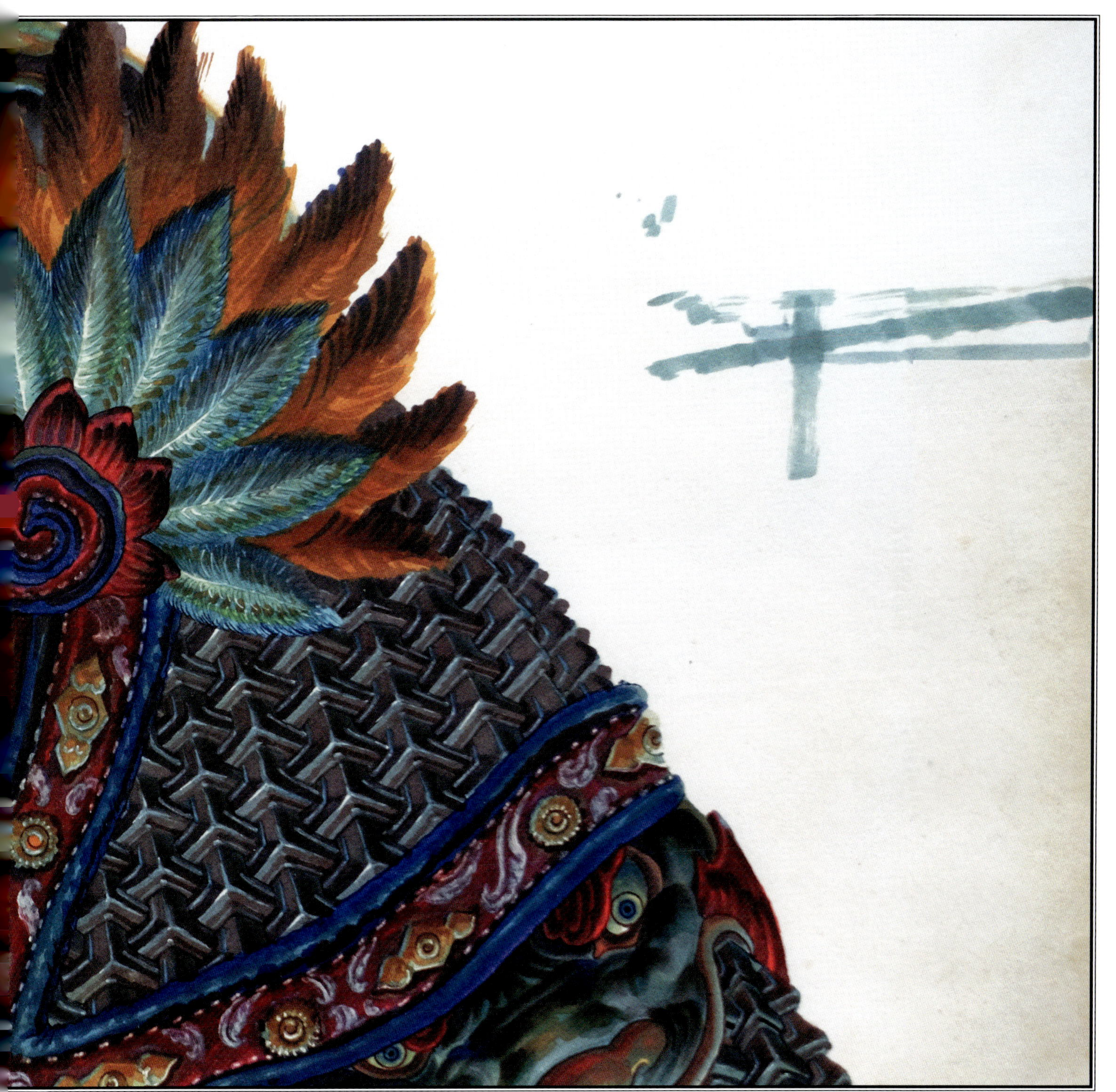

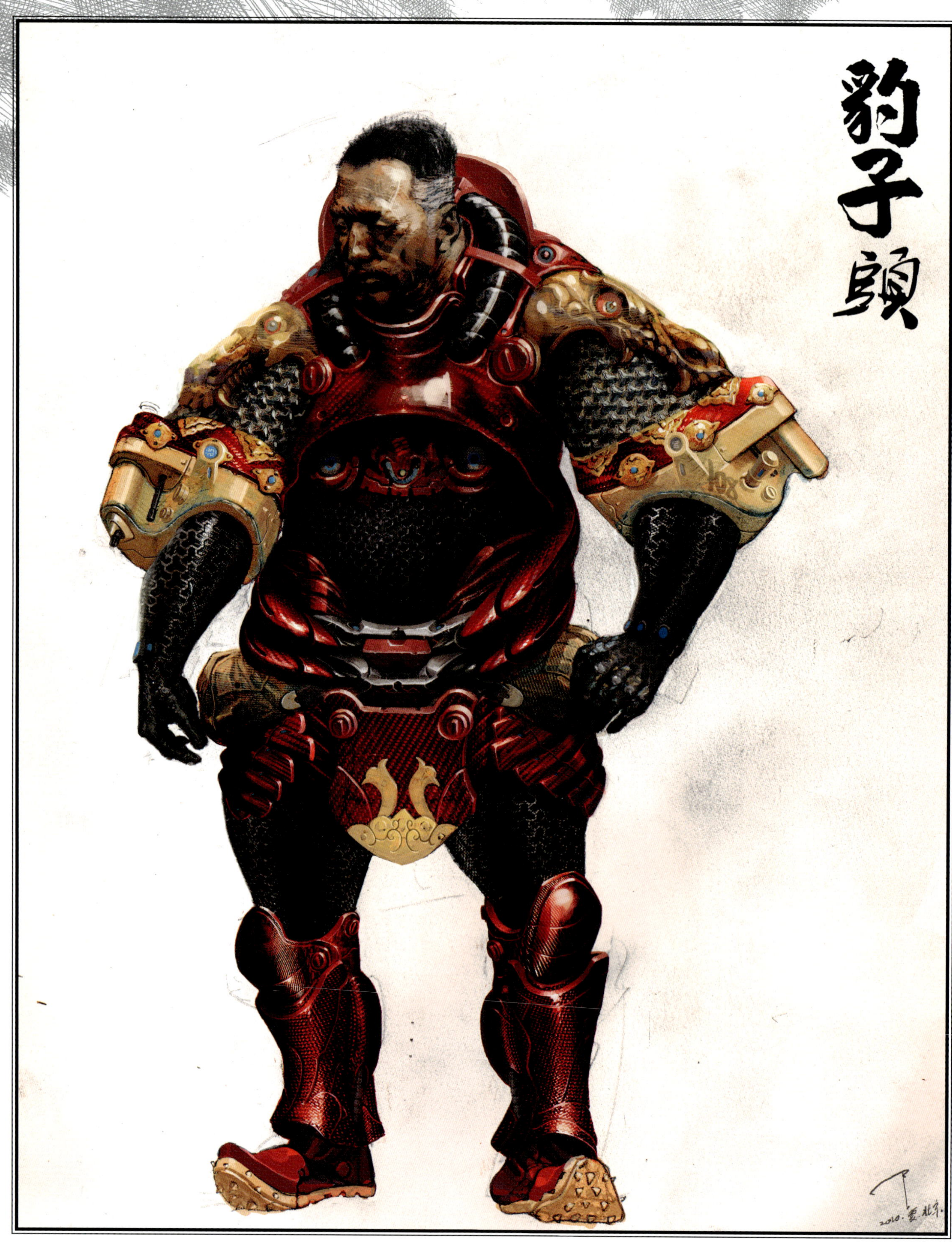

Lin Chong, "108" Design, 2010, ink pen on paper, digital composition and finalization in Photoshop.

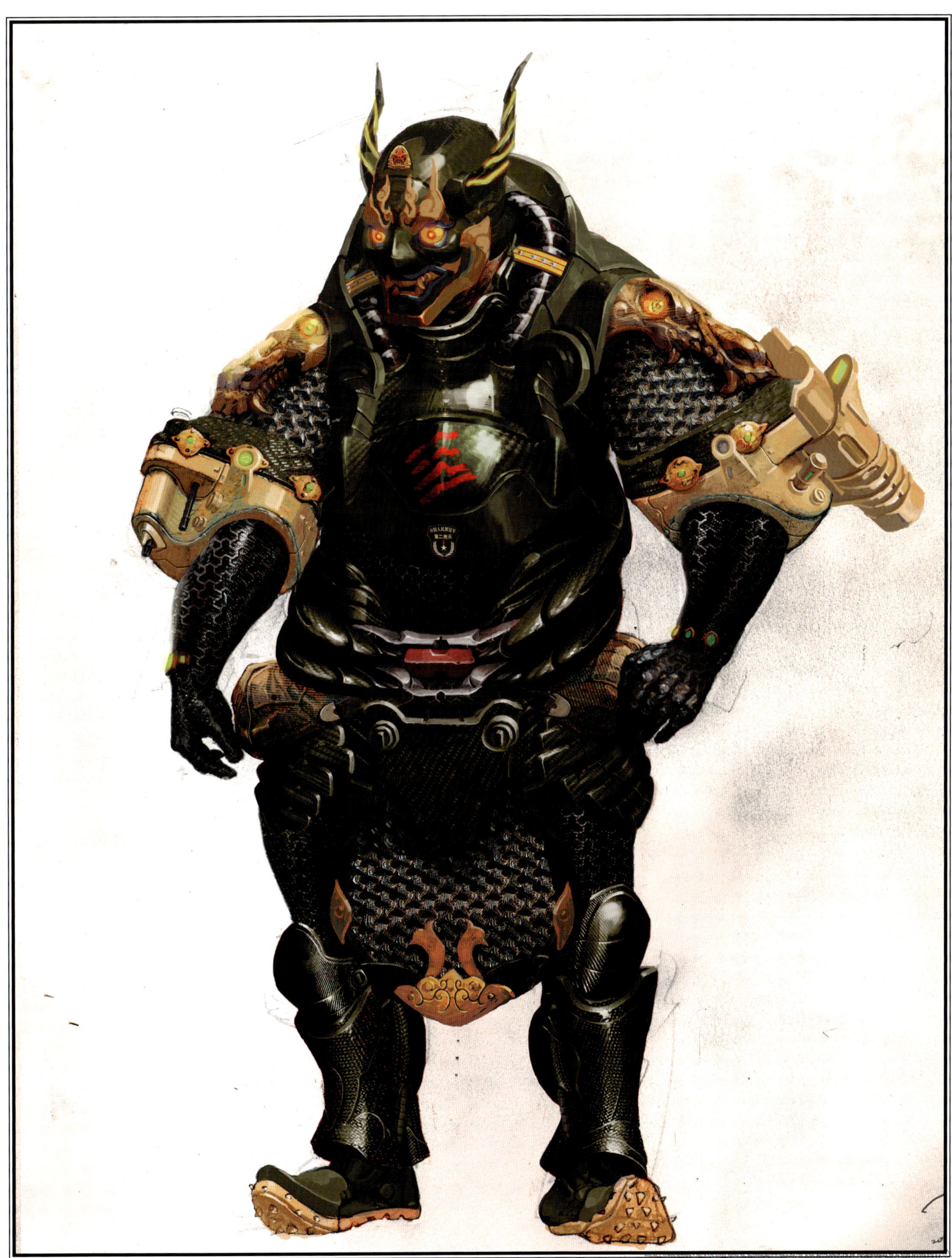

Baozi Tou, "108" Design, 2010, ink pen on paper, digital composition and Photoshop finalization.

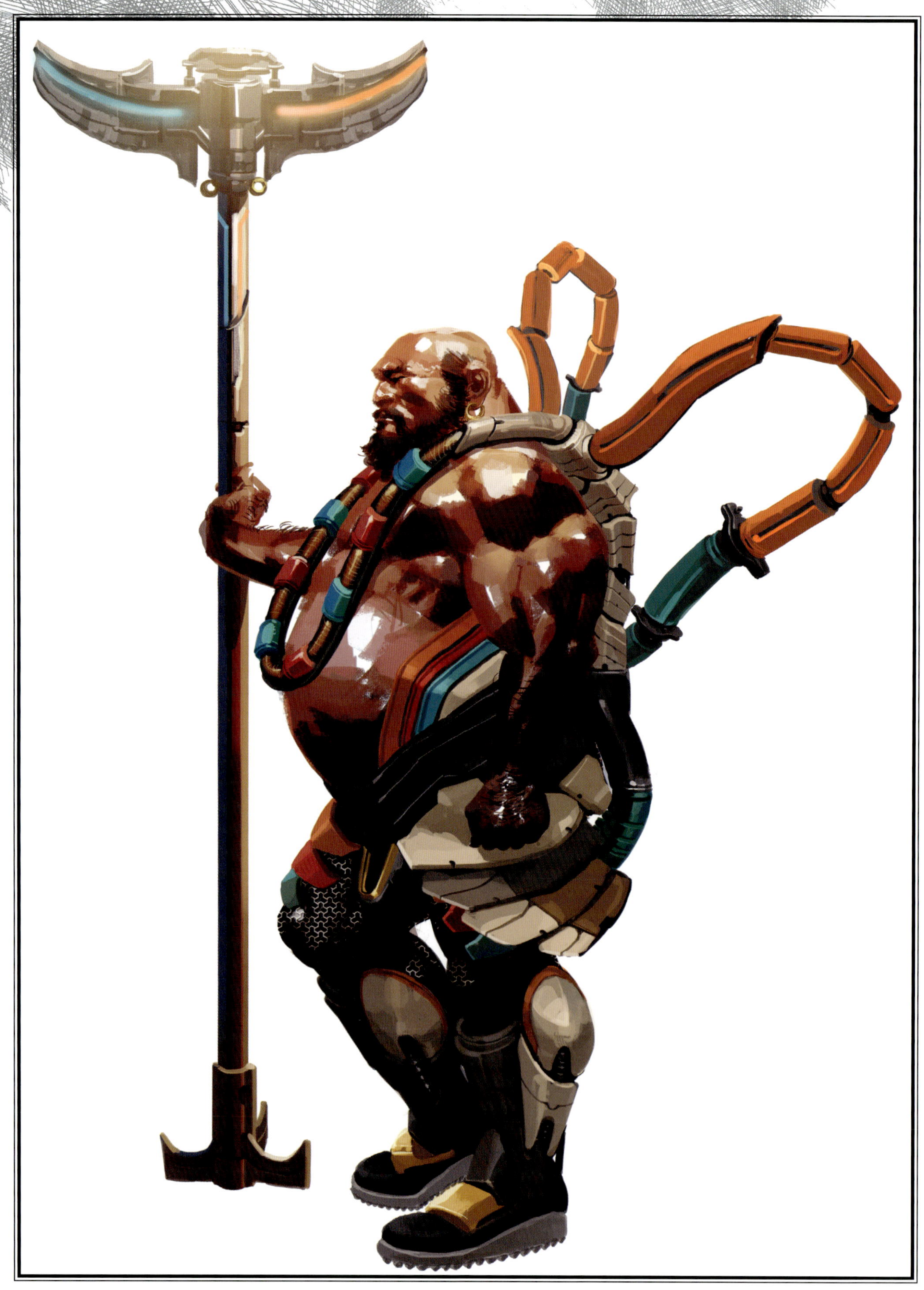

Hua He Shang, "108" Design, 2010, ink pen on paper, digital composition and Photoshop graphic finalization.

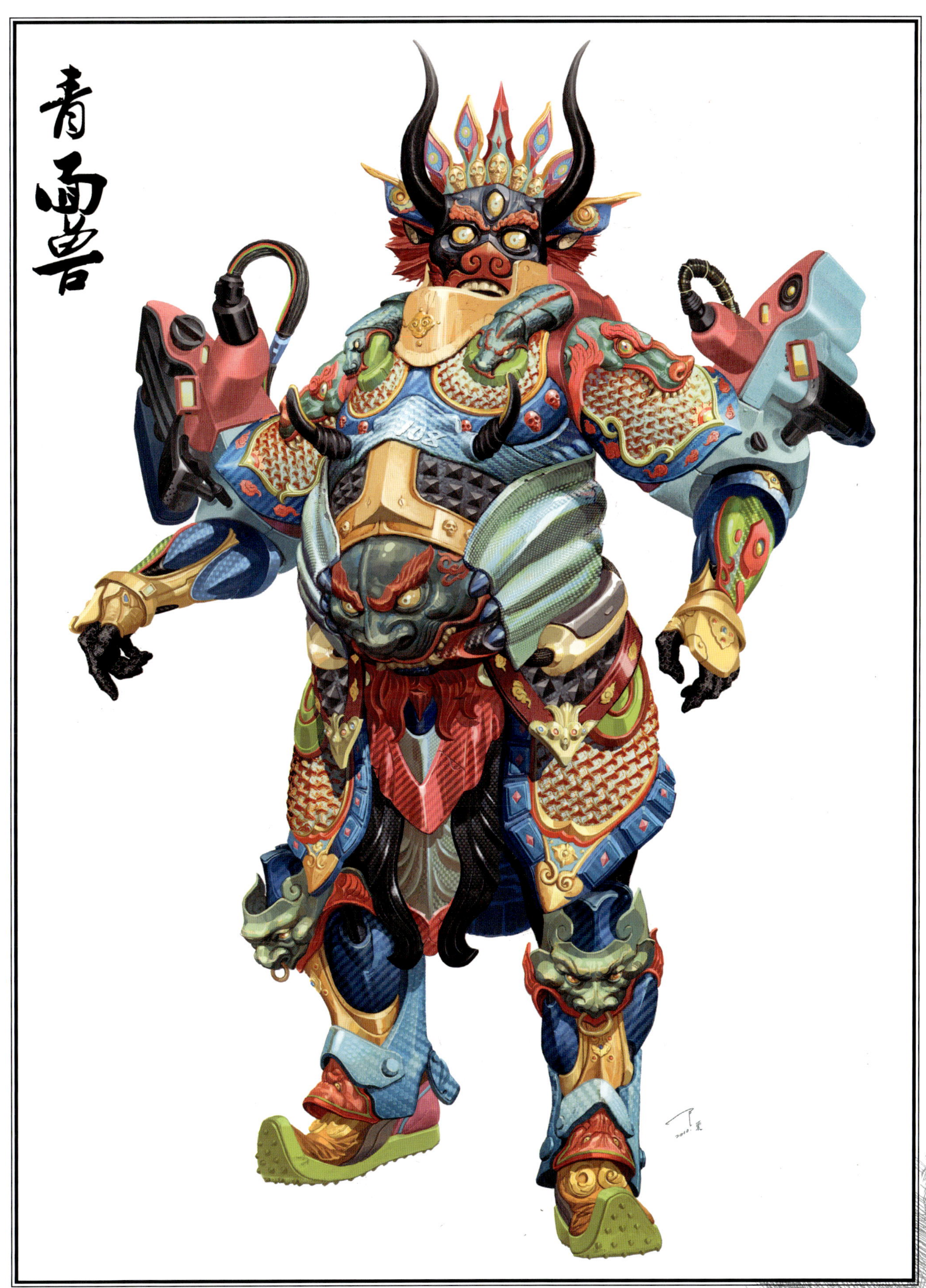

Qing Mian Shou, "108" Design, 2010, ink pen on paper, digital composition and Photoshop graphic finalization.

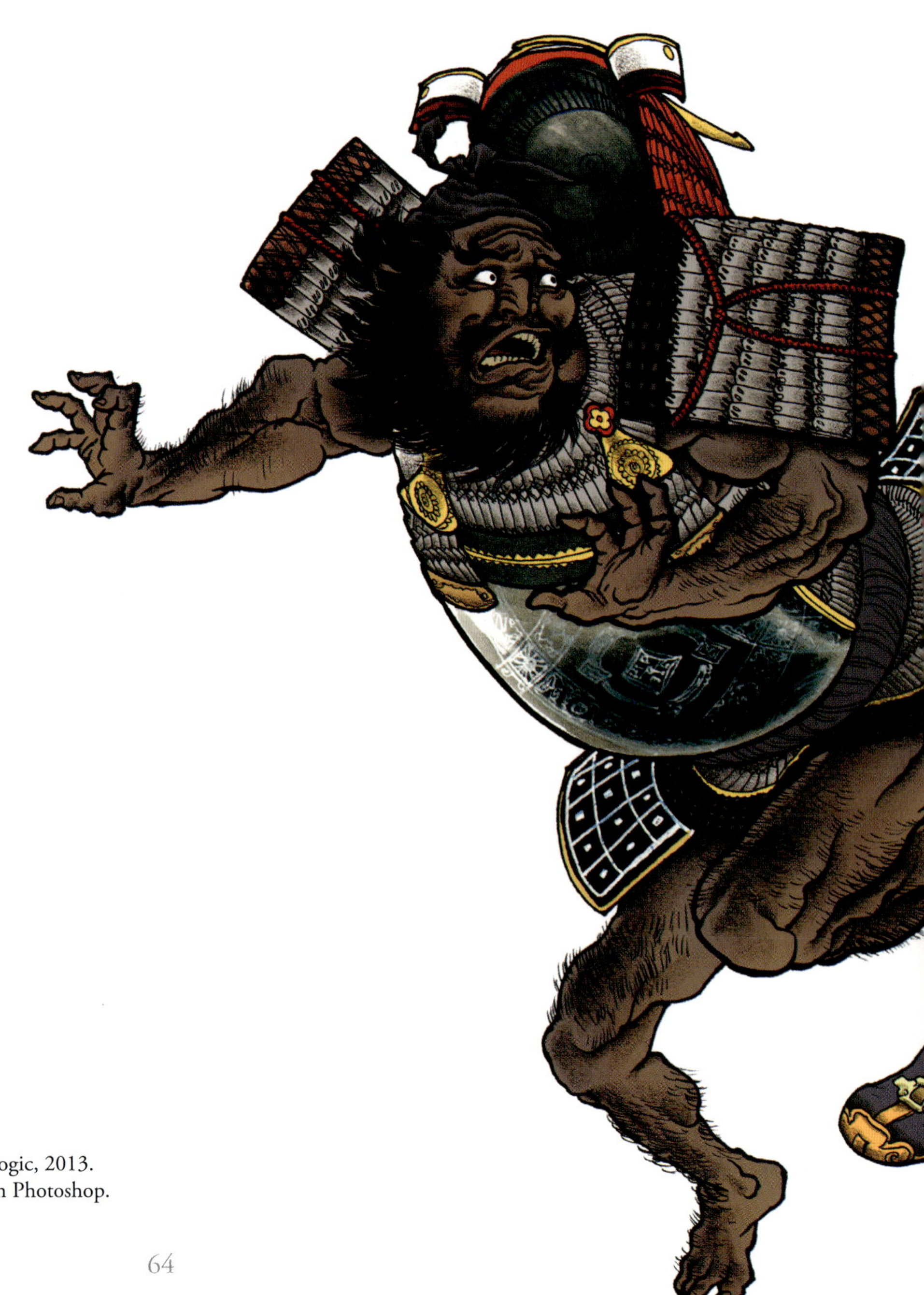

斬死鬼

Ax Demon, DVD cover for the group Lose Control of Logic, 2013.
Ink pen on paper, digital composition and finalization in Photoshop.

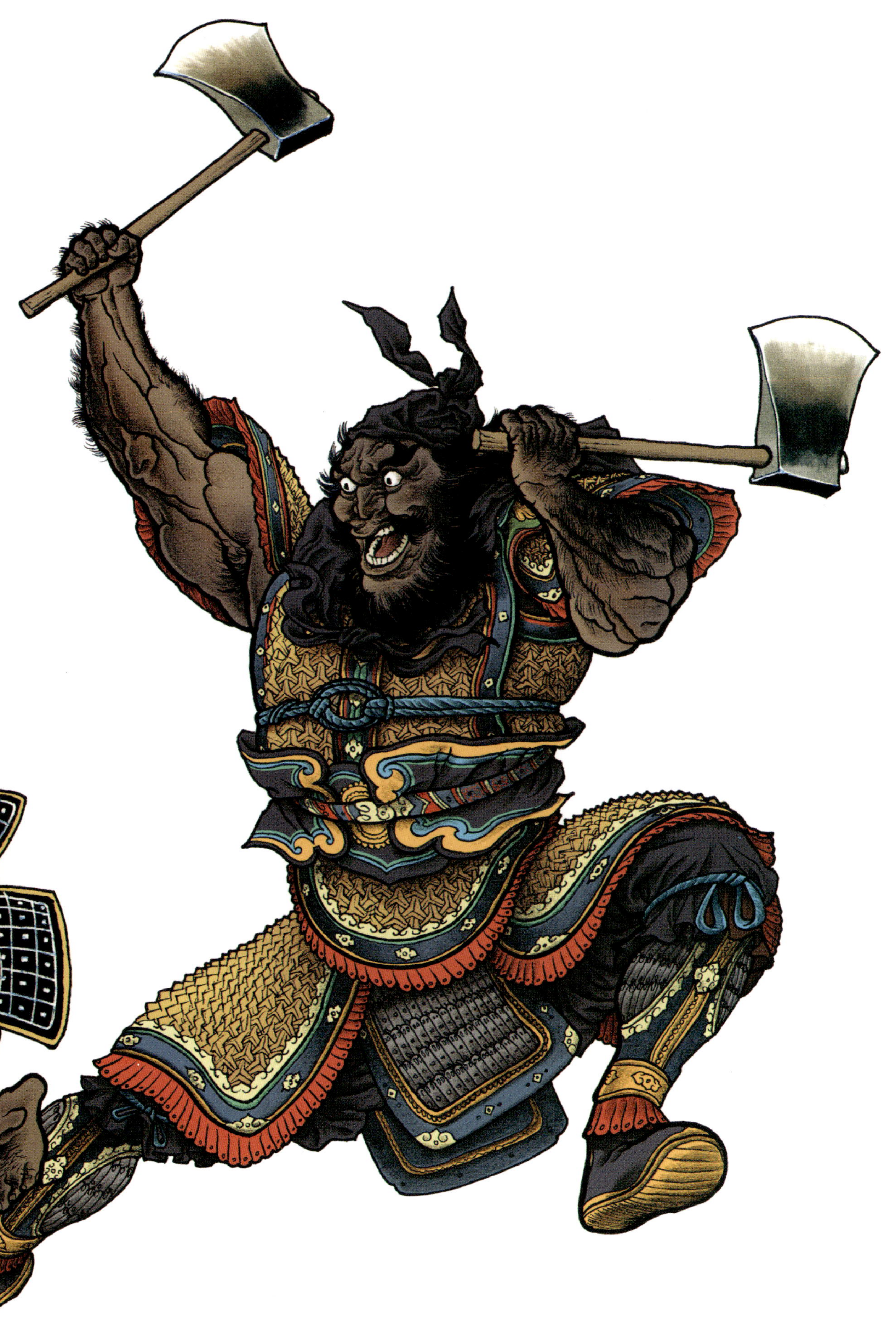

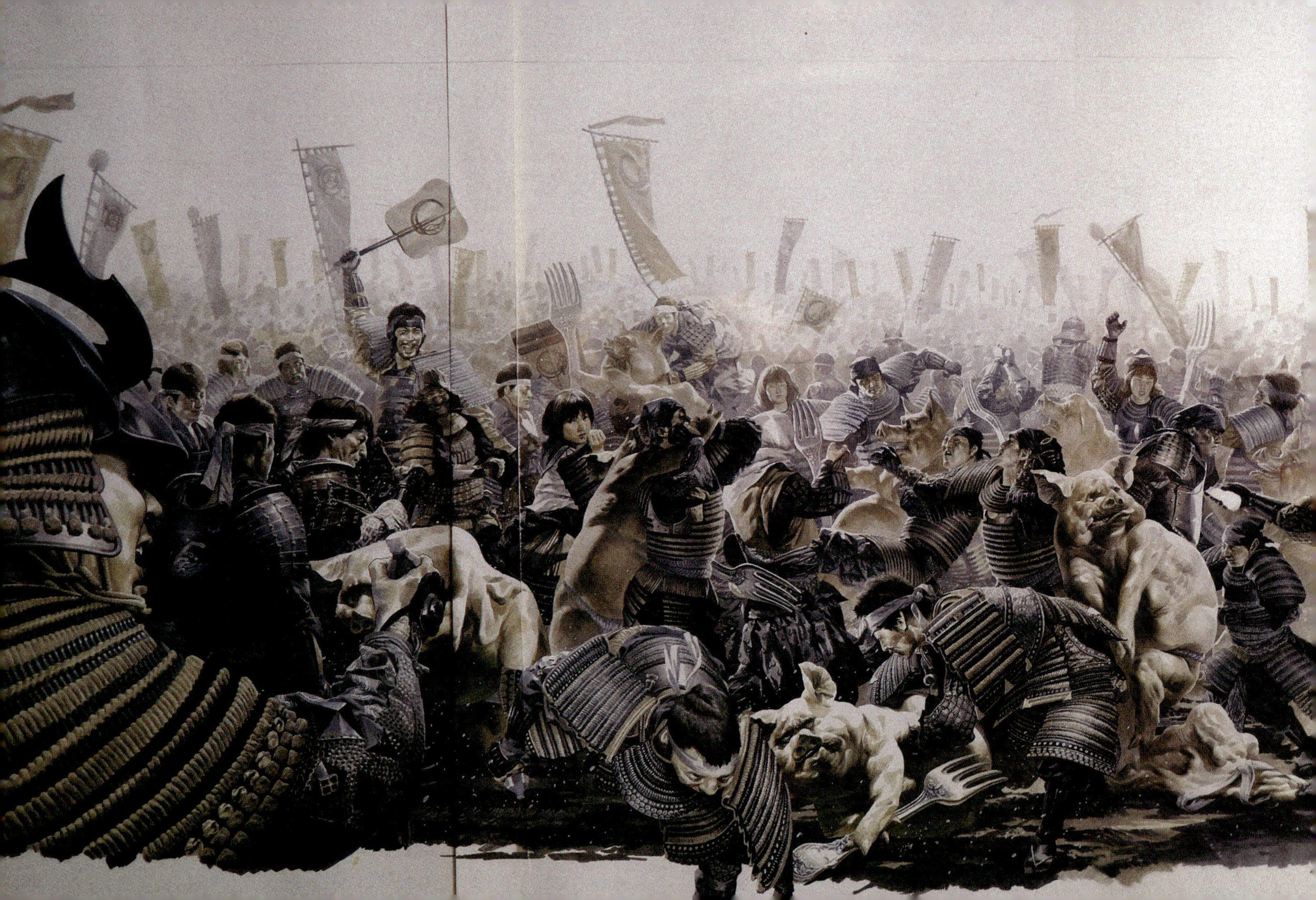

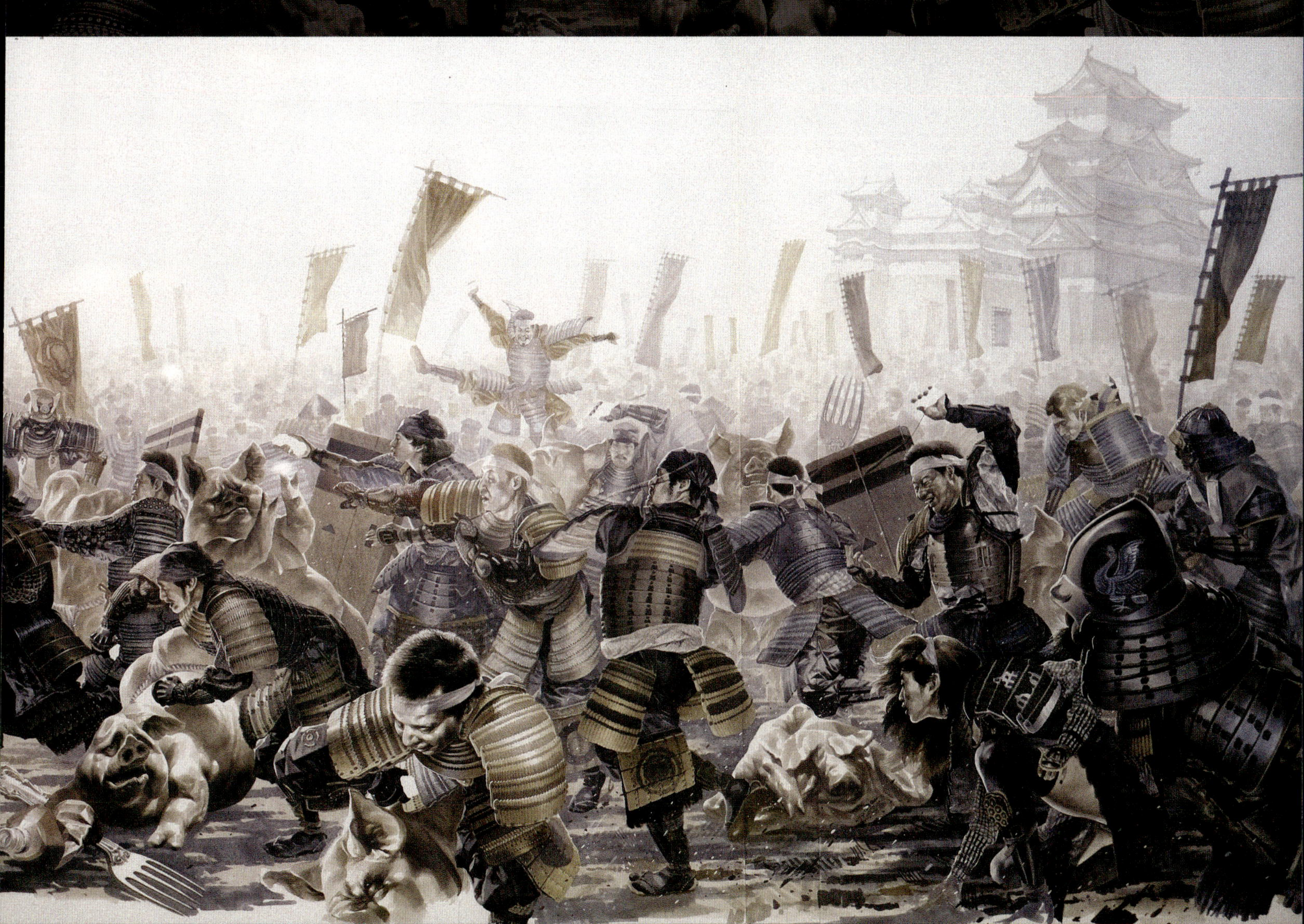

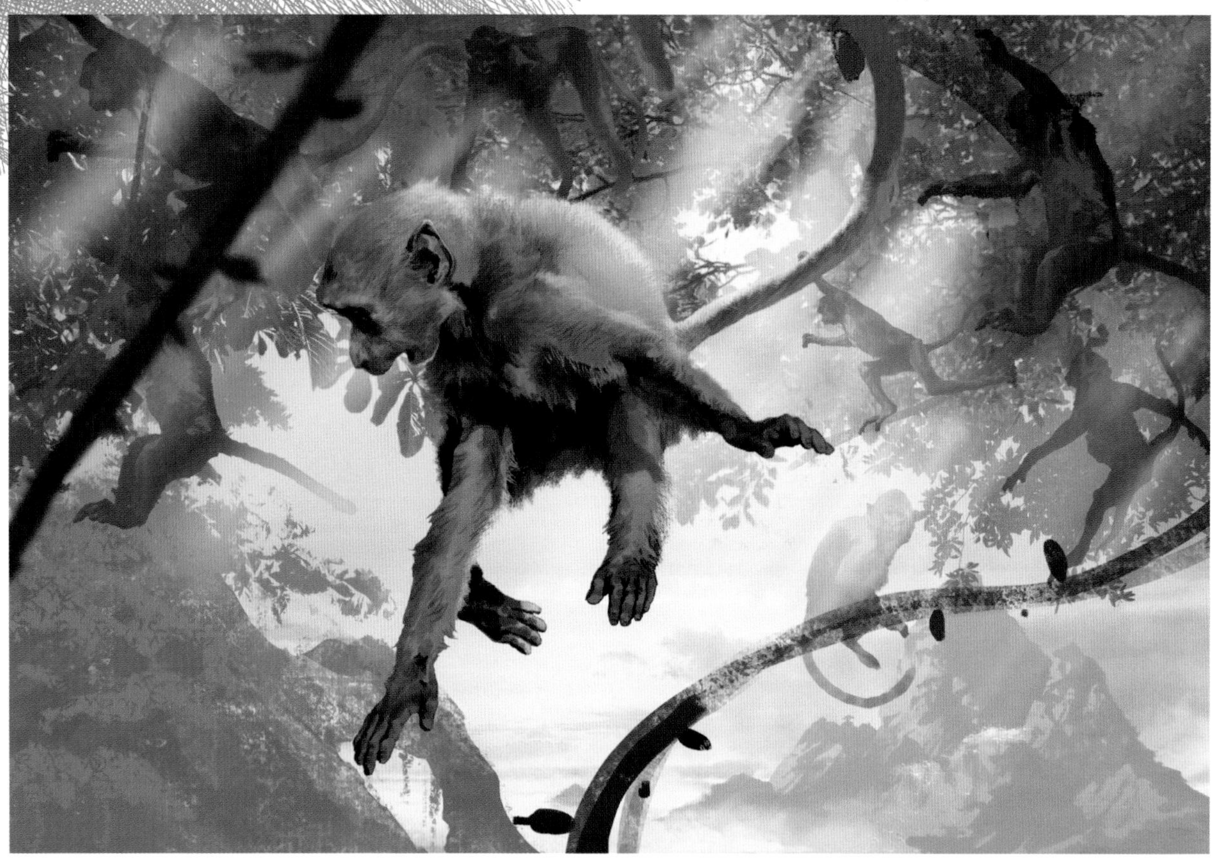

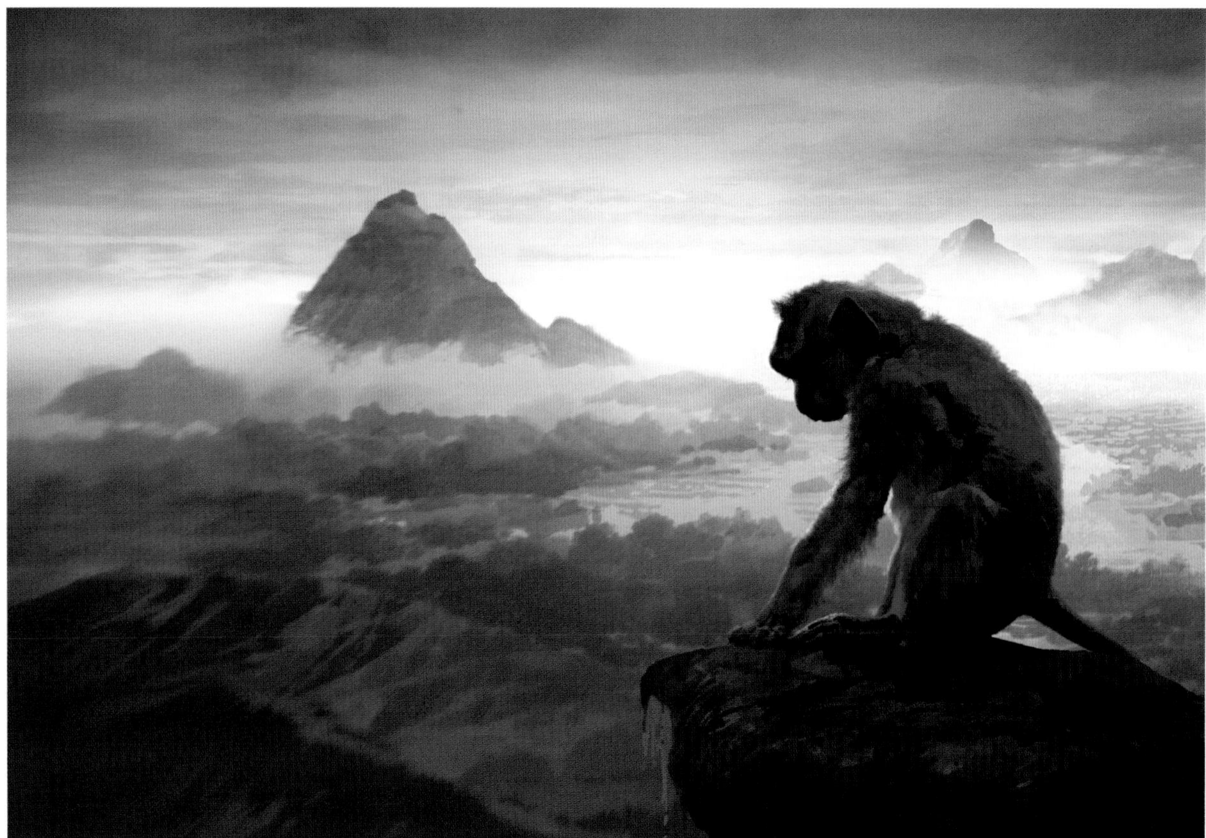

Conceptual images of the film *Xi You, Fu Yao Pian*, digital composition and graphic finalization in Photoshop.

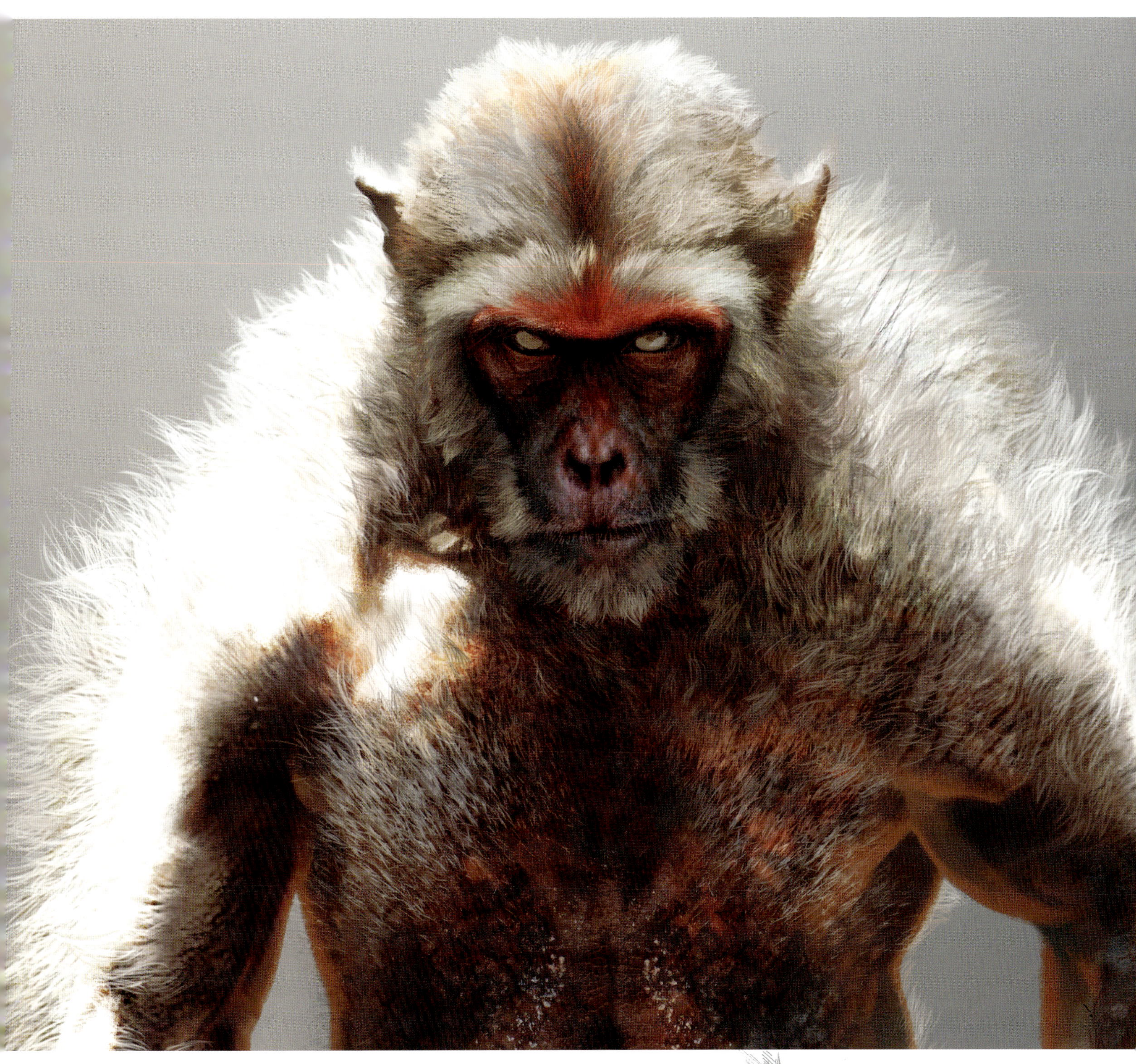

Wu Kong Australopithecus, 2015. Conceptual image from the film *Xi You, Fu Yao Pian.*
Digital composition and graphic finalization in Photoshop.

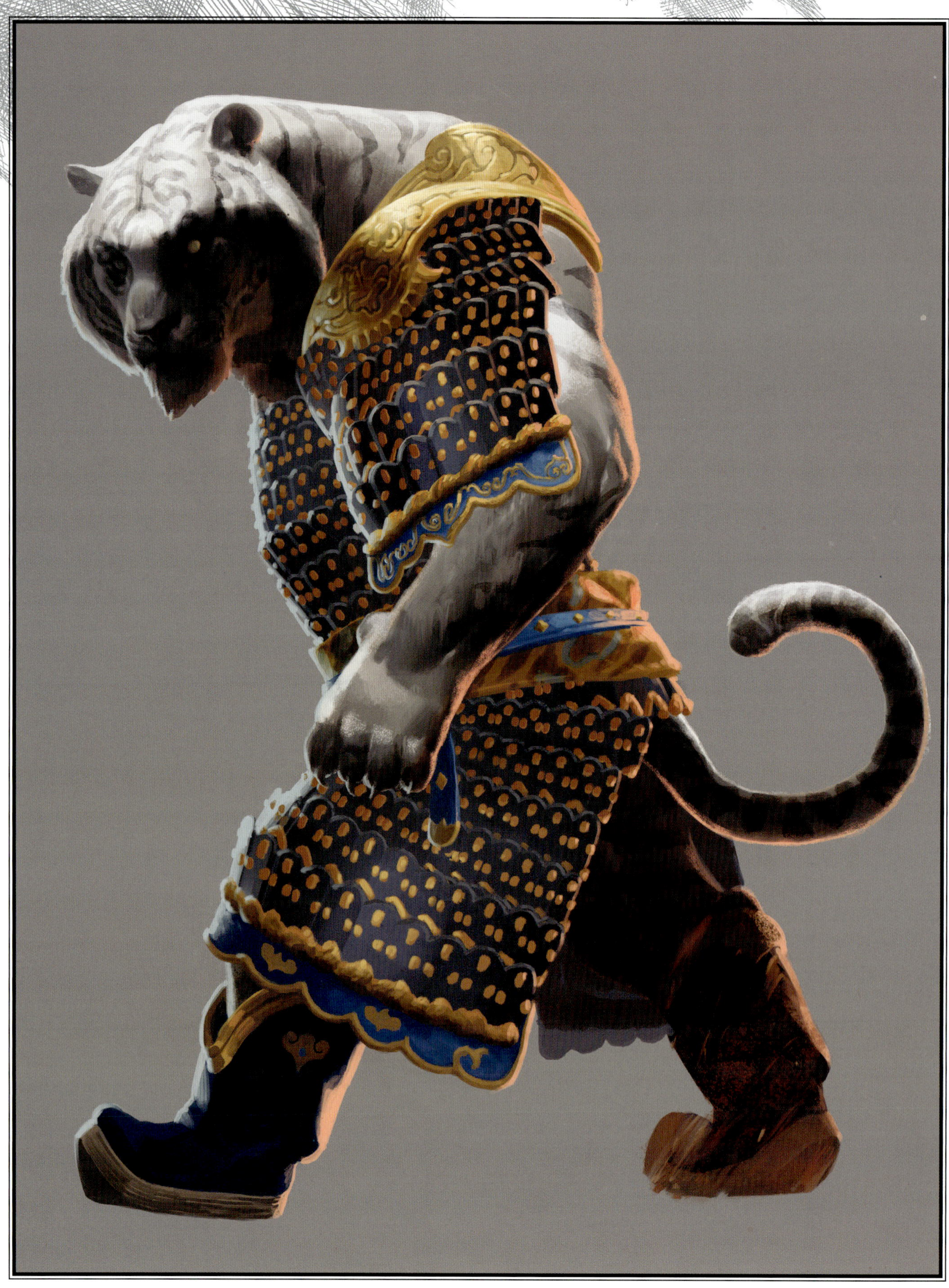

White Tiger General-in-Chief, concept image from the movie *I Don't Want to Name the Name*, 2016.
Digital composition and graphic finalization in Procreate.

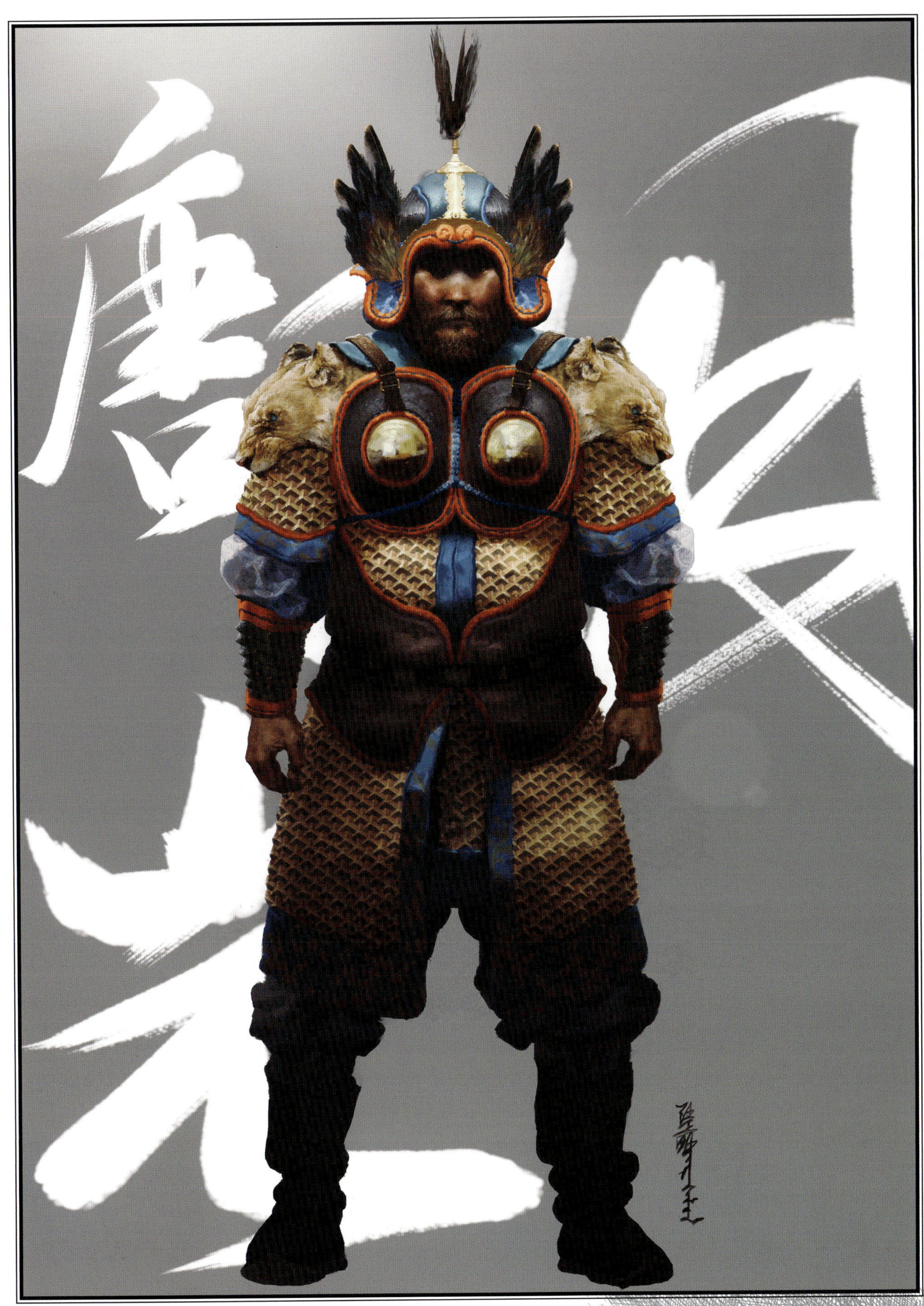

General in armor, Ming Guang County, Tang Dynasty,, 2017.
Digital composition and graphic finalization in Procreate.

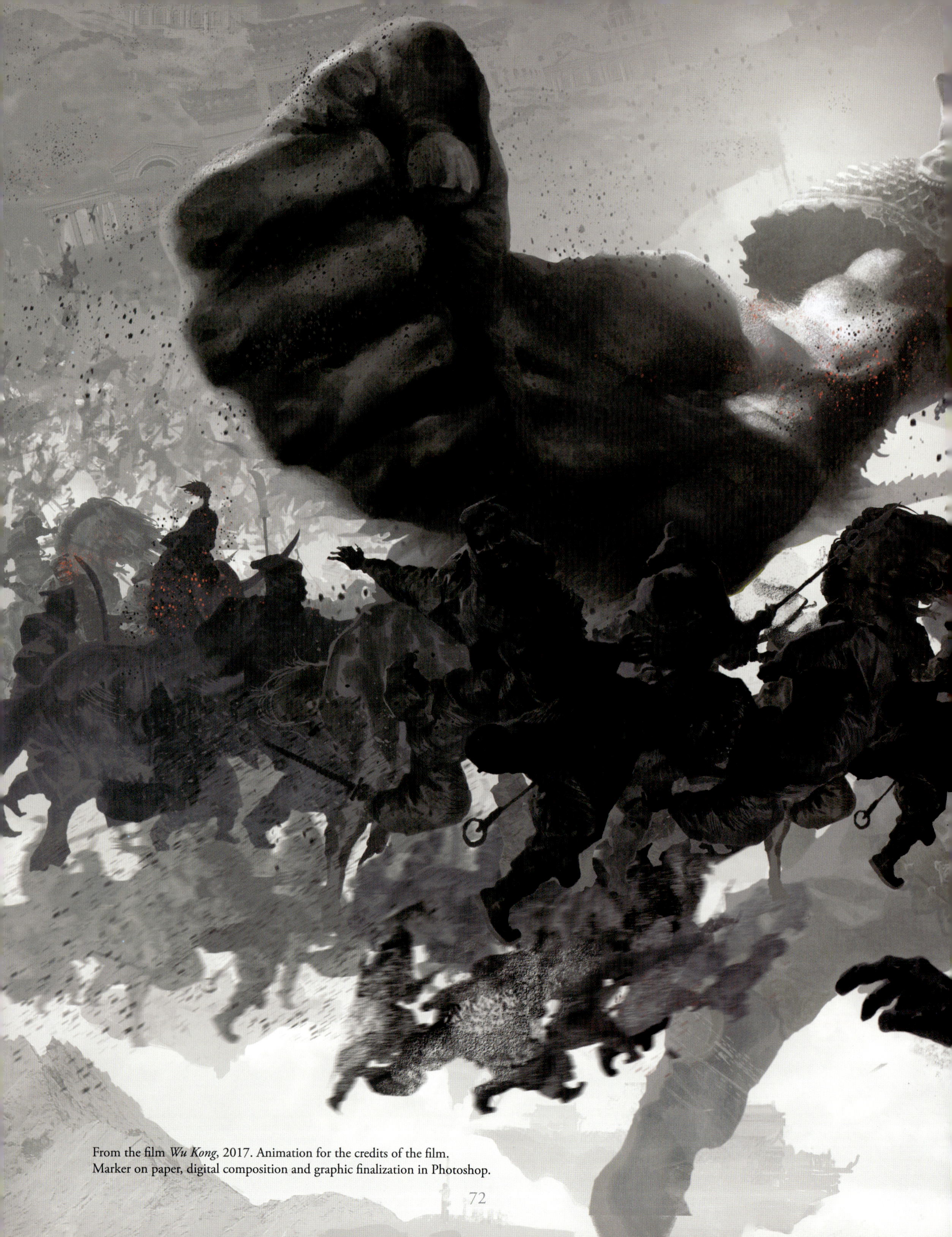

From the film *Wu Kong*, 2017. Animation for the credits of the film.
Marker on paper, digital composition and graphic finalization in Photoshop.

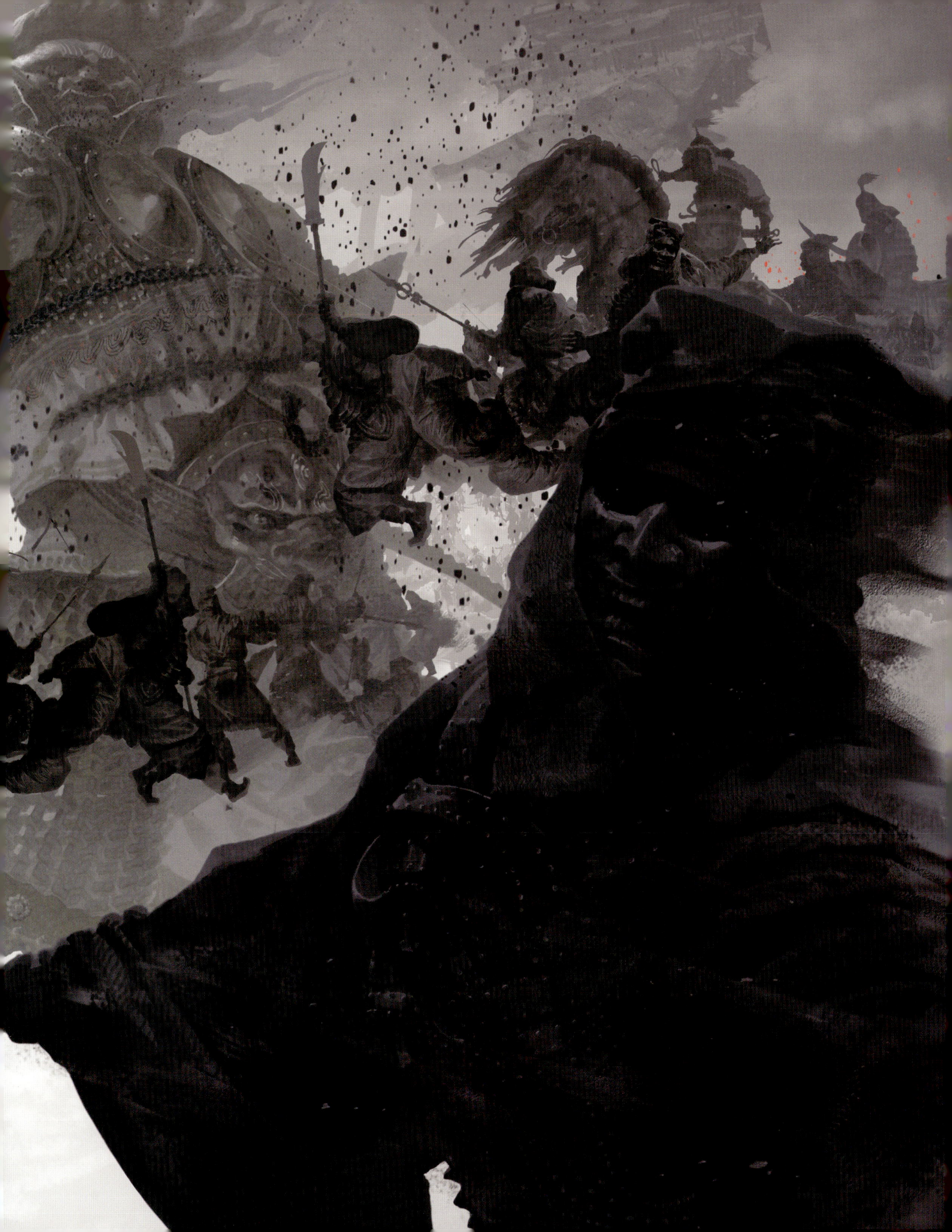

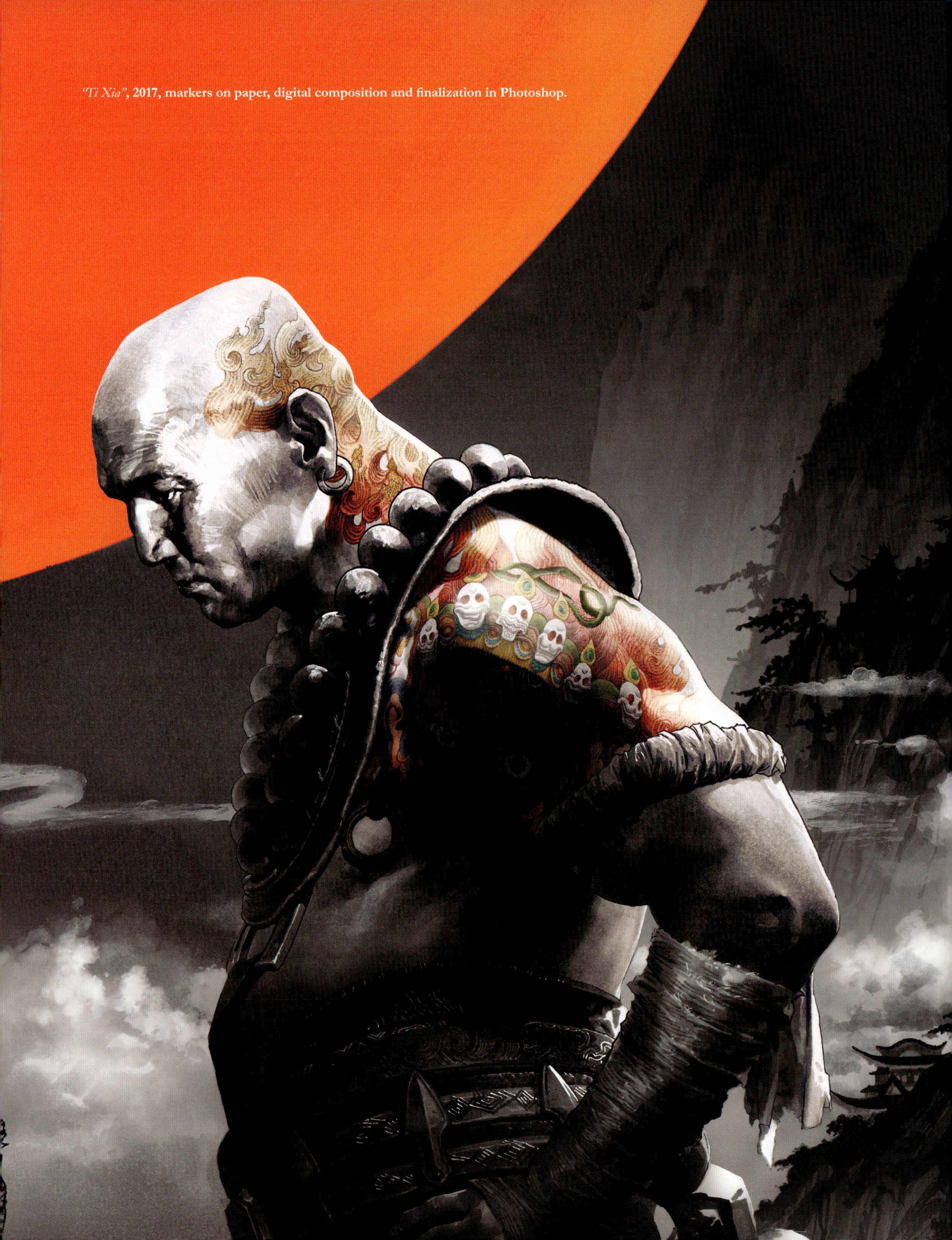

"Ti Xia", 2017, markers on paper, digital composition and finalization in Photoshop.

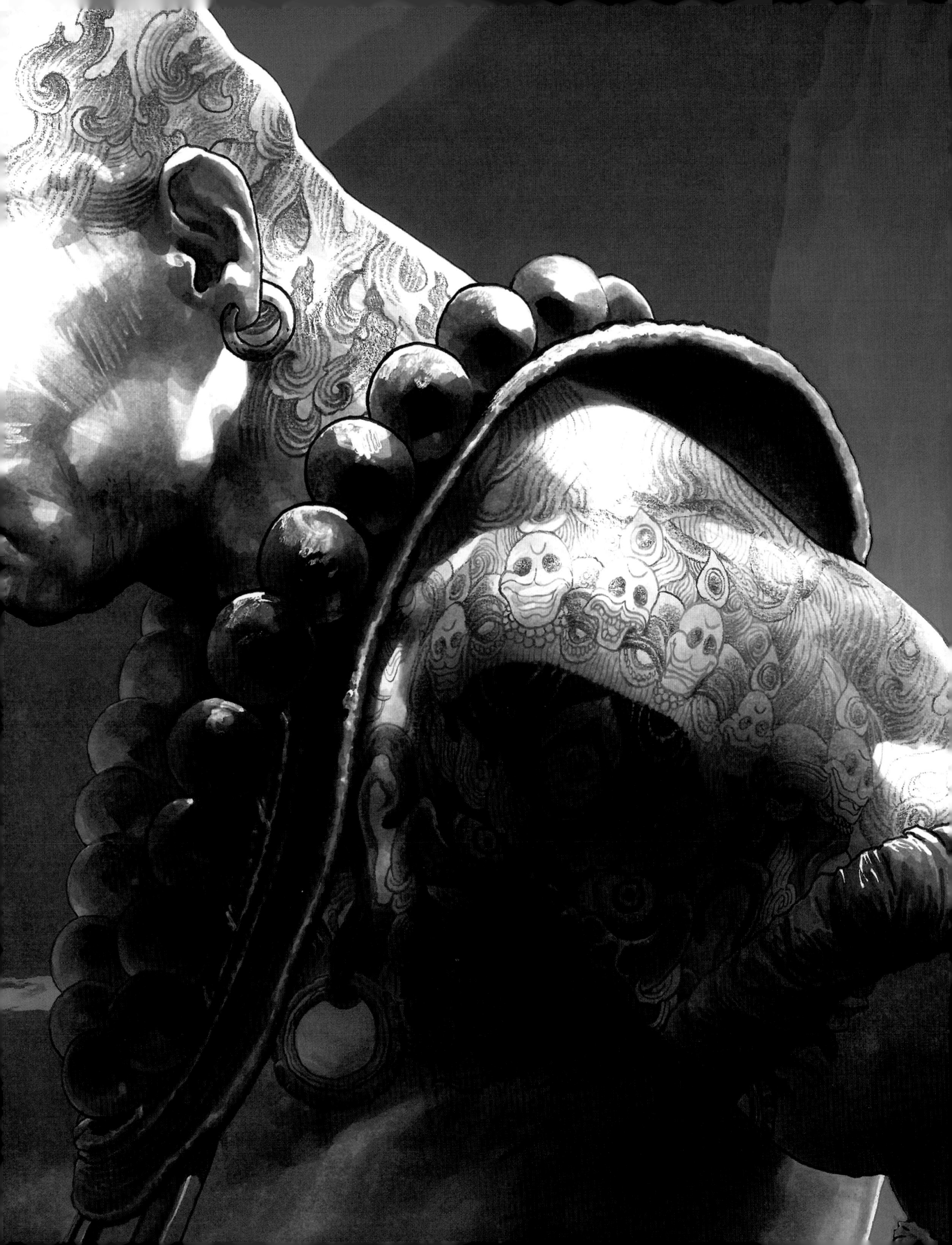

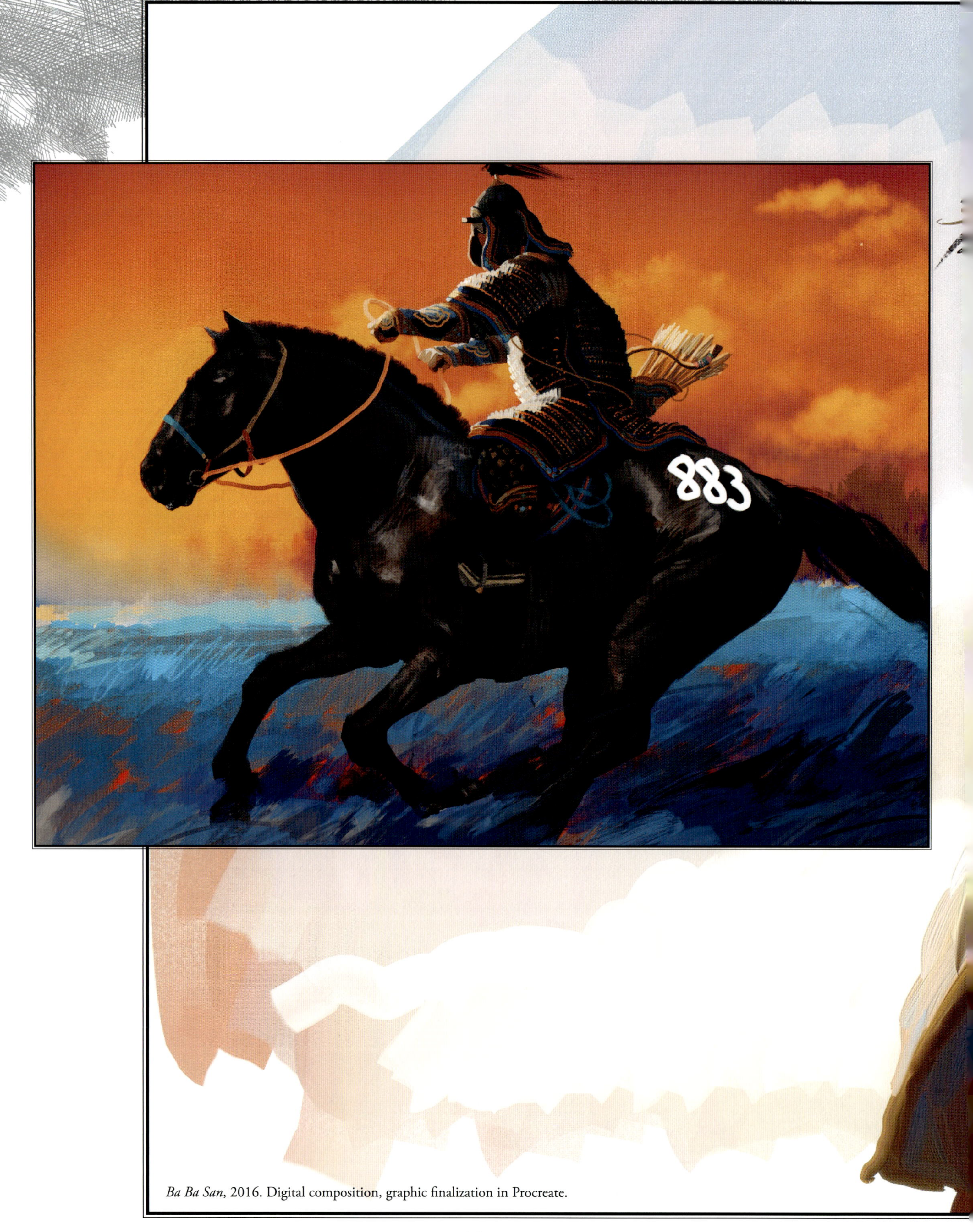

Ba Ba San, 2016. Digital composition, graphic finalization in Procreate.

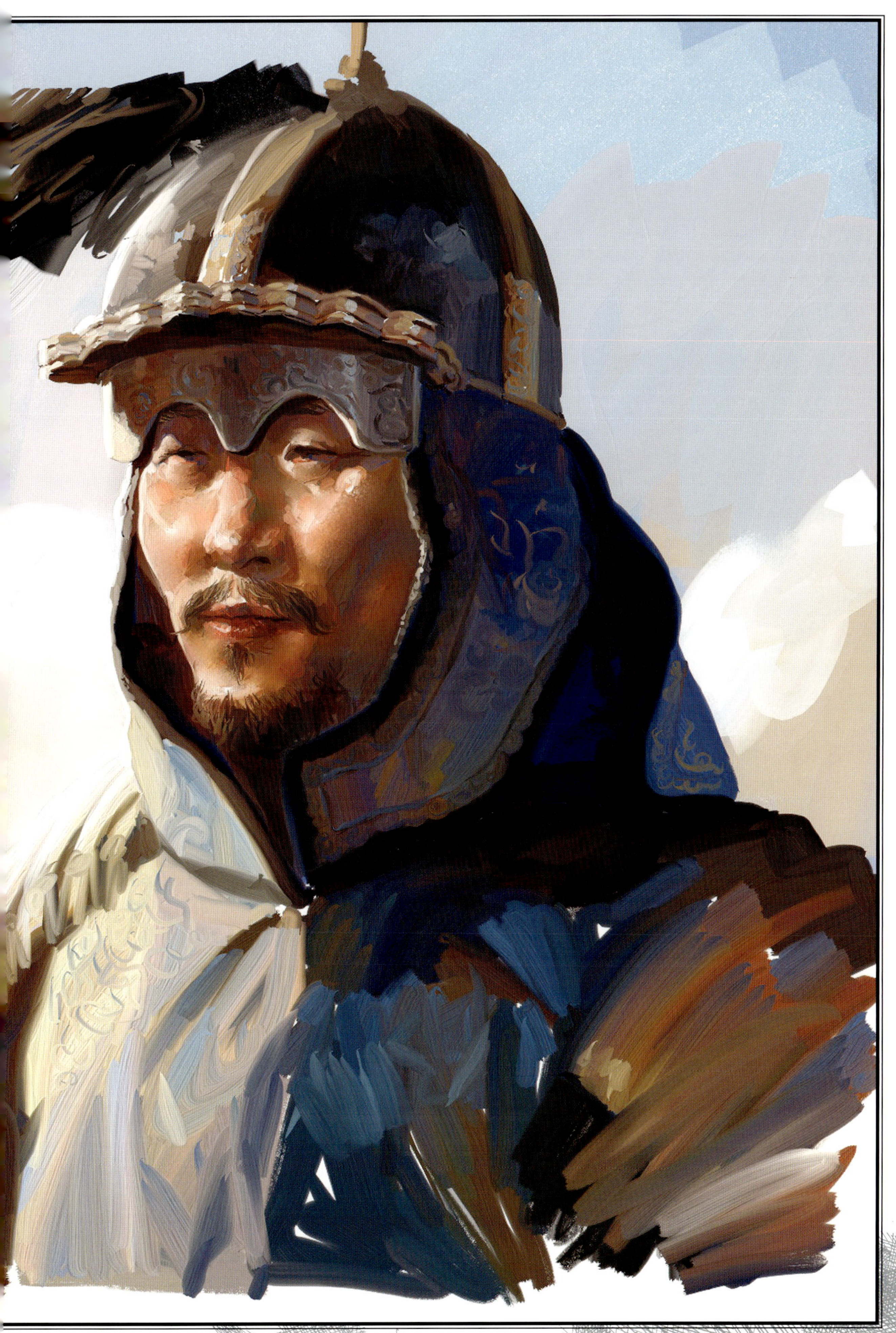

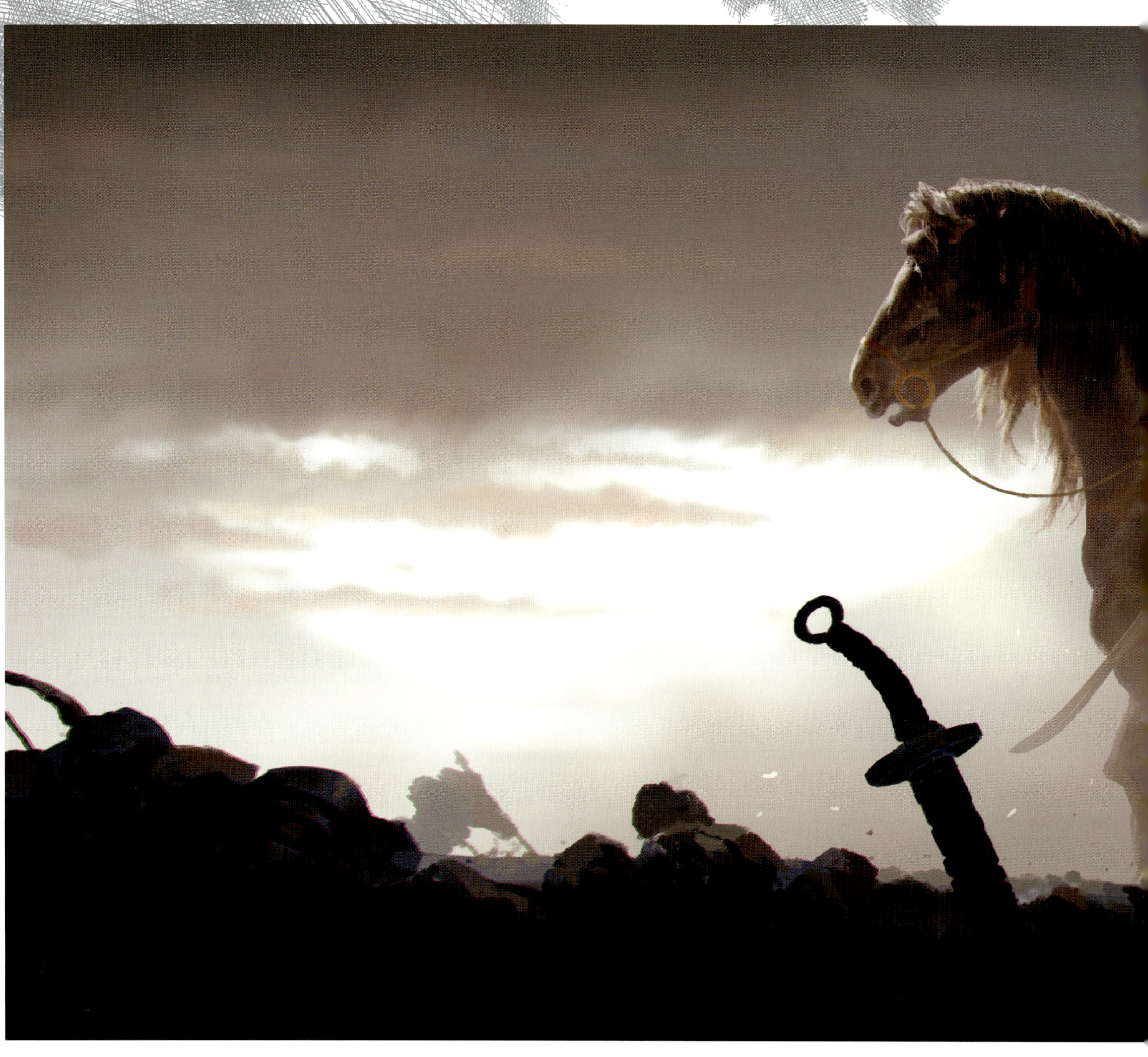

MORI, 2018. Digital composition and graphic finalization in Photoshop.

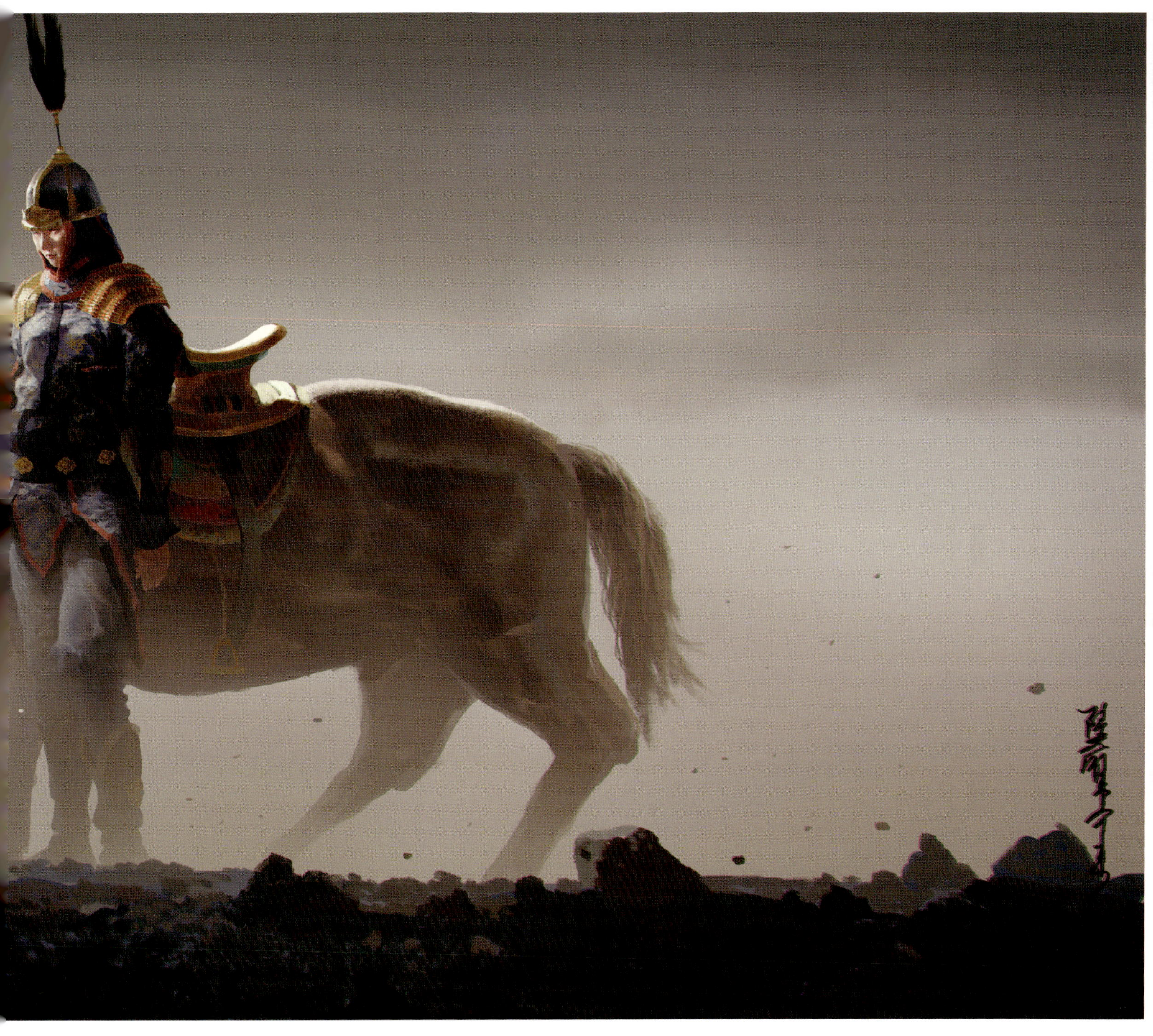

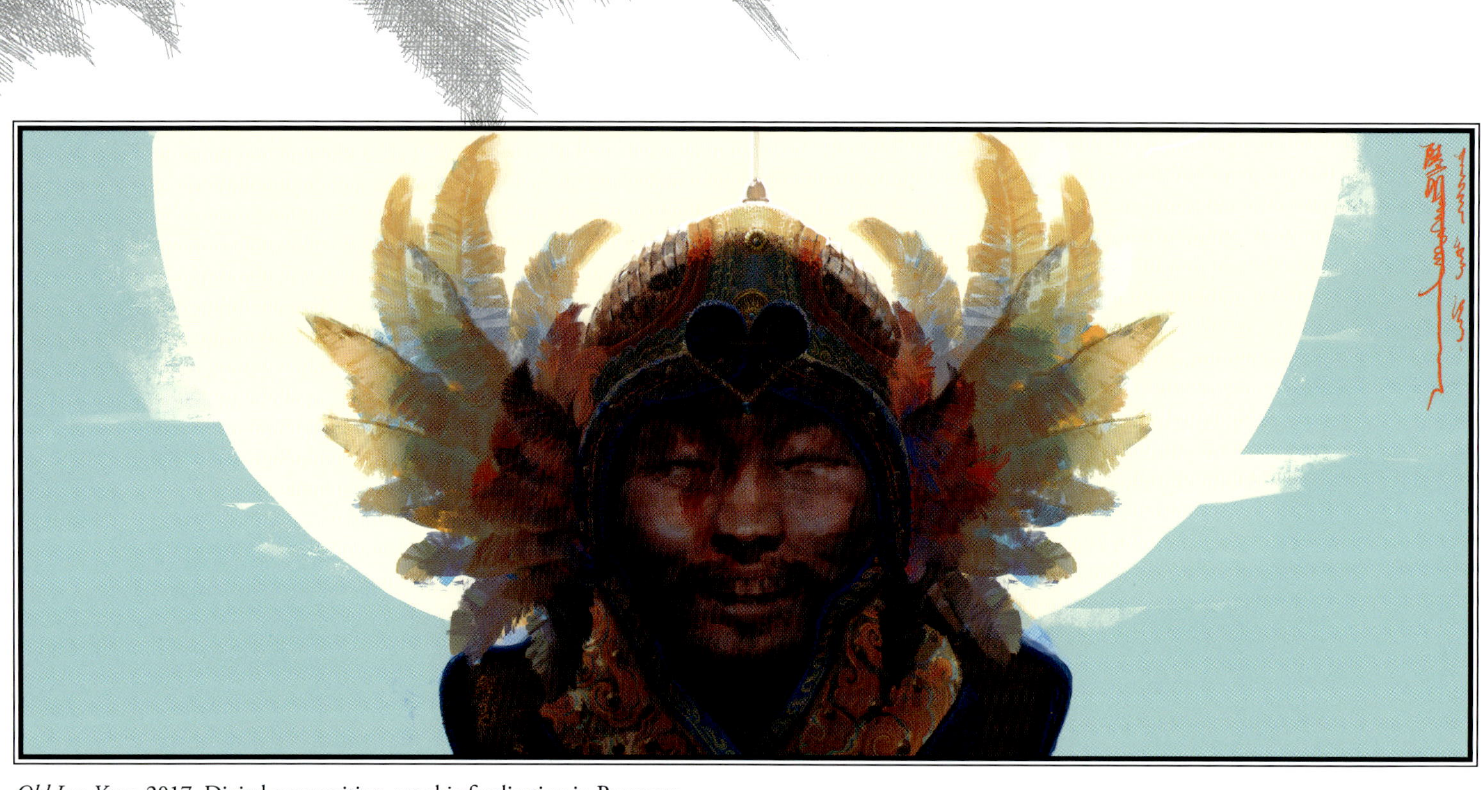

Old Luo Yang, 2017. Digital composition, graphic finalization in Procreate.

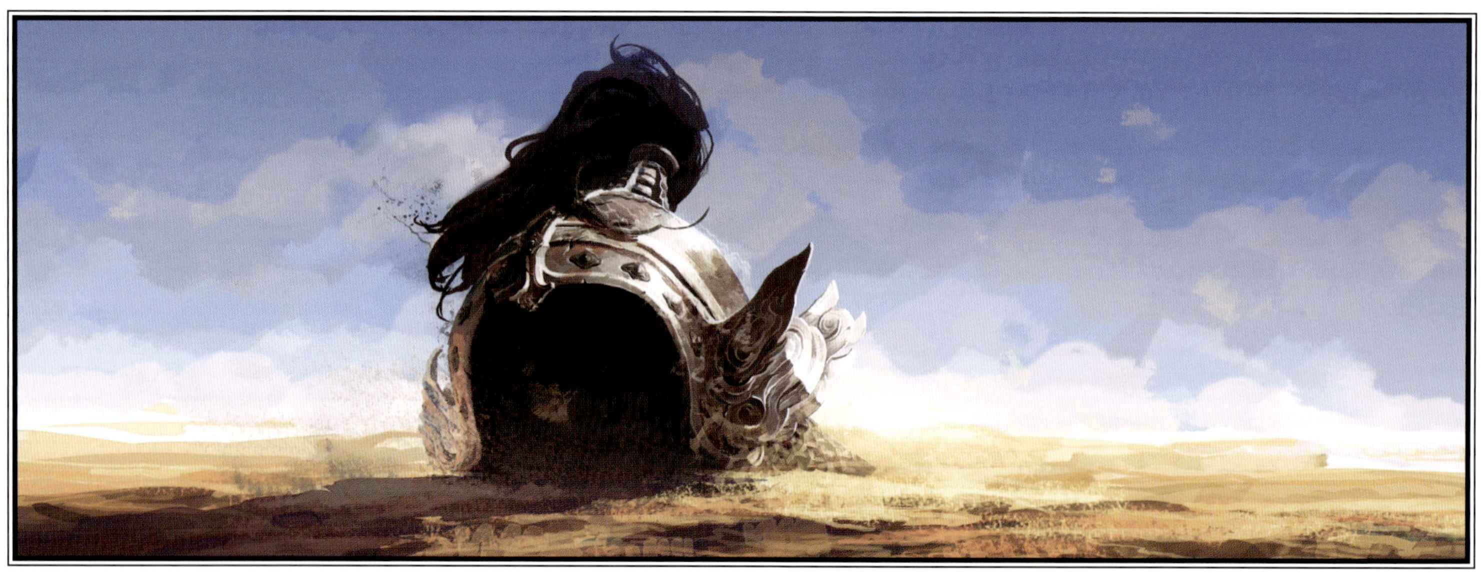

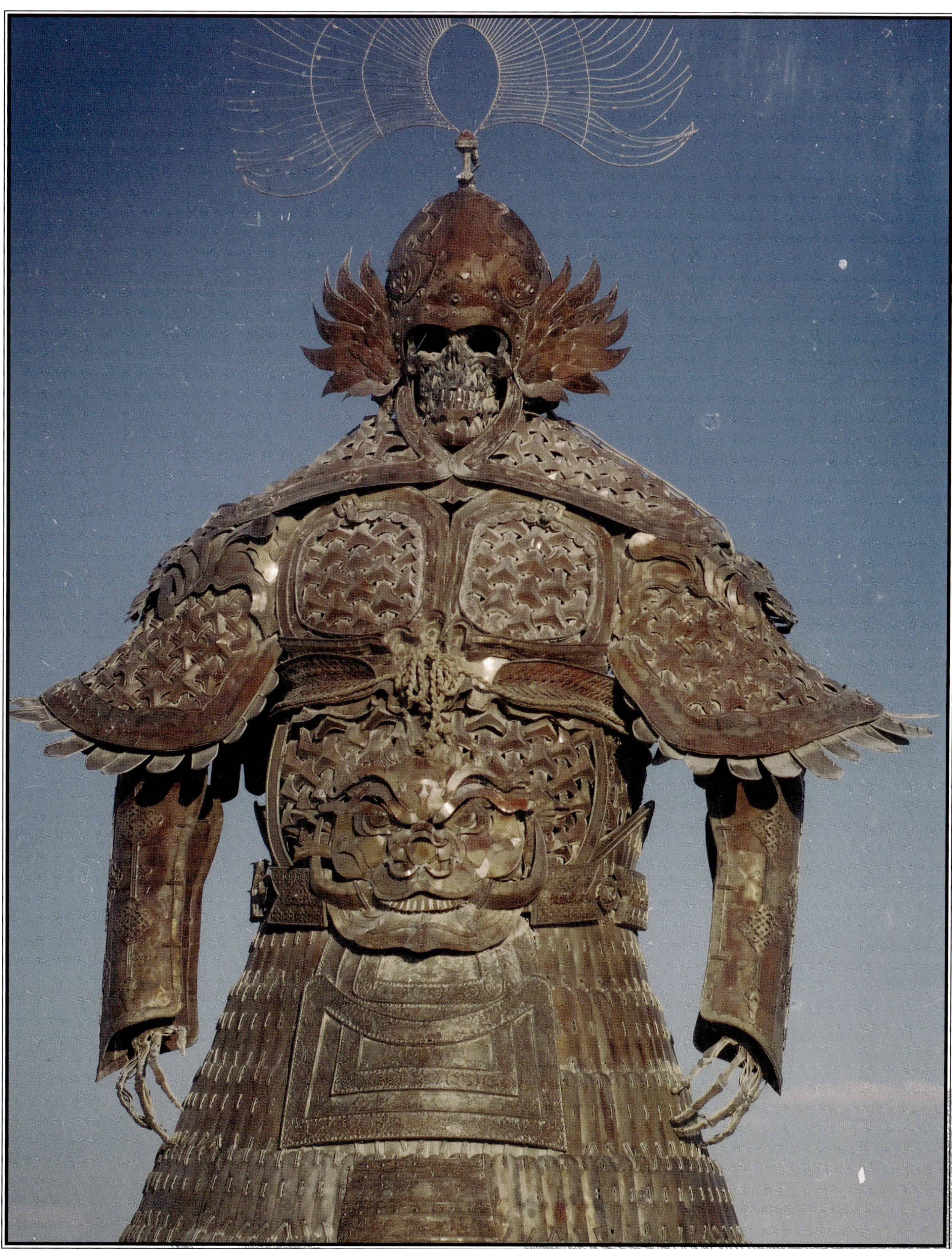

THUNDER RUMBLES…

Thunder rumbles in his chest,
Yet his face is like the deep waters of a lake.
He's in a rage.
Mortally wounded, his blood flows drop by drop.
He staggers, securing his rear, slamming his torn carcass and dragging it forward.
His body constantly bruised,
His eyes have become blind.
Under the chirping of birds in the storm.
After being crushed, he licks his wounds.
The scars from previous wounds add endlessly,
Petrified to form an indestructible black armor,
Guardian of the rebel flame
Which leaps and struggles desperately deep in his heart.

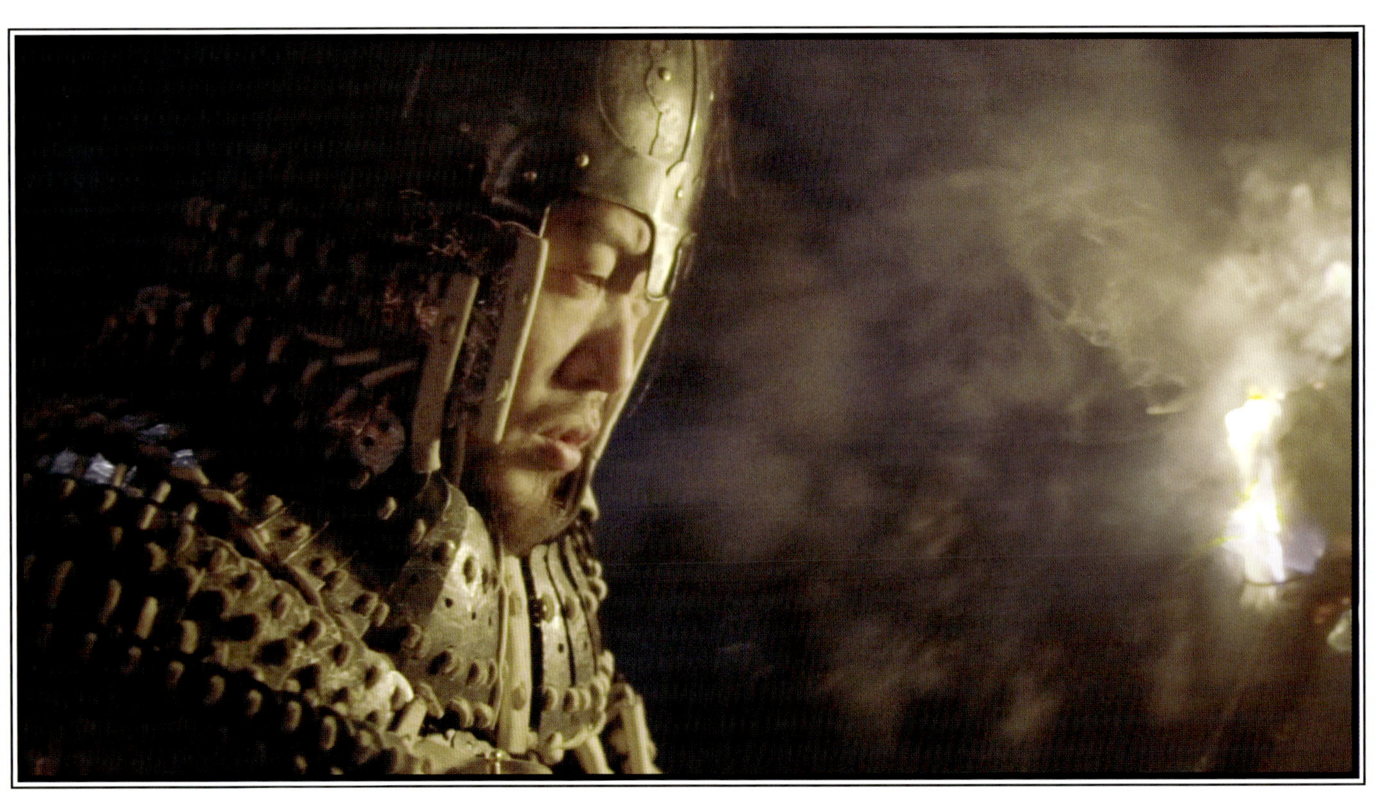

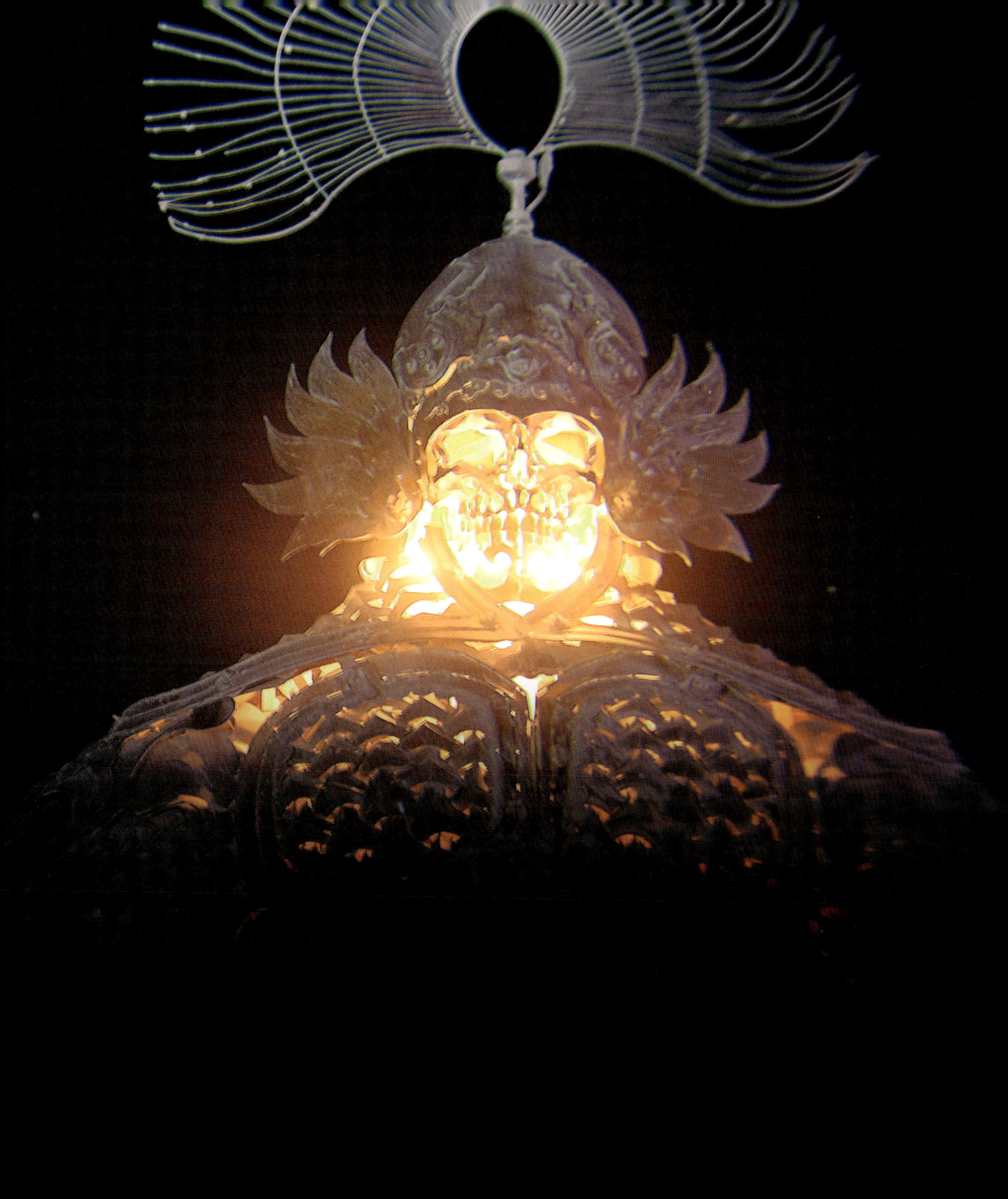

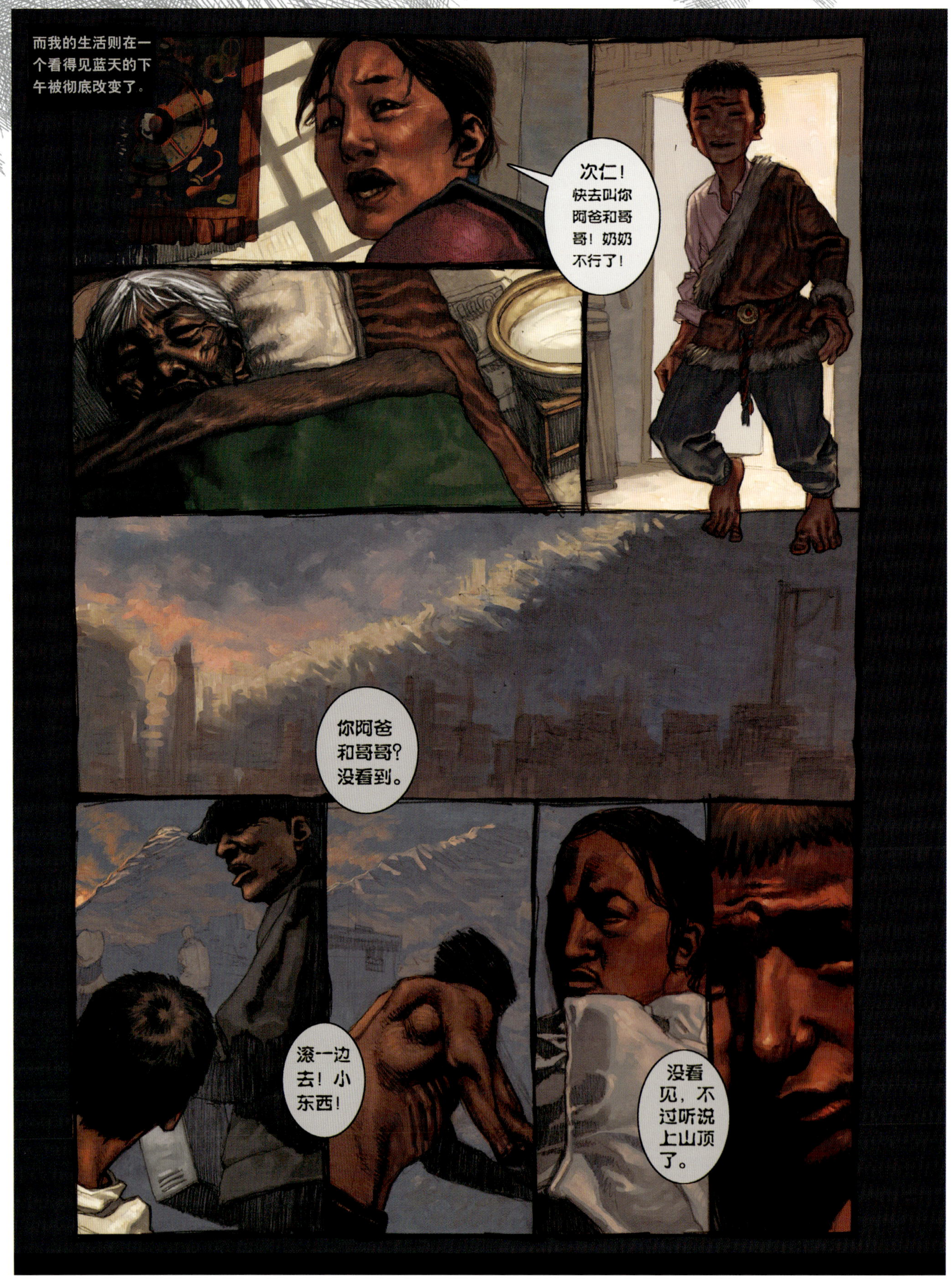

From the comic *The Discovery of the Child from the Snowy Mountains* page 2 and 3, 2002. Pen and ink on A3 paper. Digital composition and graphic finalization in Painter.

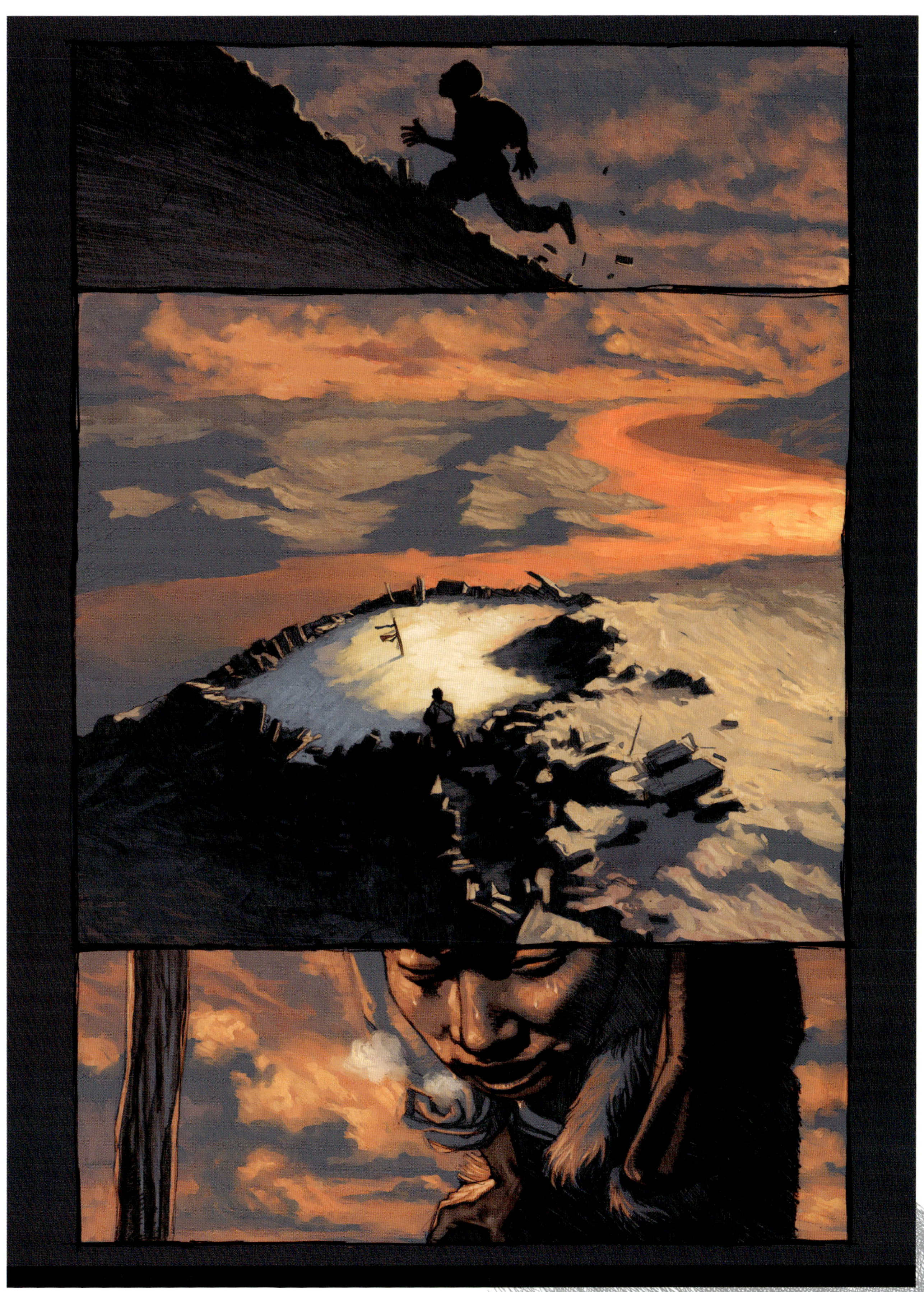

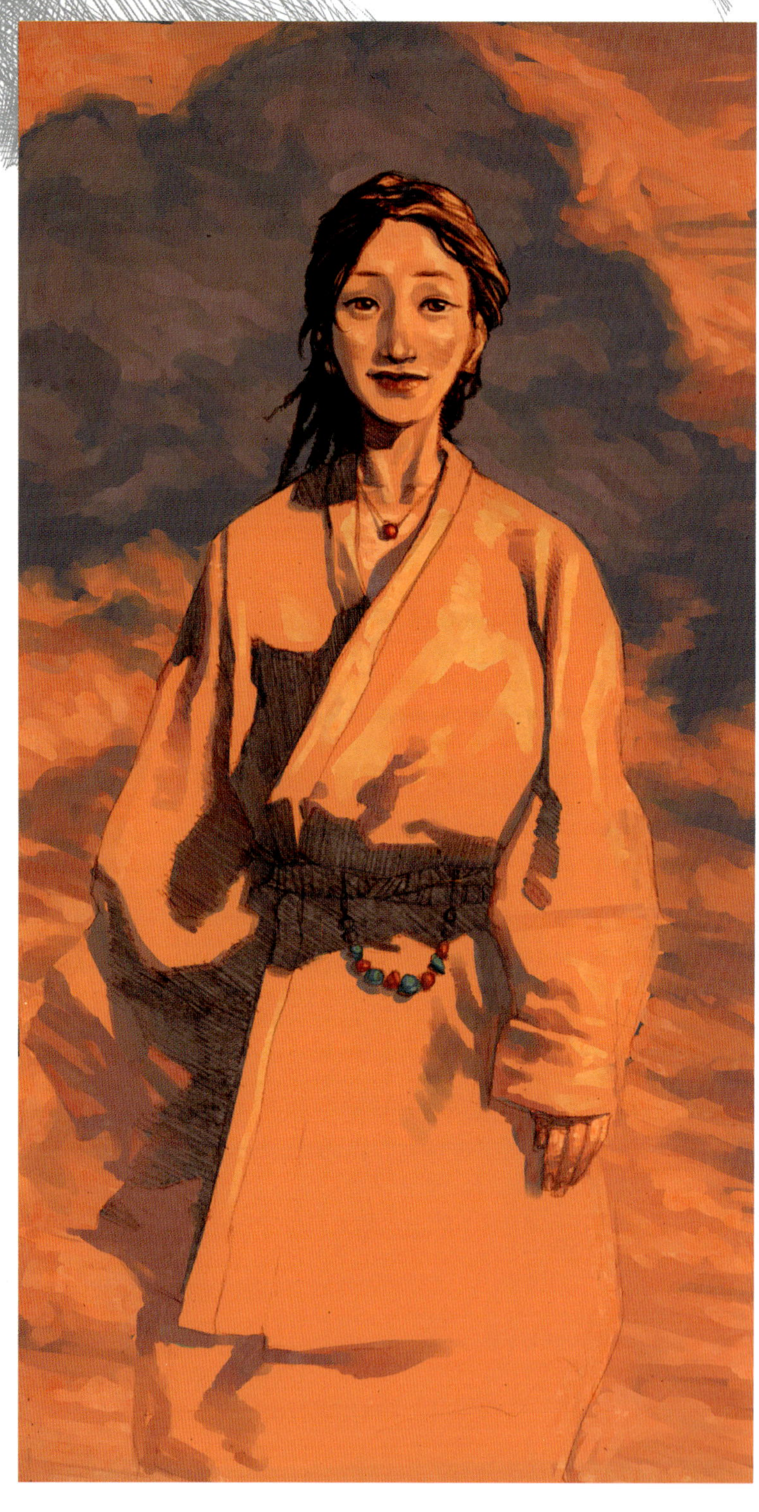

Panels from *The Discovery of the Child from the Snowy Mountains*, 2002. Pen and ink on A3 paper. Digital composition and graphic finalization in Painter.

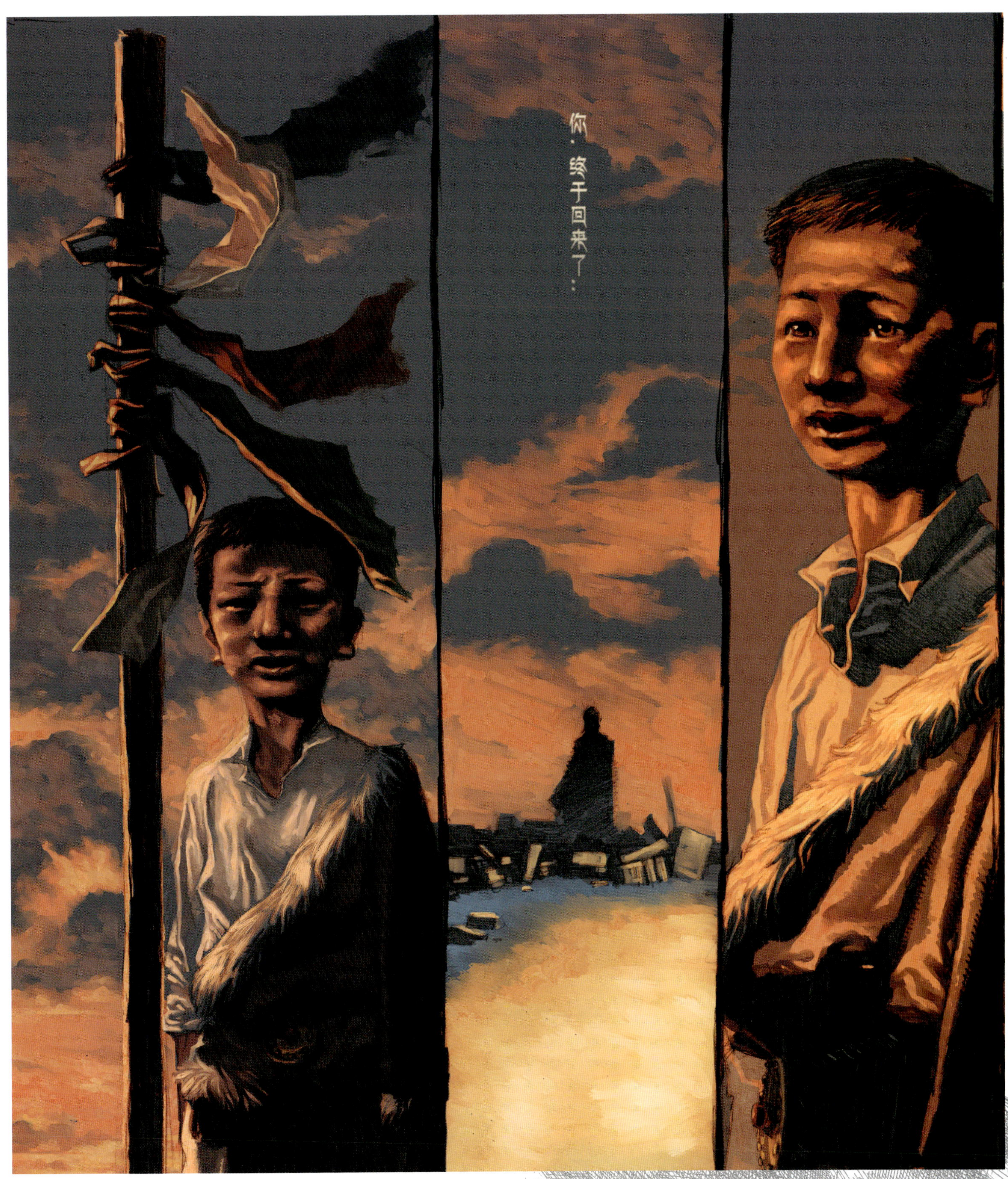

你．终于回来了．．

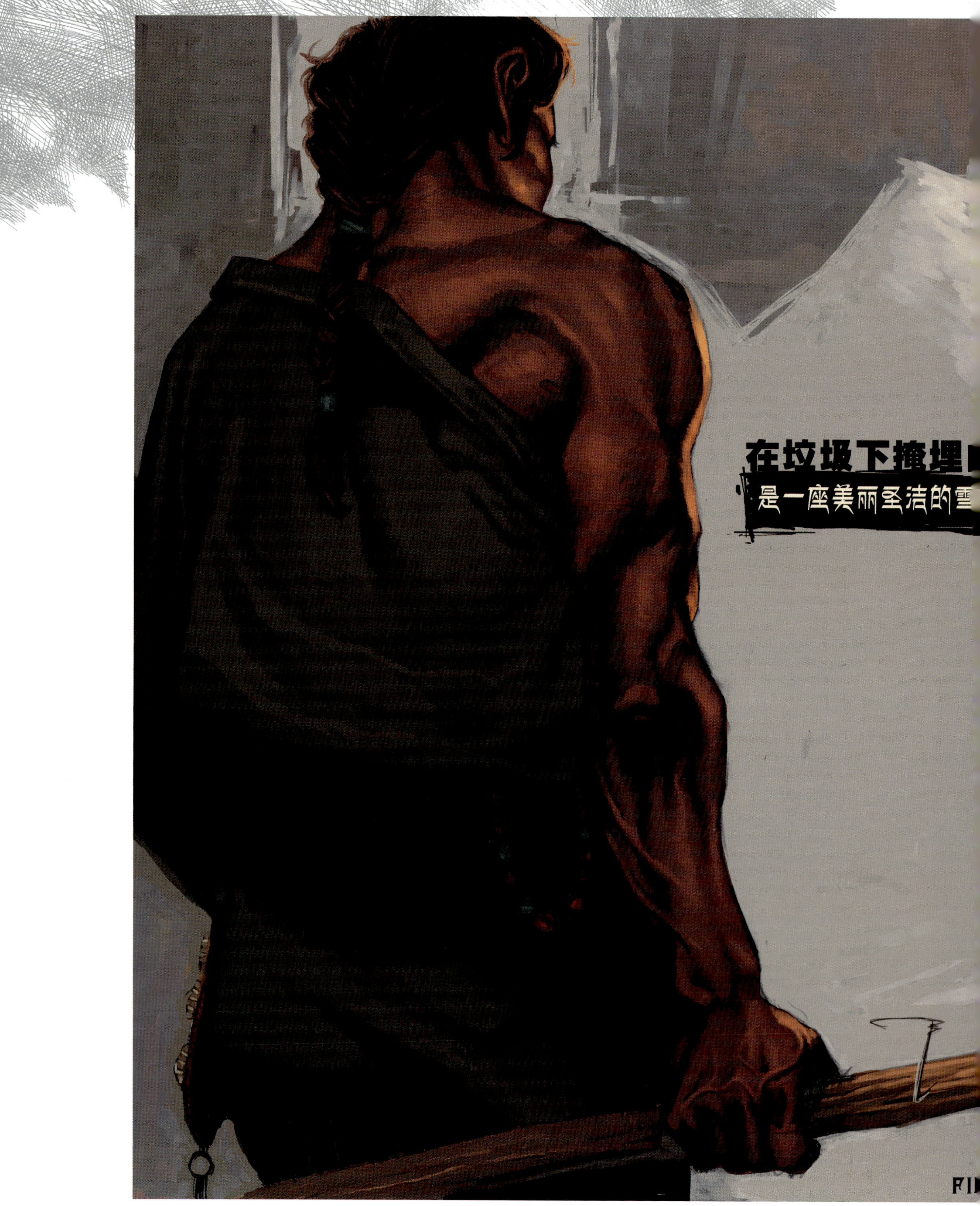

The Discovery of the Child from the Snowy Mountains page 9, 2002. Pen and ink on A3 paper. Digital composition and graphic finalization in Painter.

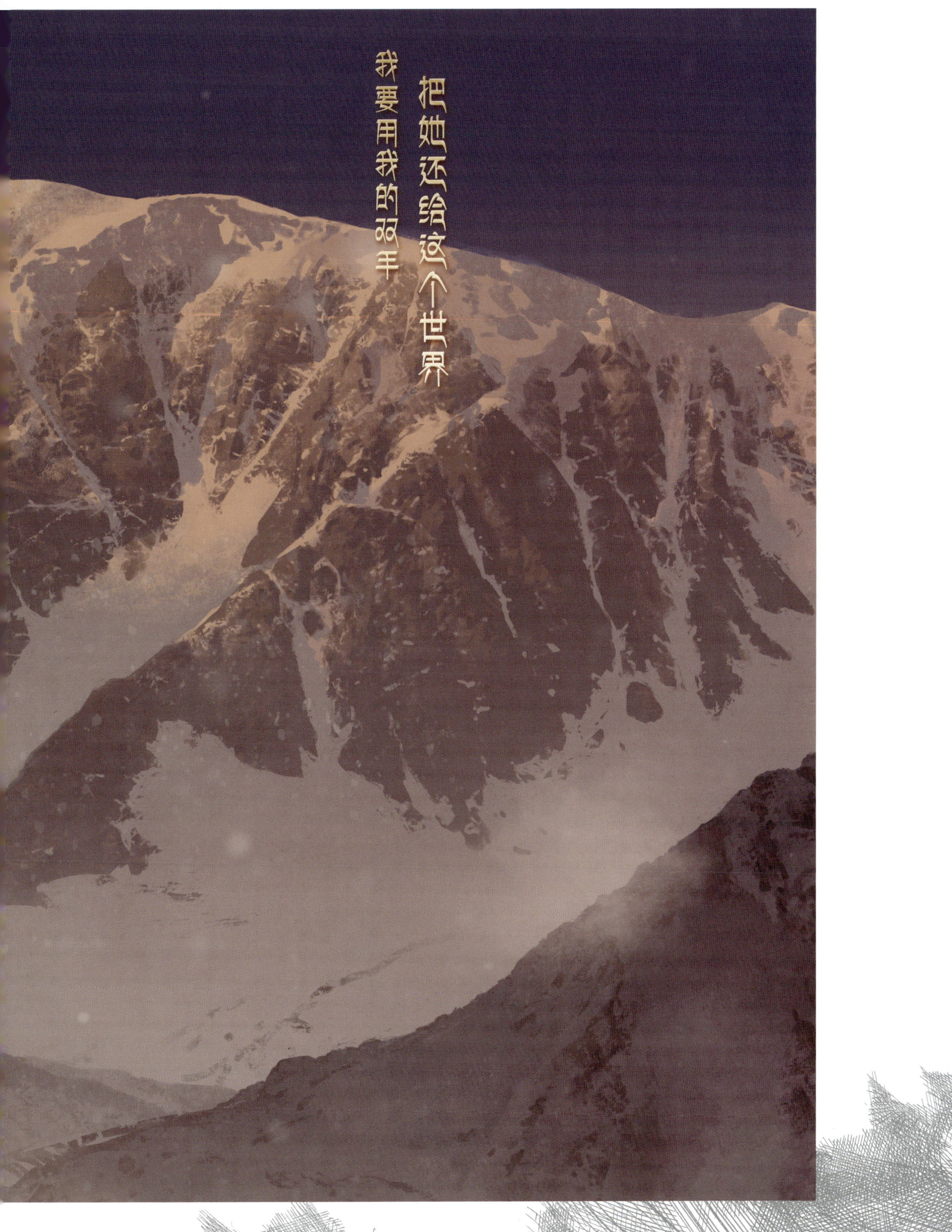
我要用我的双手
把她还给这个世界

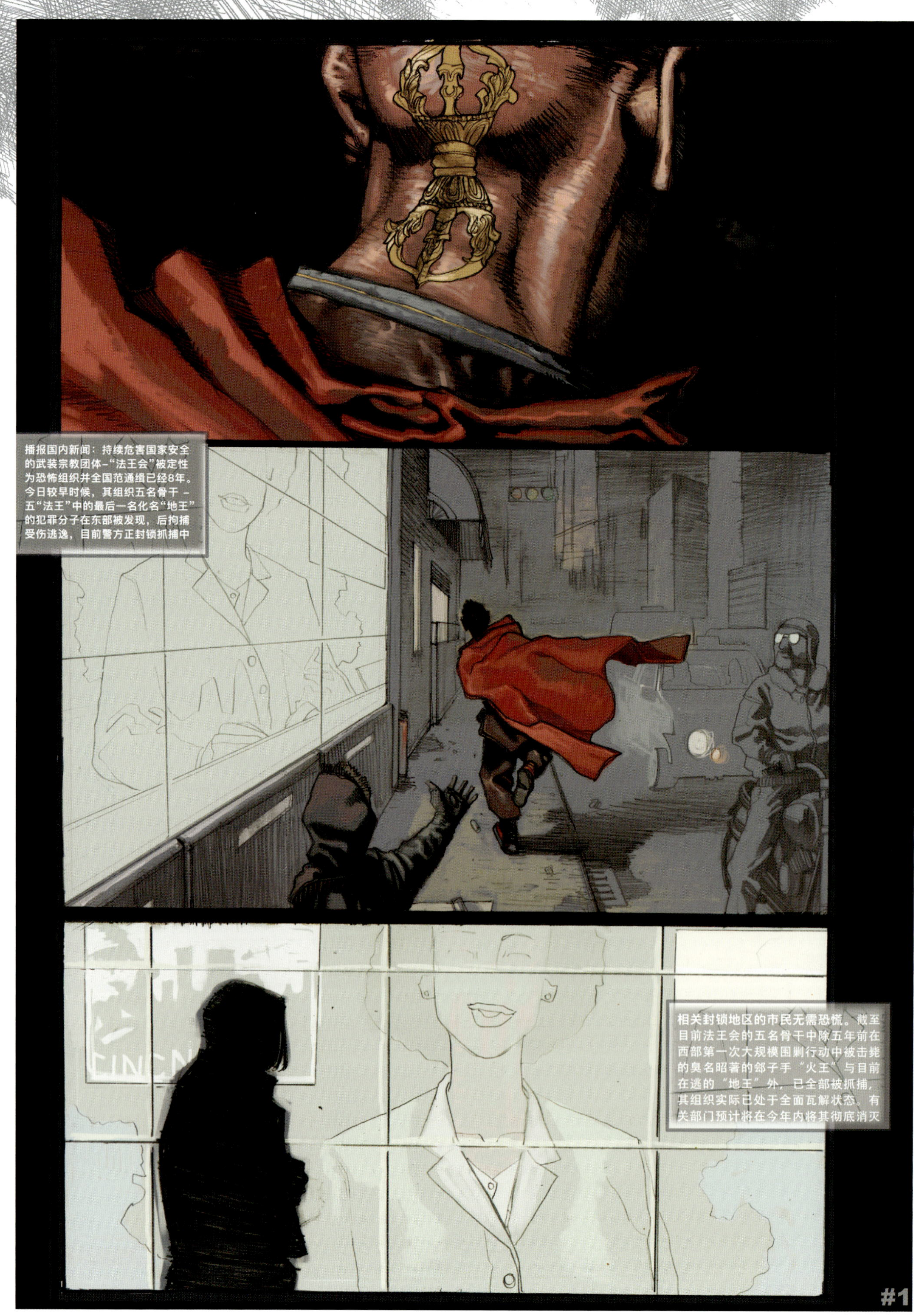

播报国内新闻：持续危害国家安全的武装宗教团体－"法王会"被定性为恐怖组织并全国范围通缉已经8年。今日较早时候，其组织五名骨干－五"法王"中的最后一名化名"地王"的犯罪分子在东部被发现，后拘捕受伤逃逸，目前警方正封锁抓捕中
相关封锁地区的市民无需恐慌。截至目前法王会的五名骨干中除五年前在西部第一次大规模围剿行动中被击毙的臭名昭著的刽子手"火王"与目前在逃的"地王"外，已全部被抓捕，其组织实际已处于全面瓦解状态。有关部门预计将在今年内将其彻底消灭
#1

From *The Discovery of the Child from the Snowy Mountains*, 2002. Pen and ink on A3 paper. Digital composition and graphic finalization in Painter.

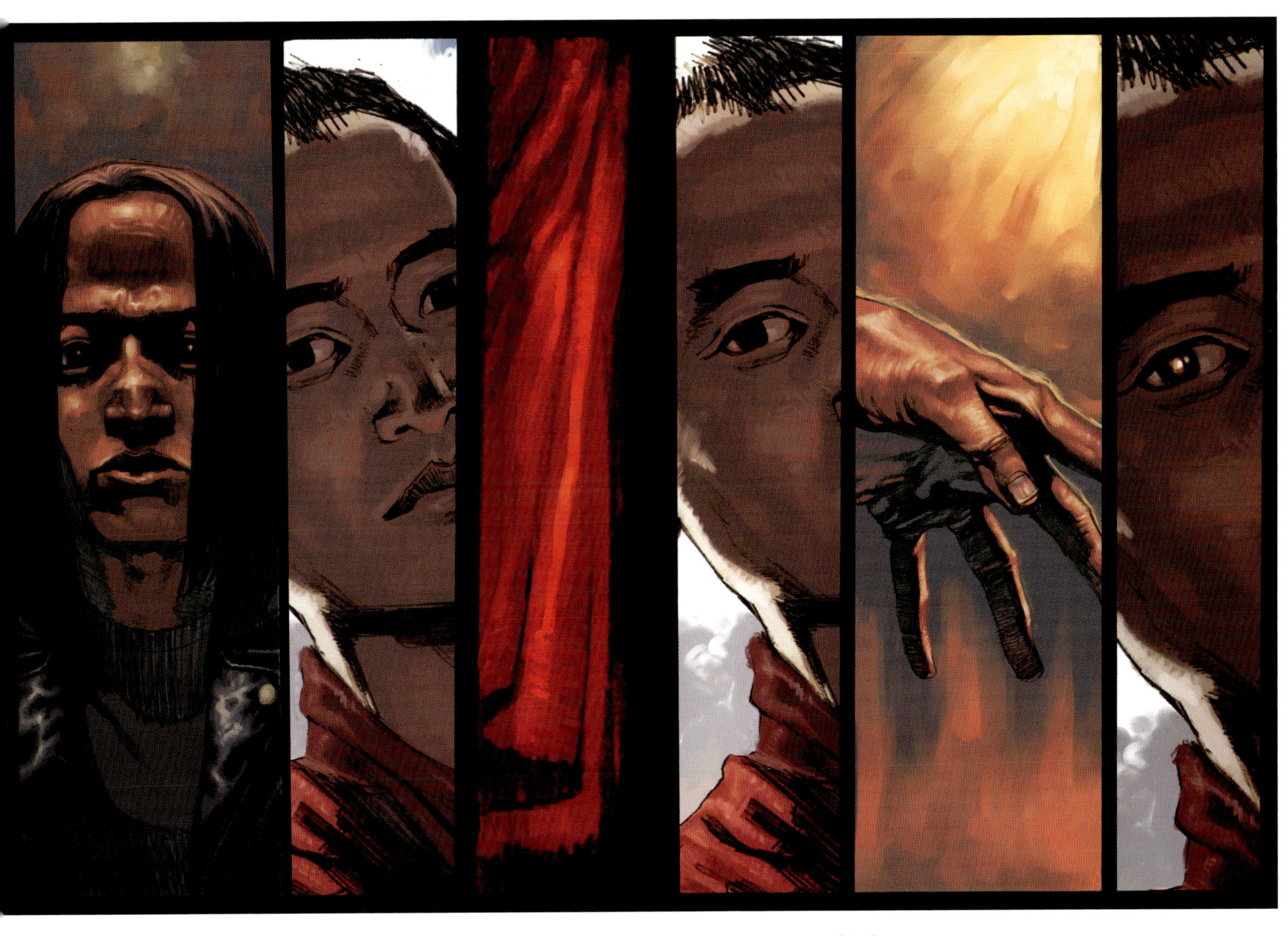

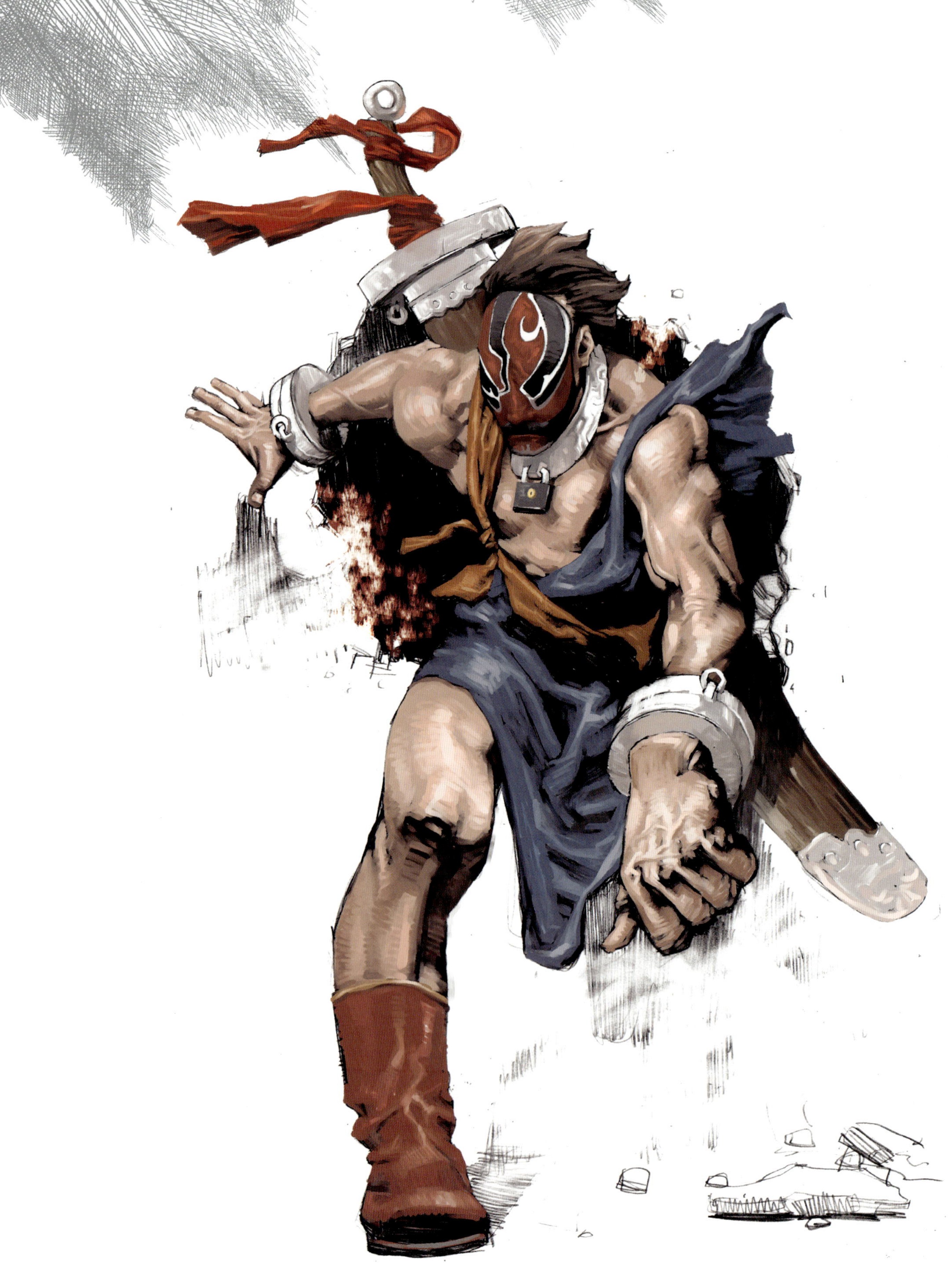

Tie Chao, 2002, Pen and ink. Digital composition and graphic finalization in Painter.

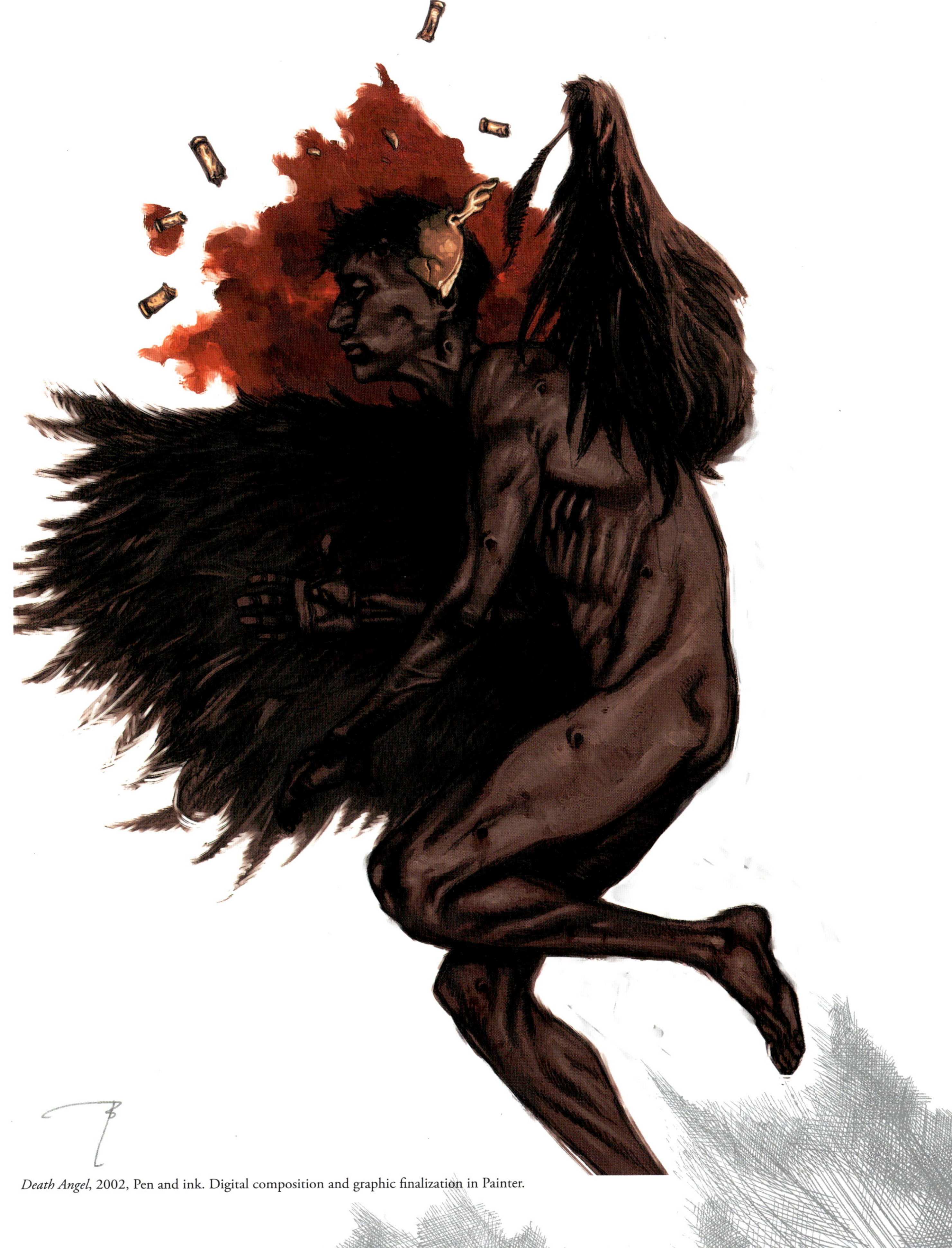

Death Angel, 2002, Pen and ink. Digital composition and graphic finalization in Painter.

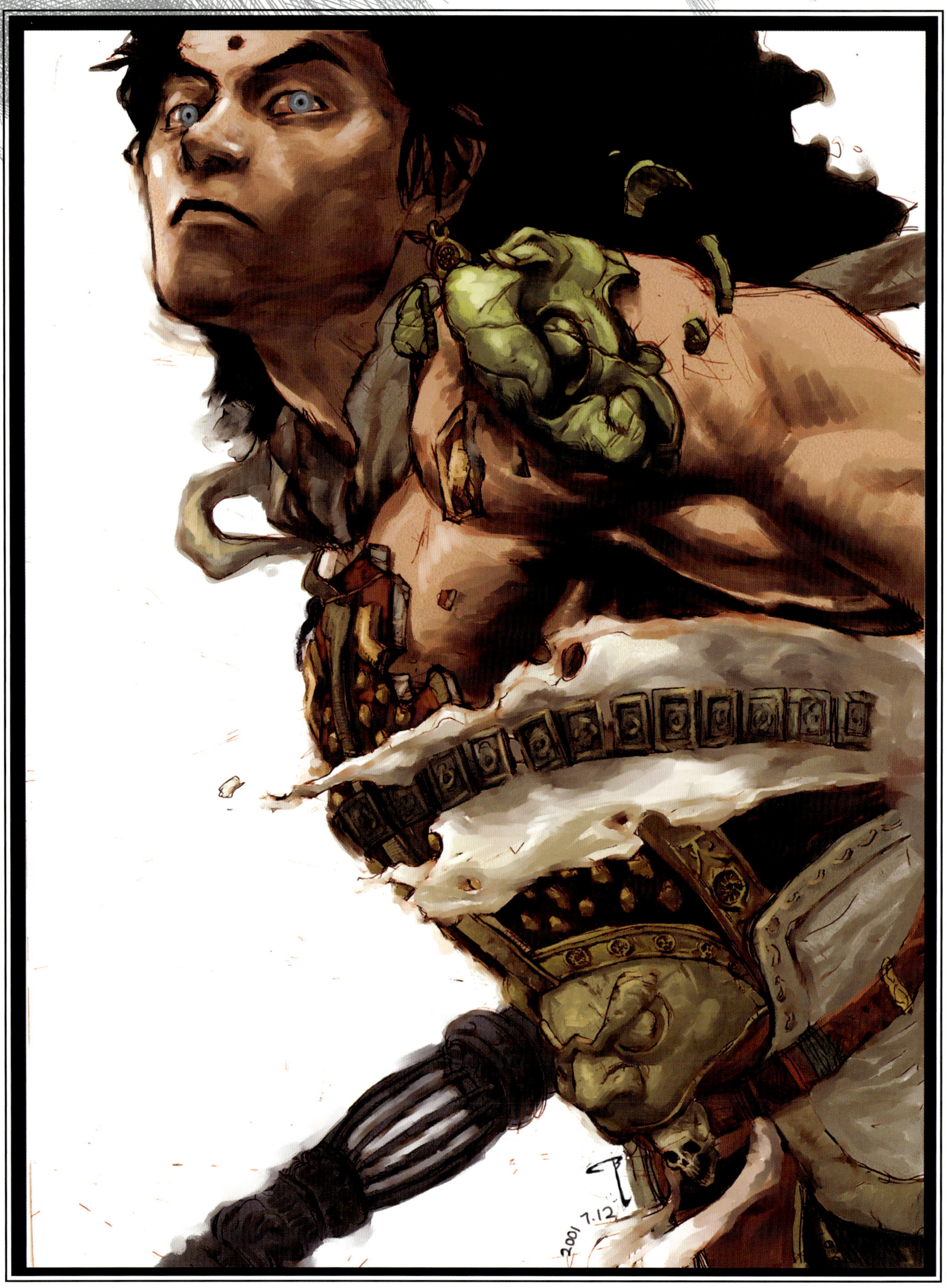

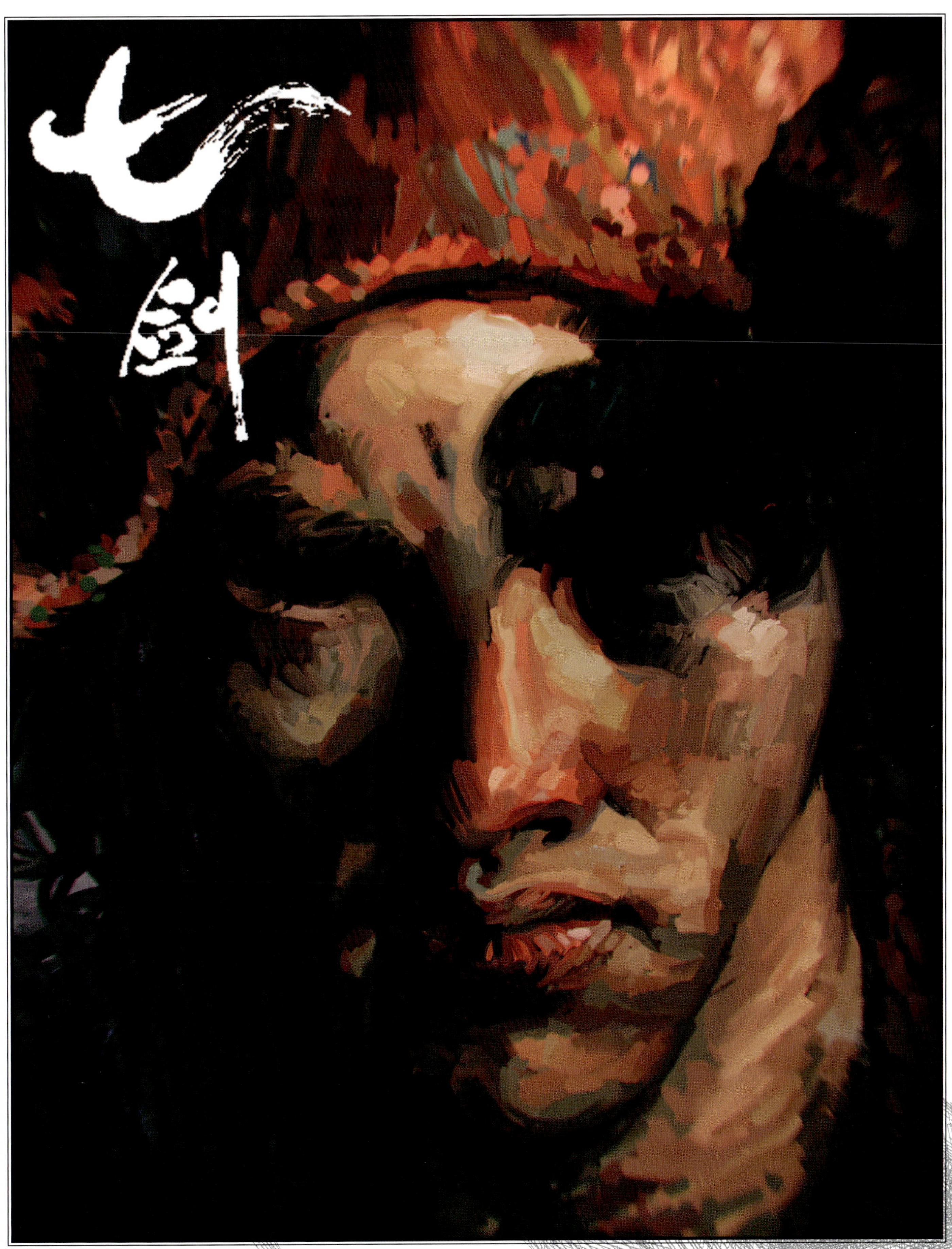

七
劍

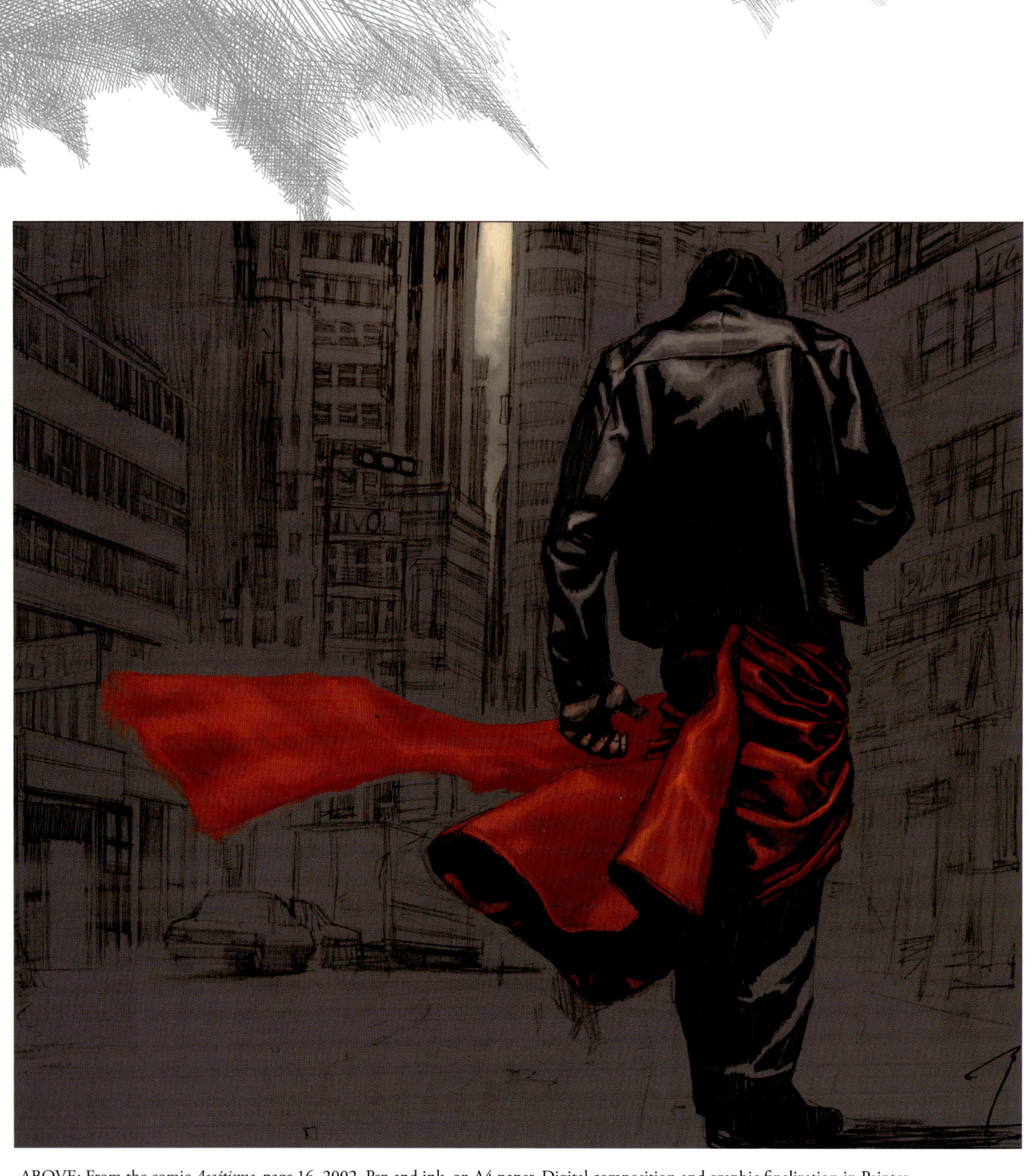

ABOVE: From the comic *Ascétisme,* page 16, 2002. Pen and ink on A4 paper. Digital composition and graphic finalization in Painter.

RIGHT*: Envol*, 2004. Pen and ink on A4 paper. Digital composition and graphic finalization in Painter.

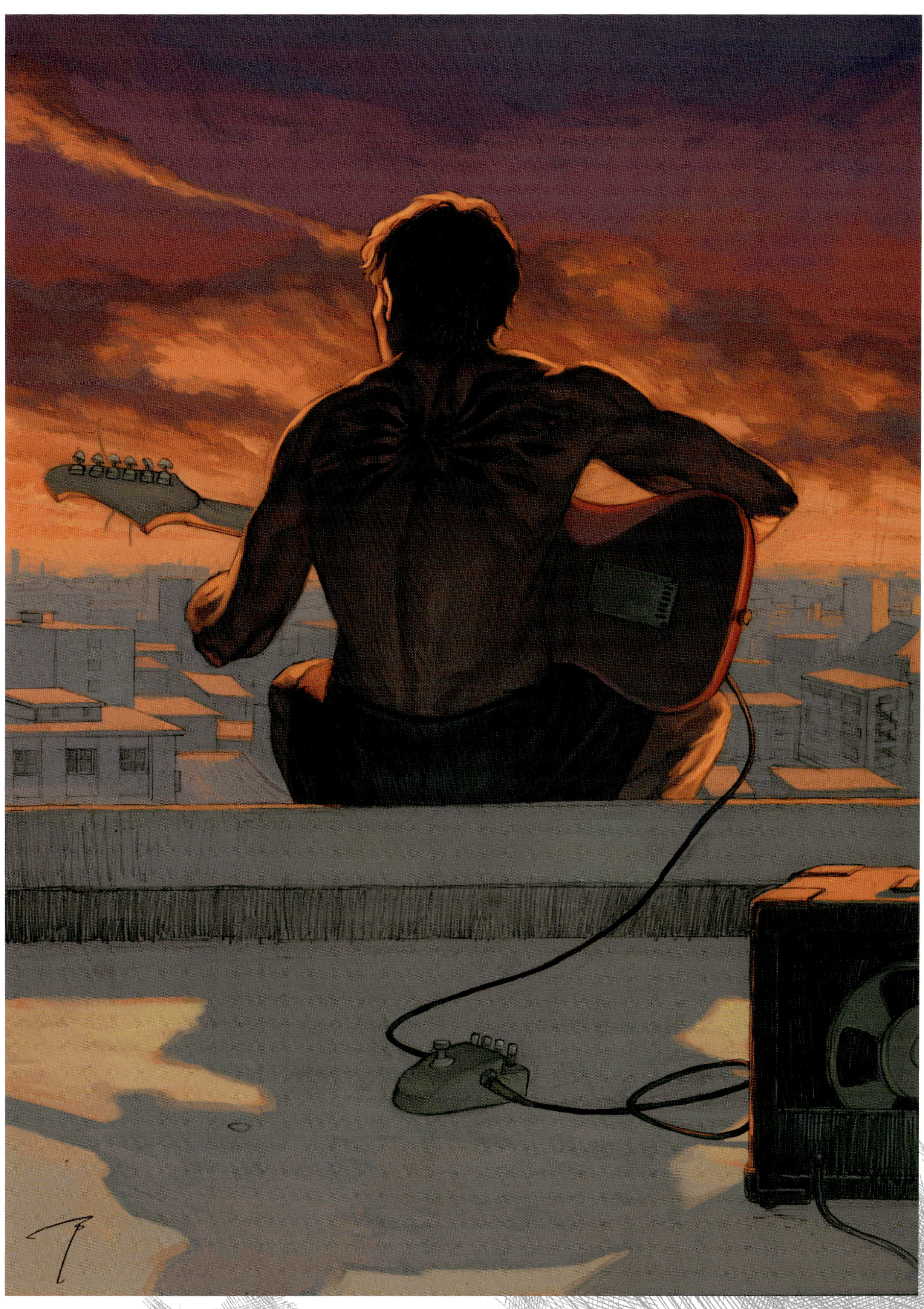

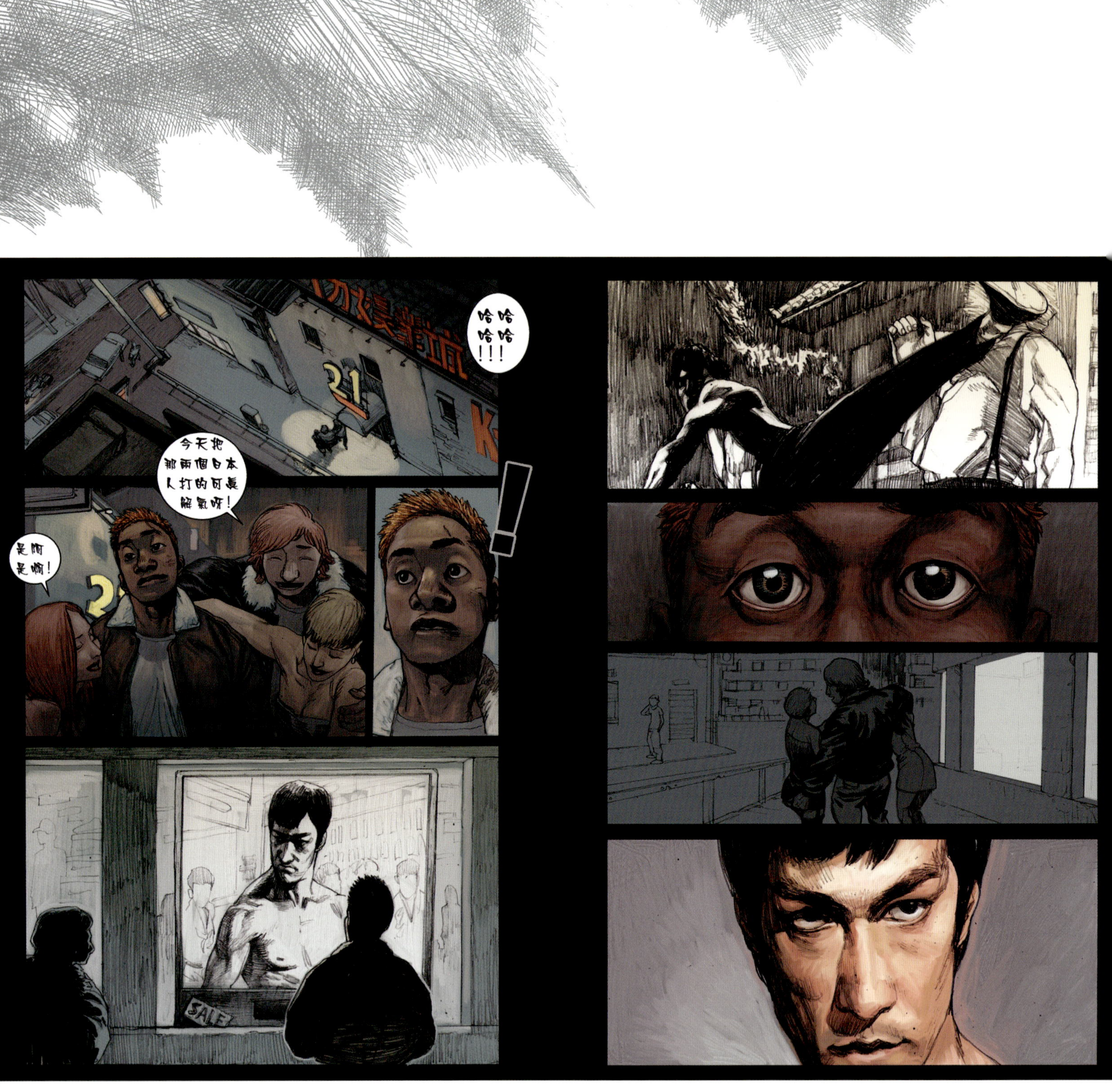

Soul of the Dragon, page 87, 2005. Pen and ink. Digital composition and graphic finalization in Painter.

2004, Digital composition and graphic finalization in Painter.

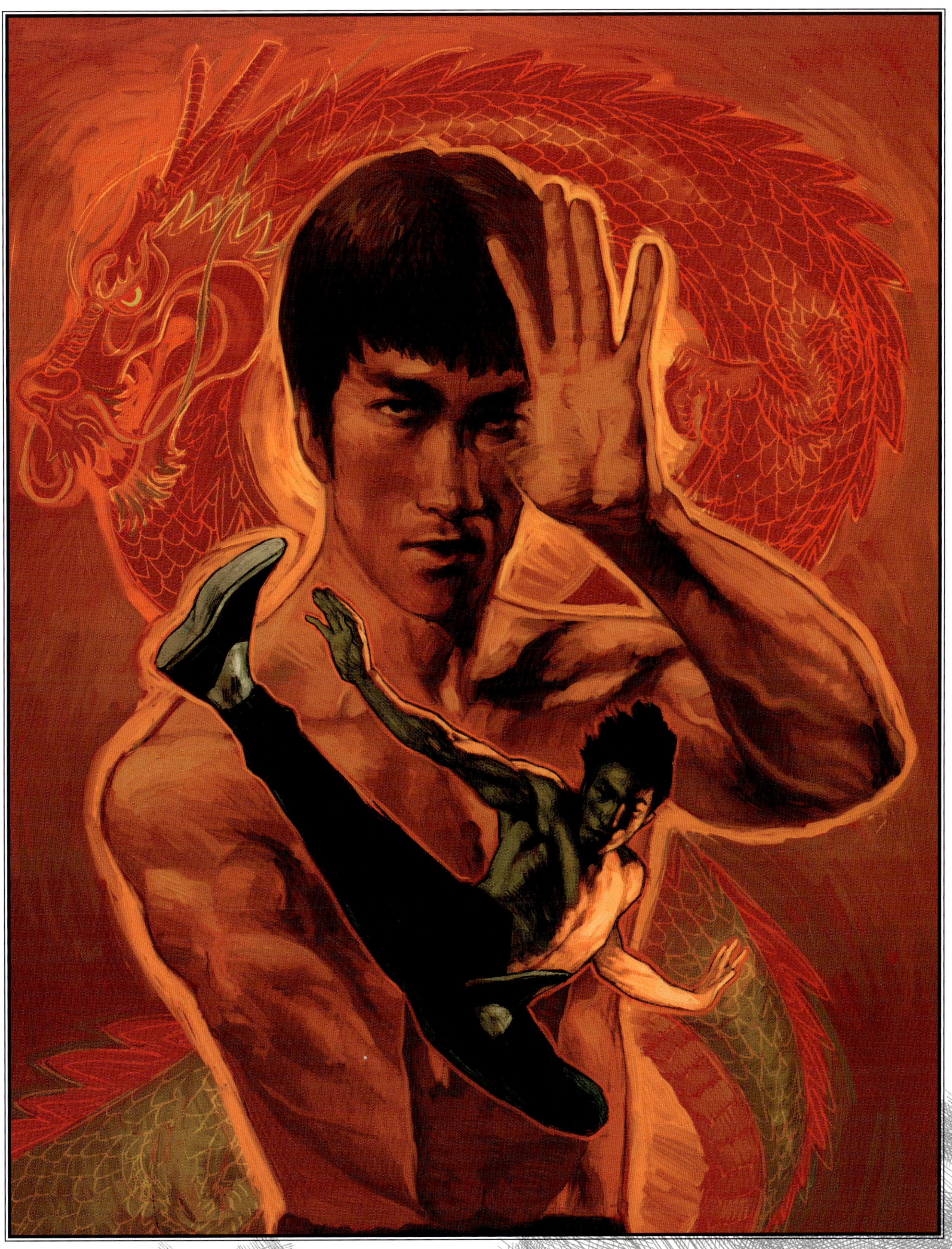

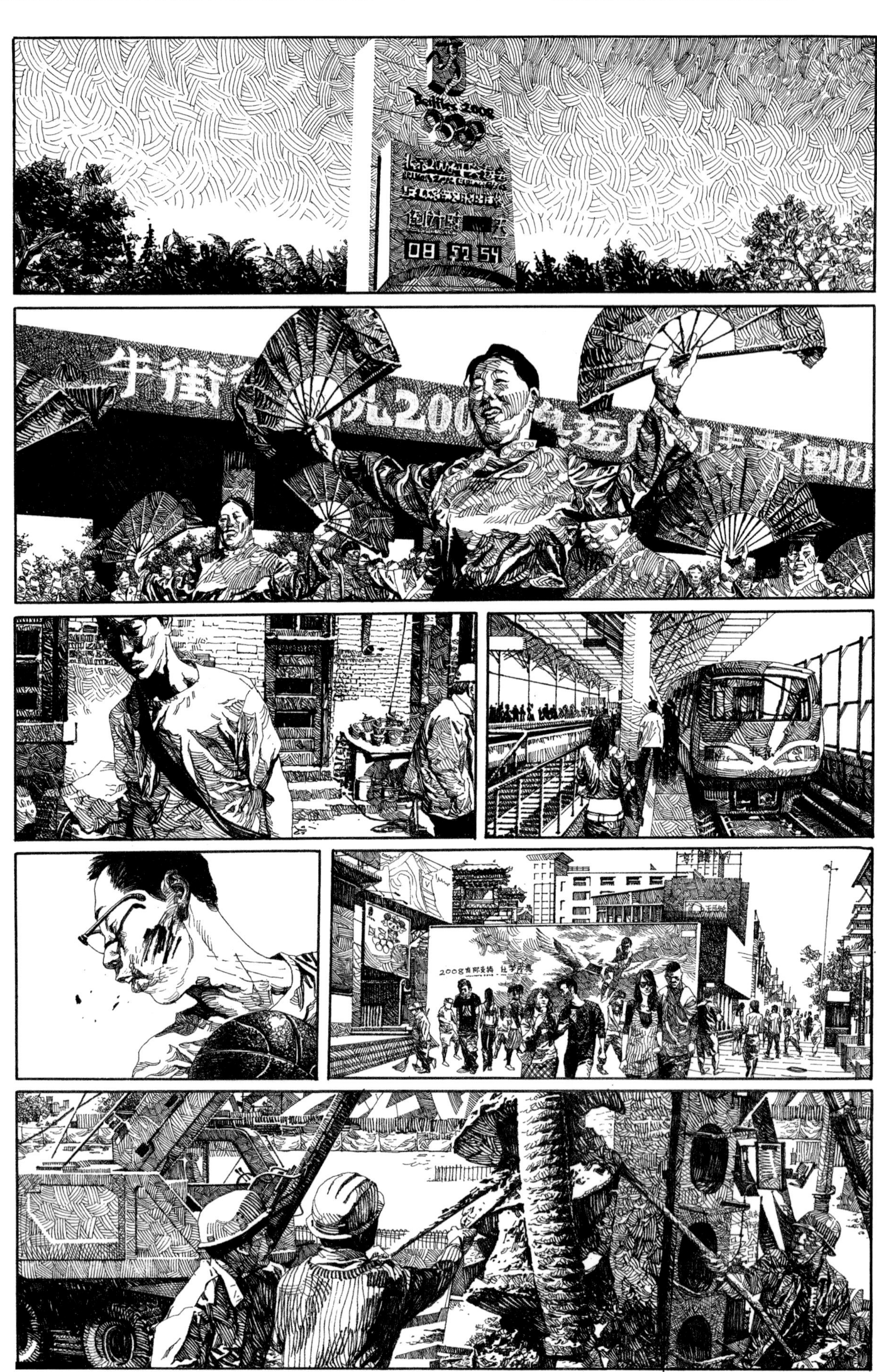

Jiao Luo by Gao Chu, 2008. Pen and ink A3 paper. Digital composition and graphic finalization in Painter.

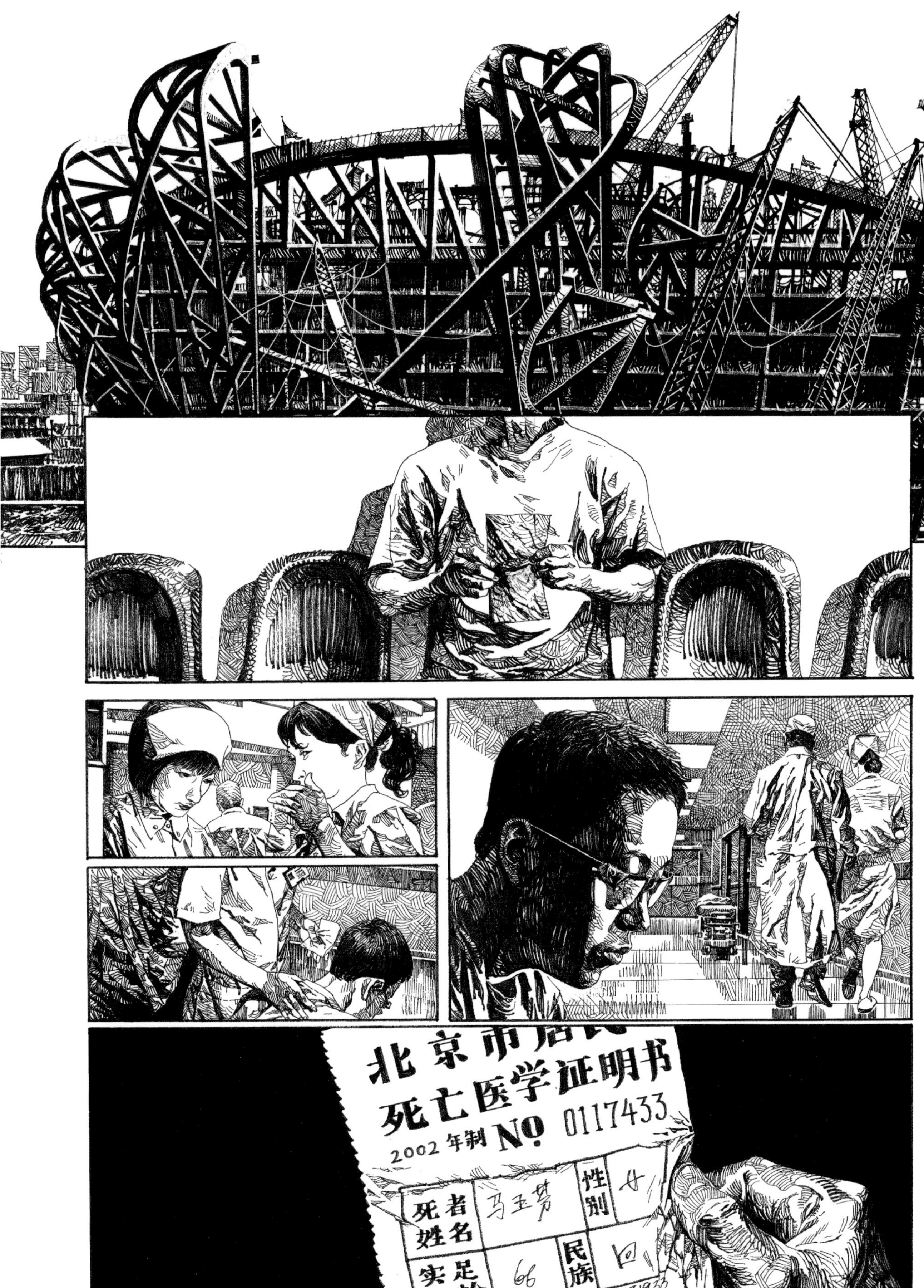

北京市居民
死亡医学证明书
2002 年制 NO 0117433
死者姓名 马玉芬
性别 女
实足年龄 66
民族 回

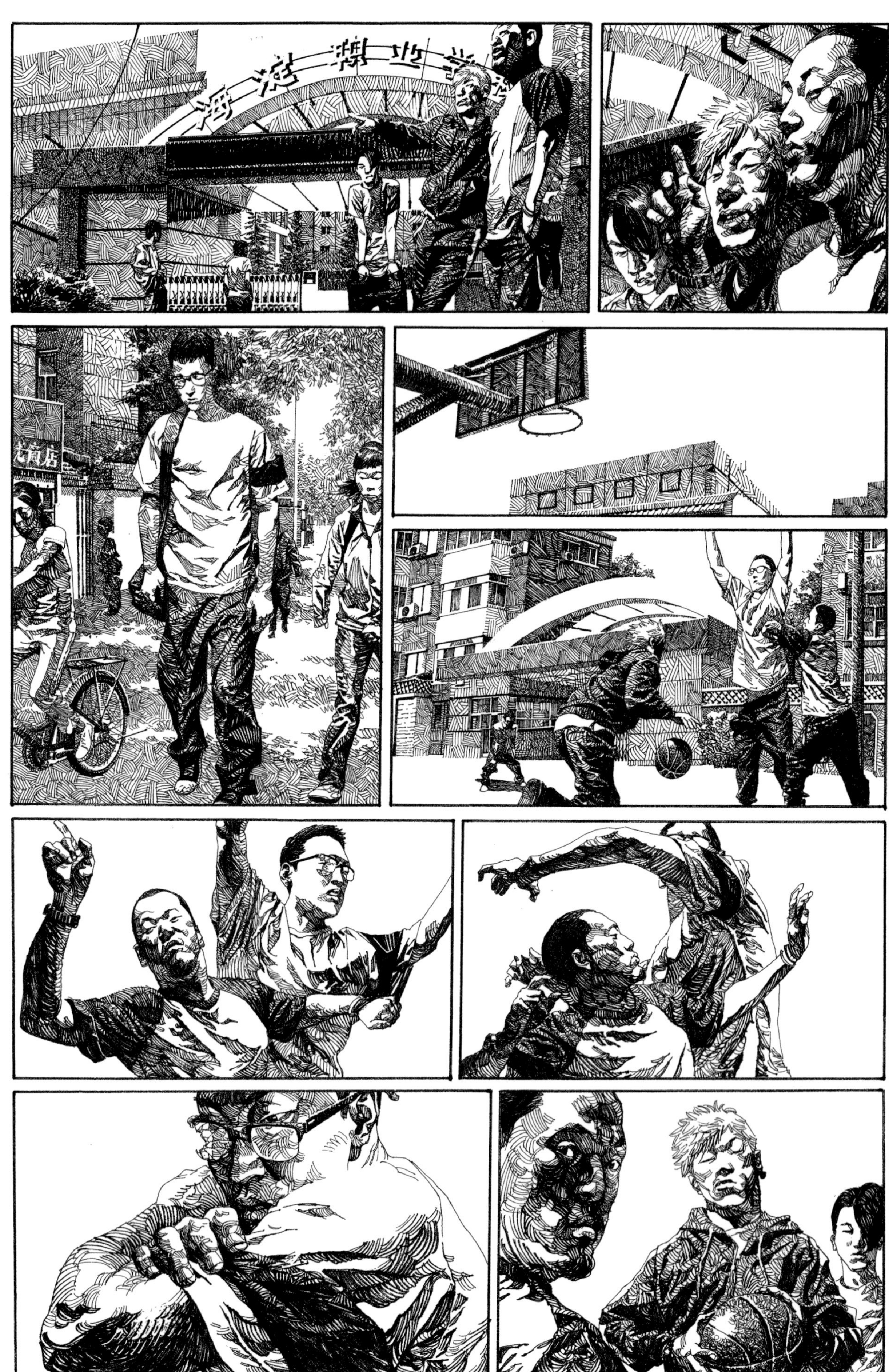

Jiao Luo by Gao Chu, 2008. Pen and ink A3 paper. Digital composition and graphic finalization in Painter.

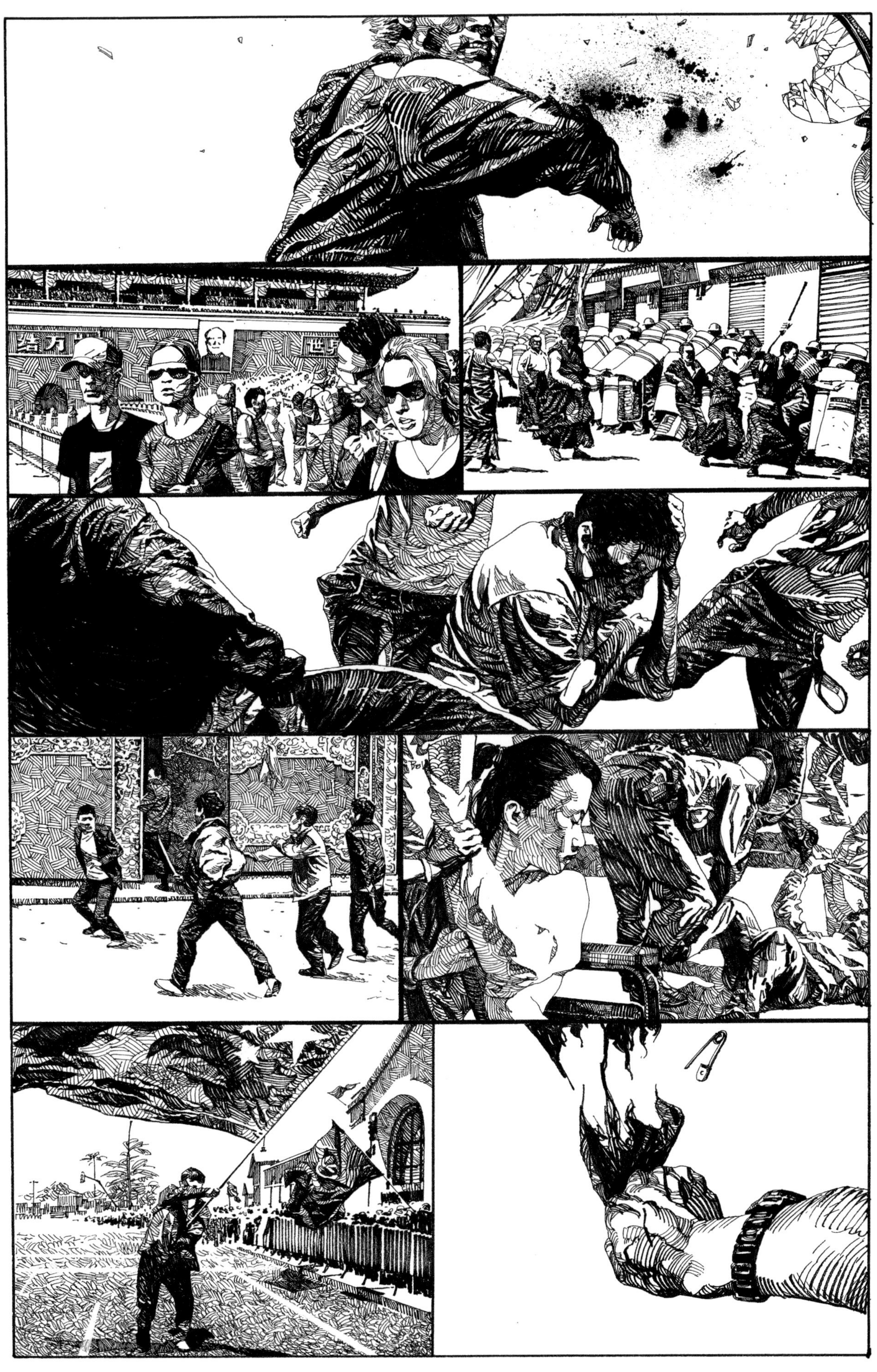

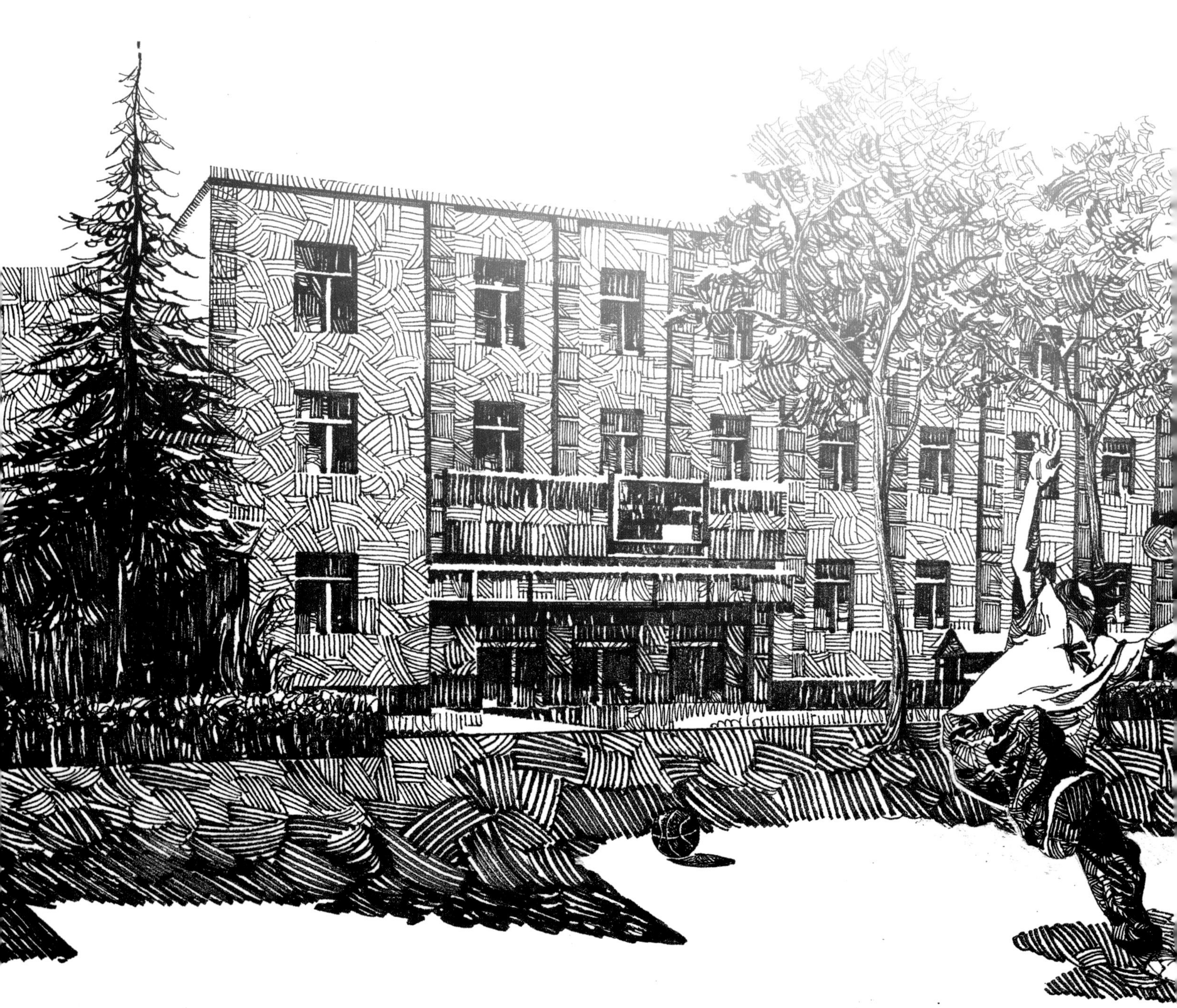

Jiao Luo by Gao Chu, 2008. Pen and ink A3 paper. Digital composition and graphic finalization in Painter.

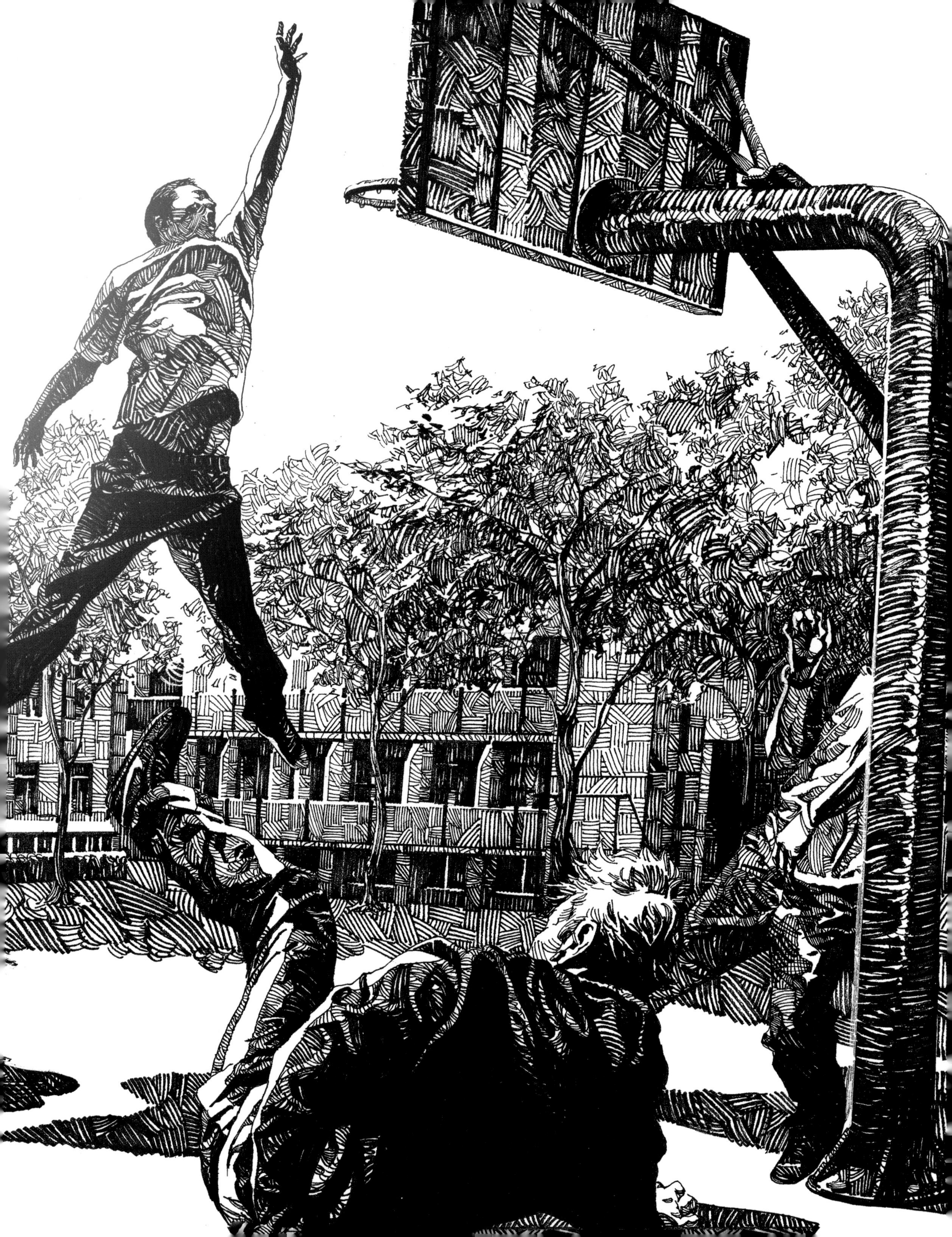

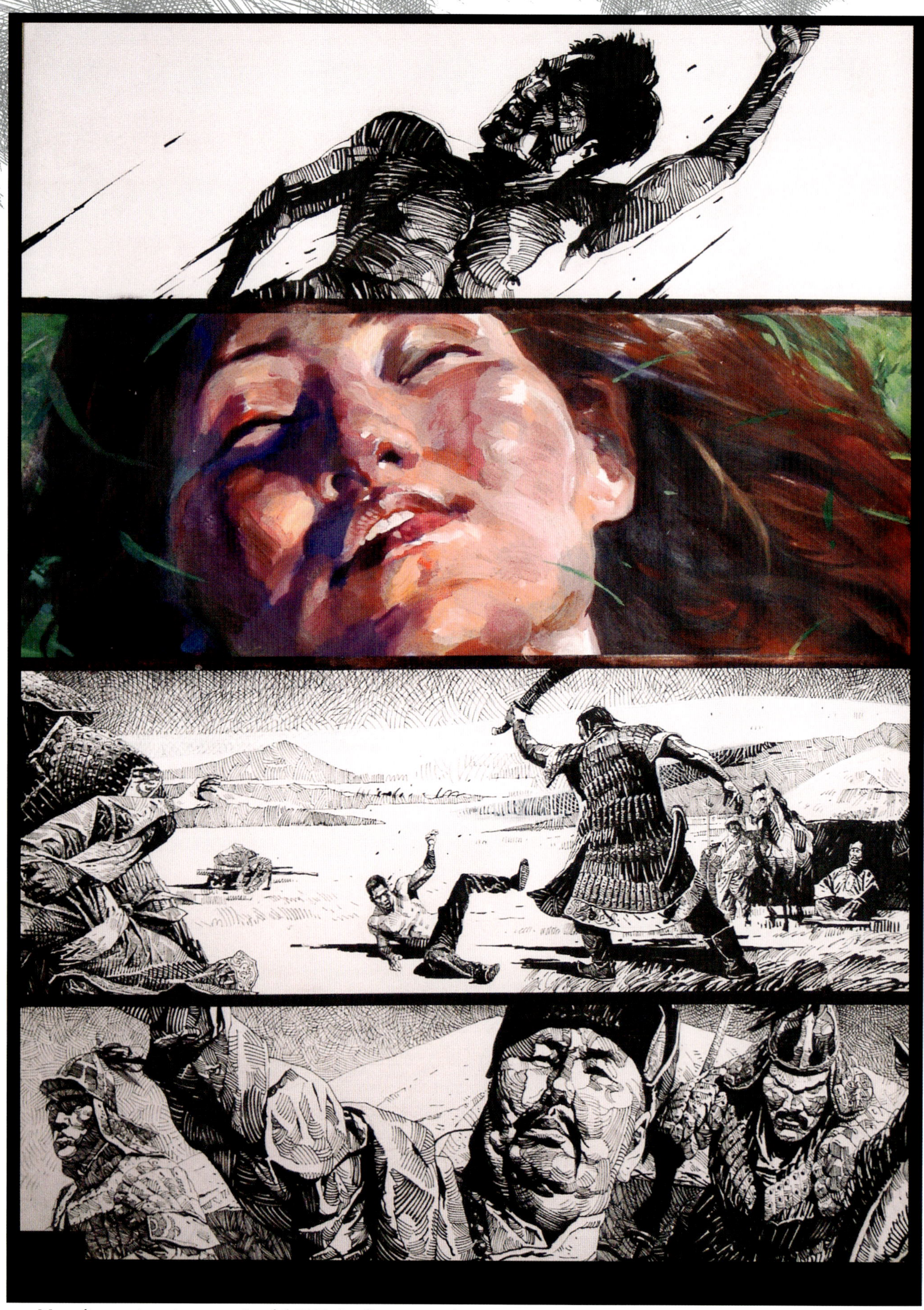

Mongolian comic project, pages 5 and 6, 2010. Acrylic on watercolor paper.

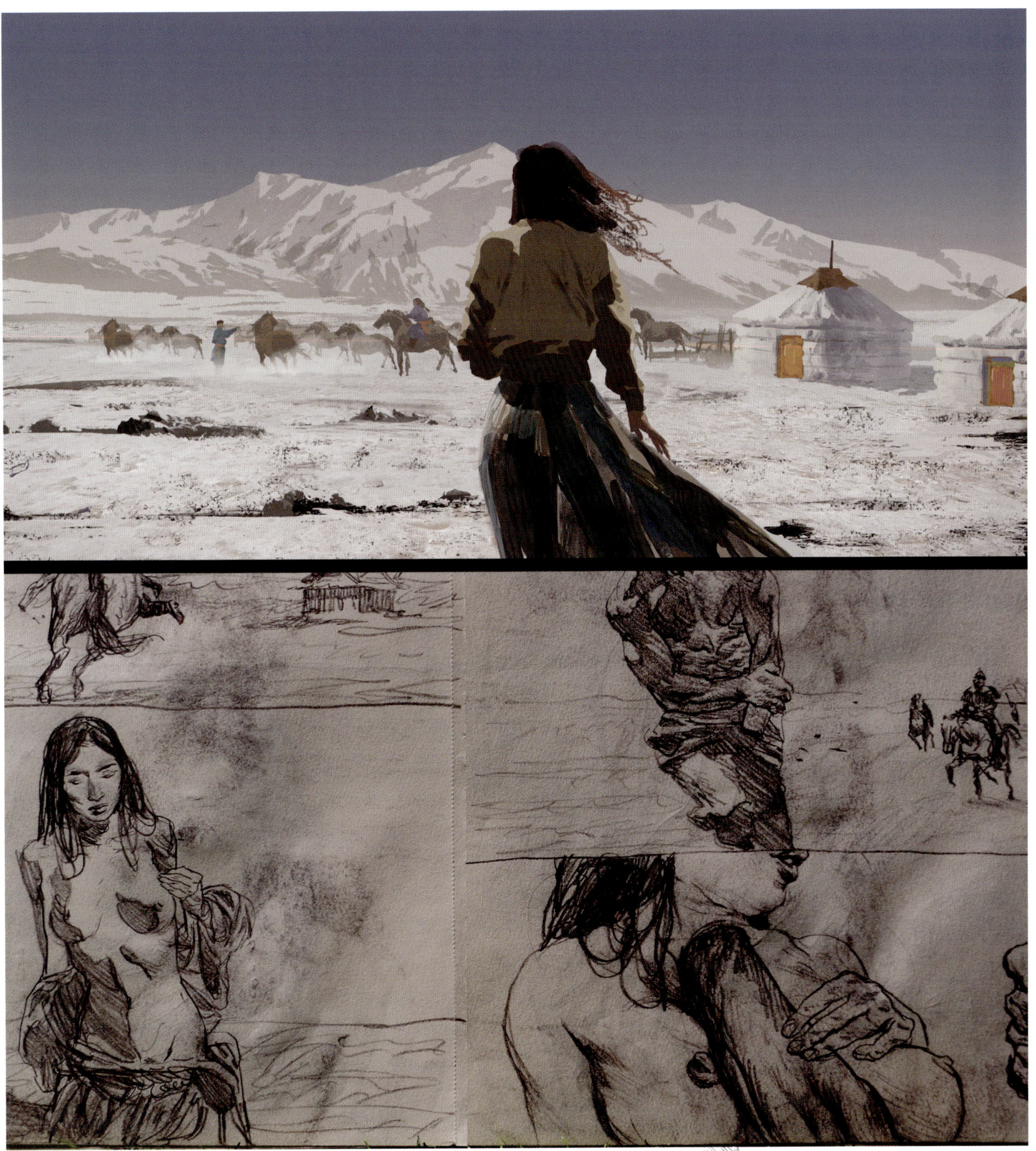

Mongolian comic project, pages 5 and 6, 2010. Acrylic on watercolor paper.

CLARITY

(Written on my birthday night)

Do not doubt.
You came into this world full of pride, strength filling your veins,
After running through disaster together, we lick the hot blood and laugh heartily.
Do not doubt.
You are stupid, you do not know how to count, you have no notion of time,
You refuse to become one of those assholes who live aimlessly and resign themselves to their own fate.
Do not doubt.
You will feel isolated, you will feel the cold,
For the sun shines in the darkest and iciest parts of this universe.
Do not doubt.
Your strength will always allow you to face a pack of wolves,
Your pride and your persistence will make you face the loneliness and the cold,
You will not stop spreading your heat to love,
Then, each time, you will be massacred by lightning!
Once again you will pick up the pieces of your body in the field
And you will reassemble them in the brazier of your heart.
The scars you keep accumulating will form your armor.
It is possible that the overwhelming loneliness will make you age.
After being generous, you may find yourself in dire straits.
But you won't regret anything.
You are still young, maybe you will be forever.
Of course, trials make you grow old before their time, but they will always be renewed.
Use your strength to fight,
Use your frankness and your honesty to struggle, use your purity to awaken everything.
Do not doubt, you are a sun!
So shine!

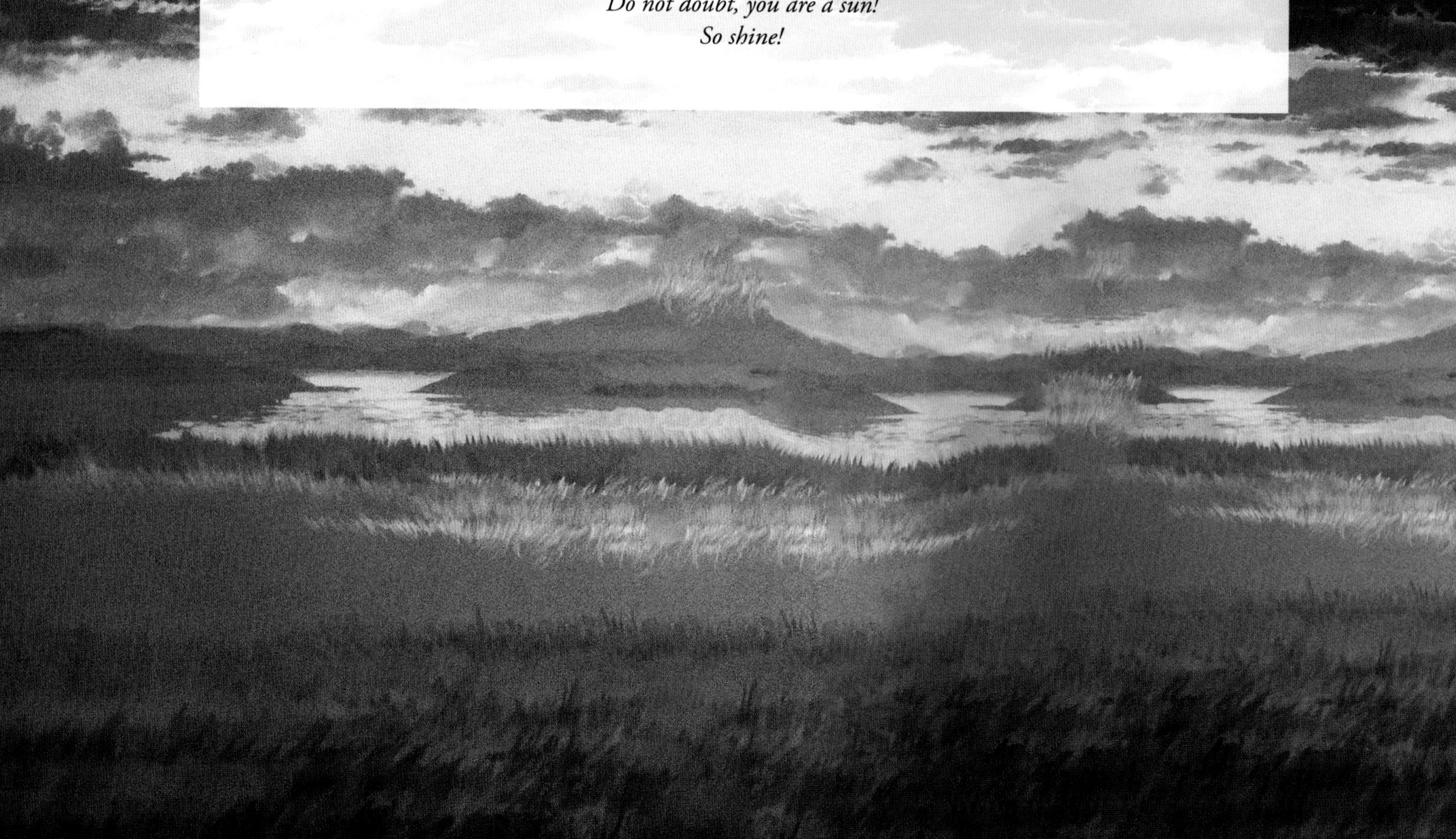

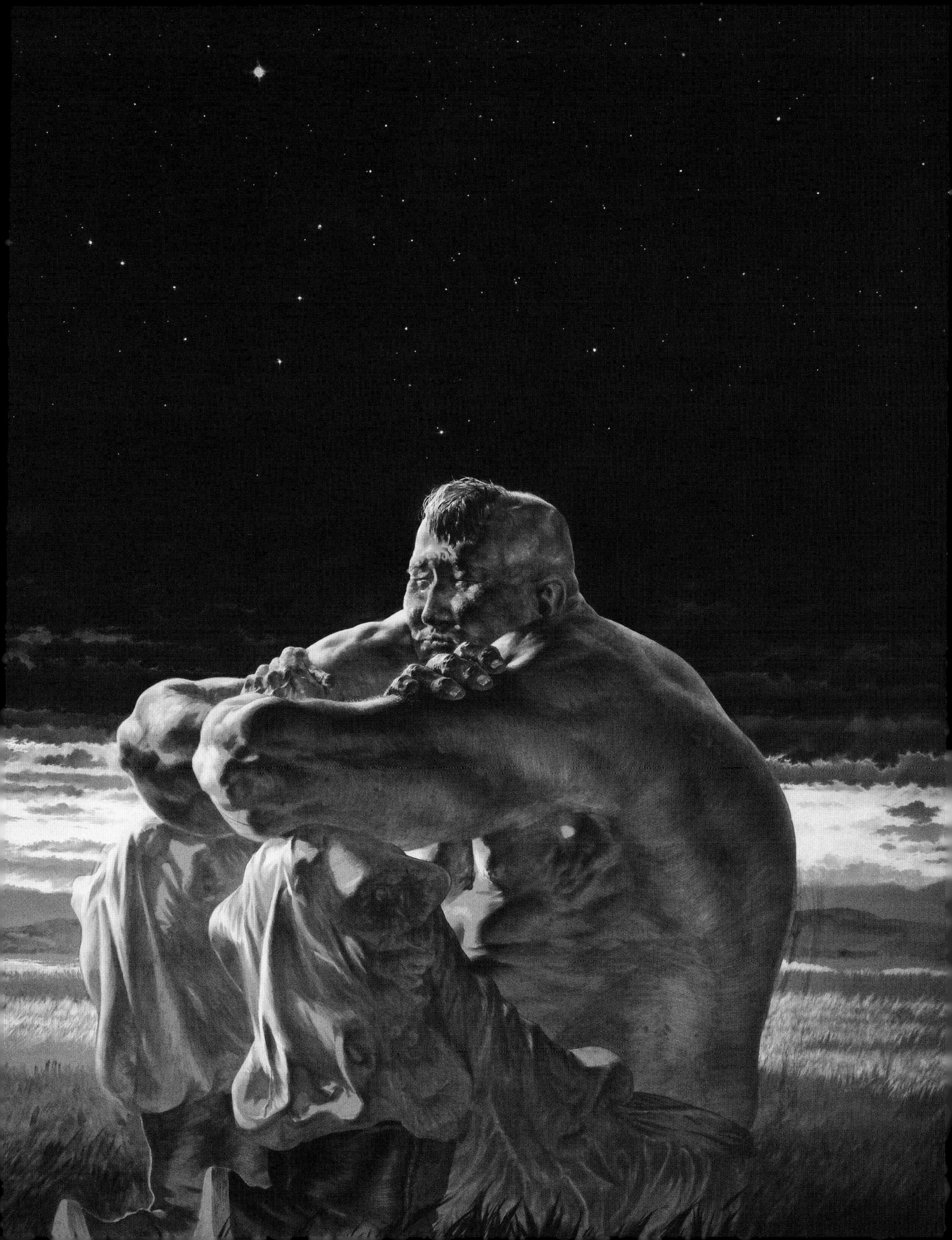

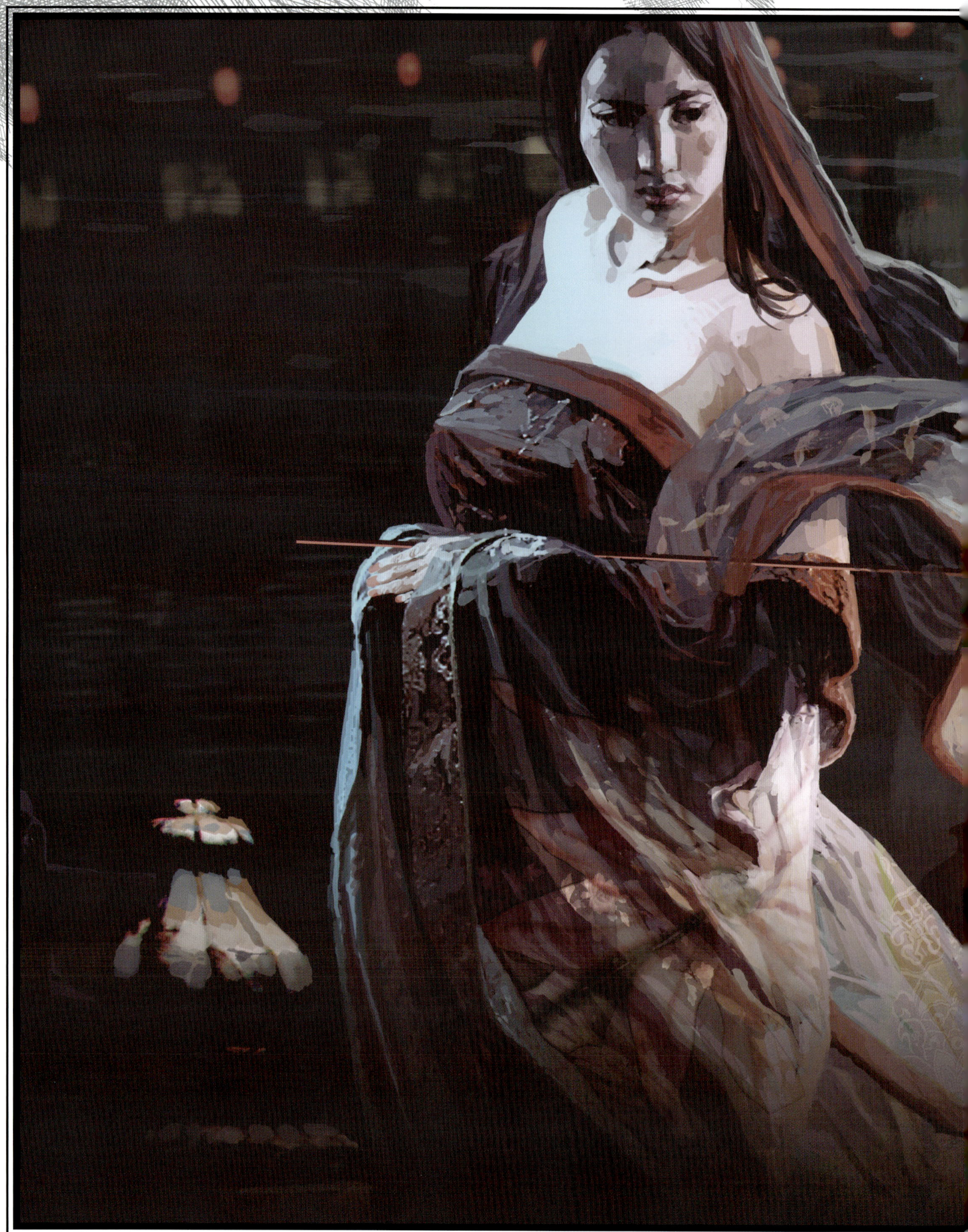

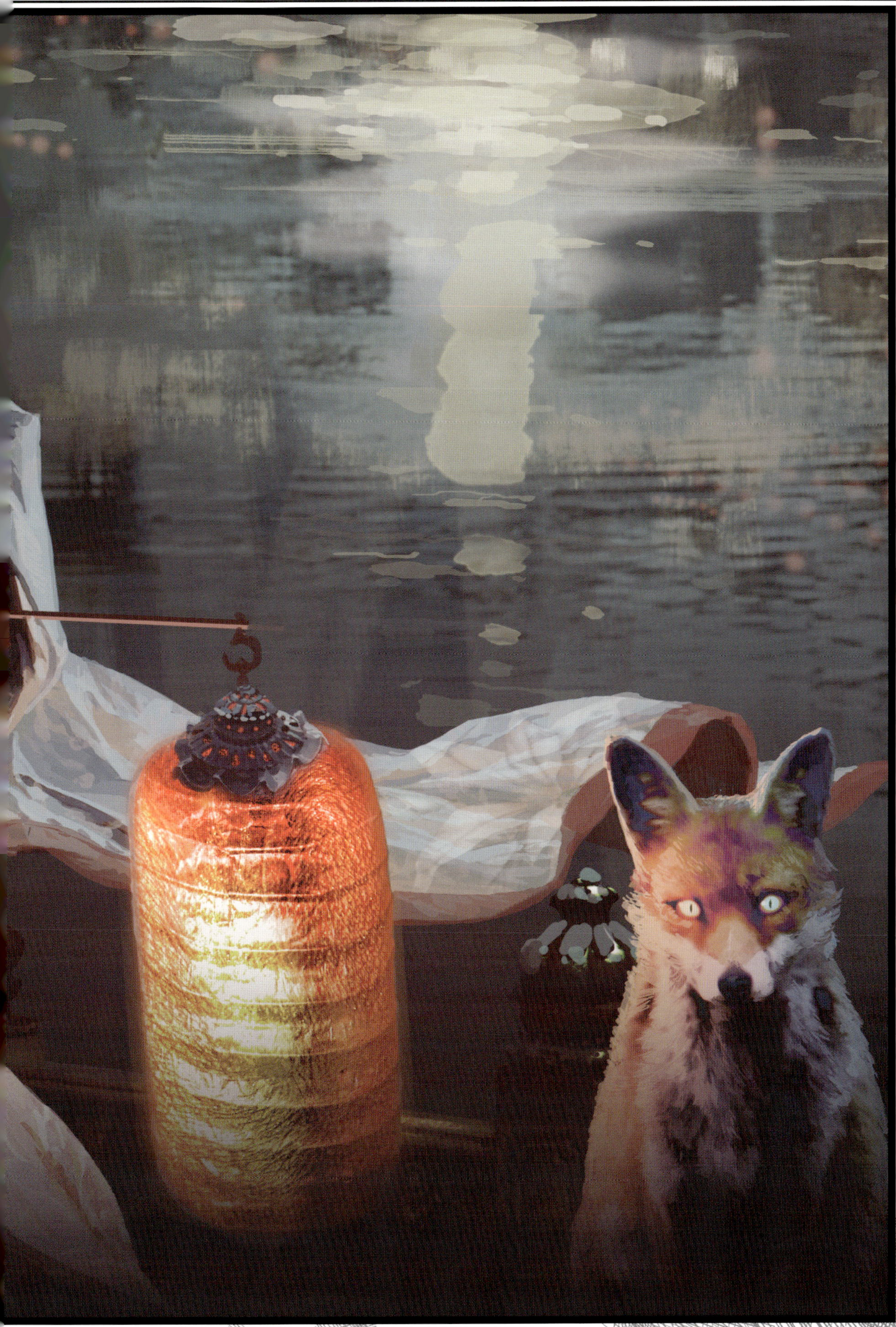

Untitled, 2010,
Art Rage +
Photoshop.

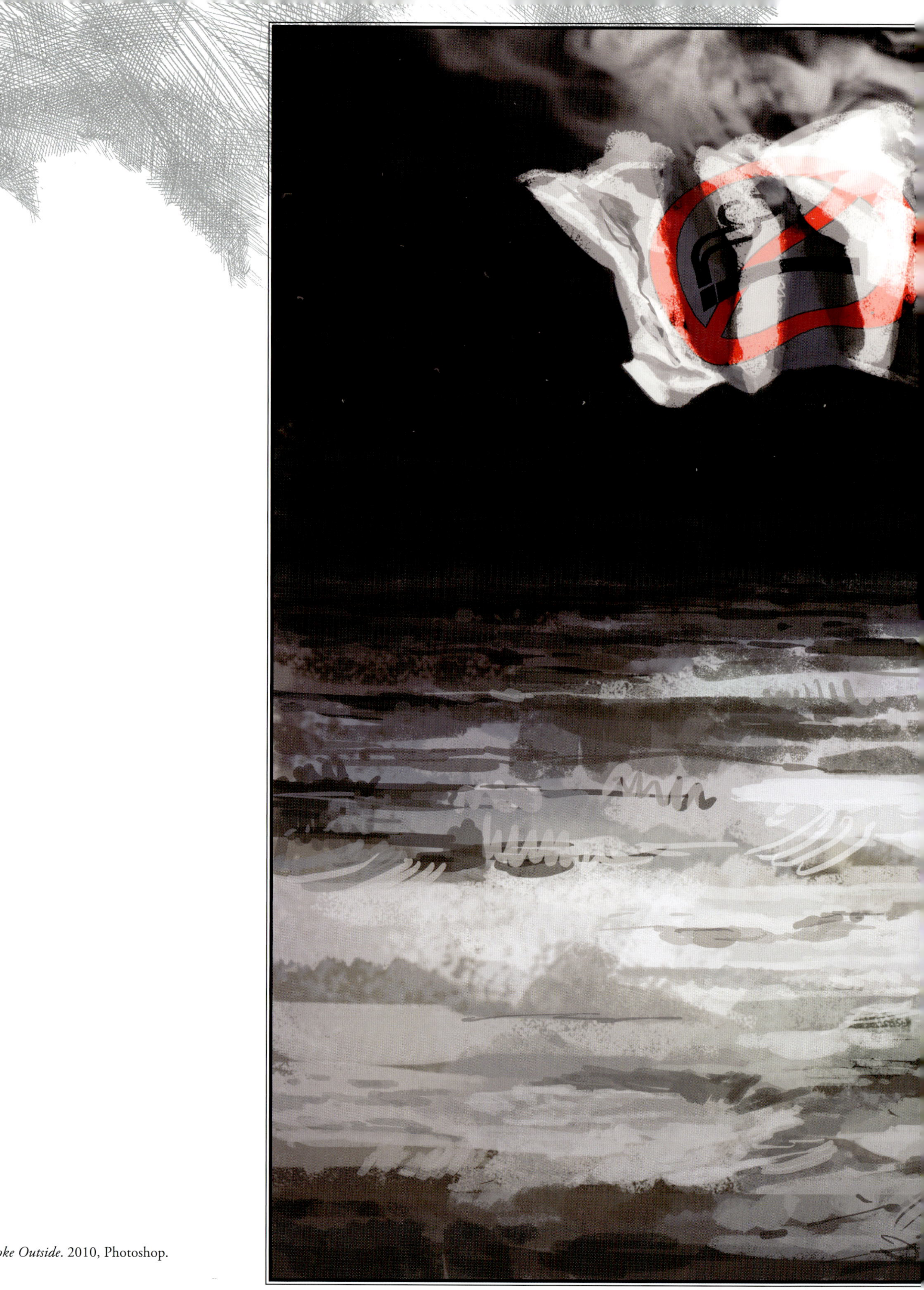

Smoke Outside. 2010, Photoshop.

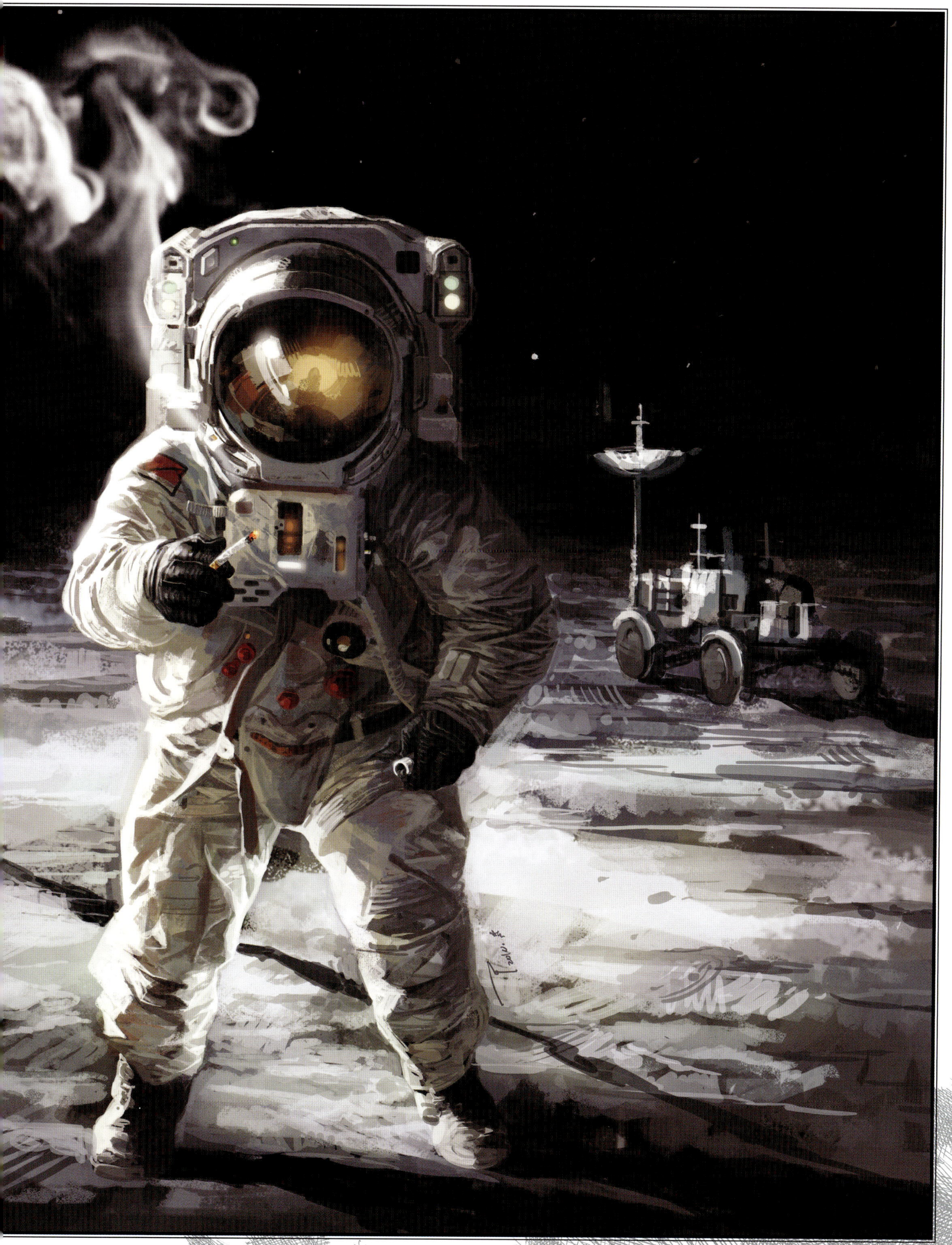

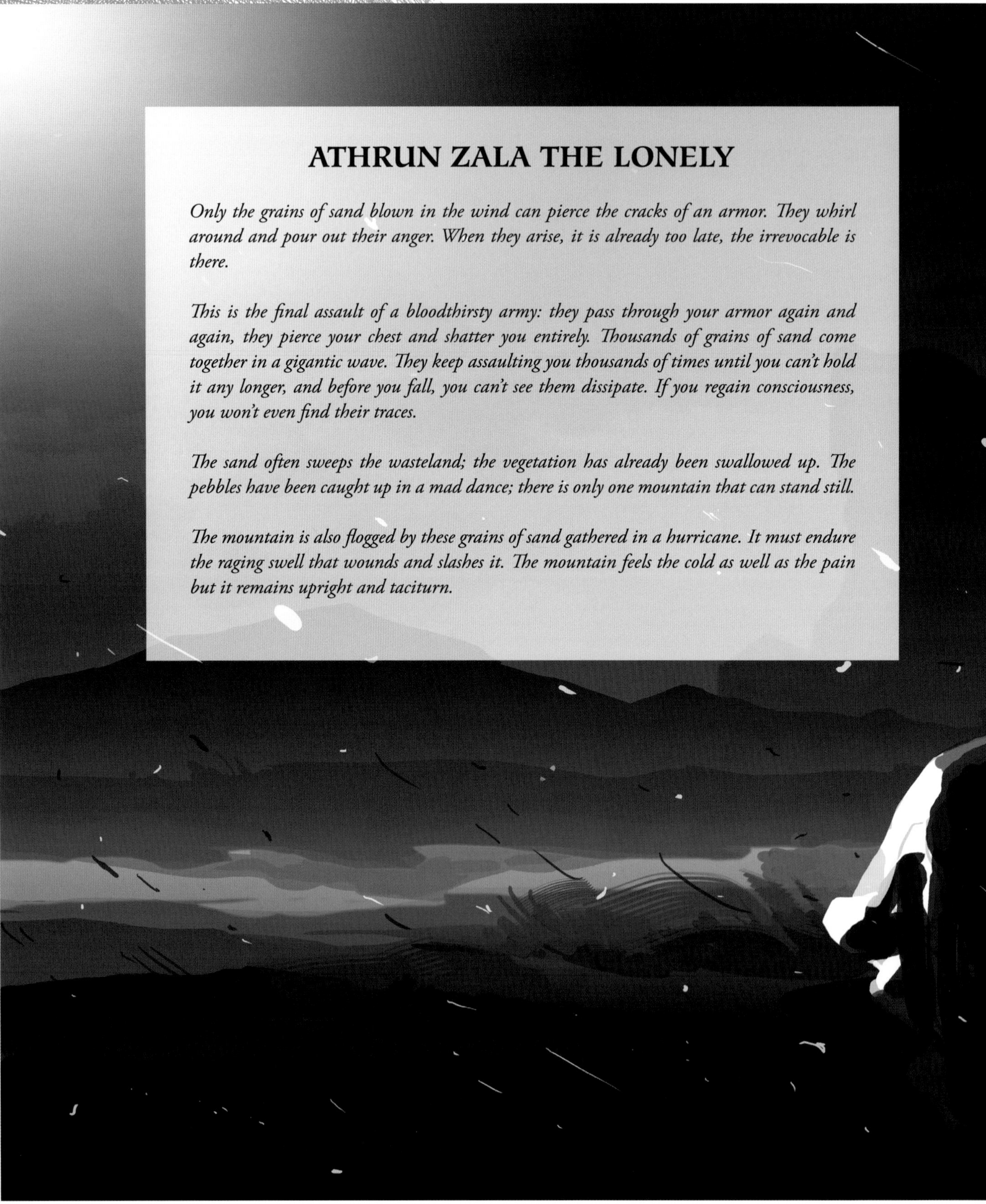

ATHRUN ZALA THE LONELY

Only the grains of sand blown in the wind can pierce the cracks of an armor. They whirl around and pour out their anger. When they arise, it is already too late, the irrevocable is there.

This is the final assault of a bloodthirsty army: they pass through your armor again and again, they pierce your chest and shatter you entirely. Thousands of grains of sand come together in a gigantic wave. They keep assaulting you thousands of times until you can't hold it any longer, and before you fall, you can't see them dissipate. If you regain consciousness, you won't even find their traces.

The sand often sweeps the wasteland; the vegetation has already been swallowed up. The pebbles have been caught up in a mad dance; there is only one mountain that can stand still.

The mountain is also flogged by these grains of sand gathered in a hurricane. It must endure the raging swell that wounds and slashes it. The mountain feels the cold as well as the pain but it remains upright and taciturn.

Lonely Araslan. 2014, Photoshop.

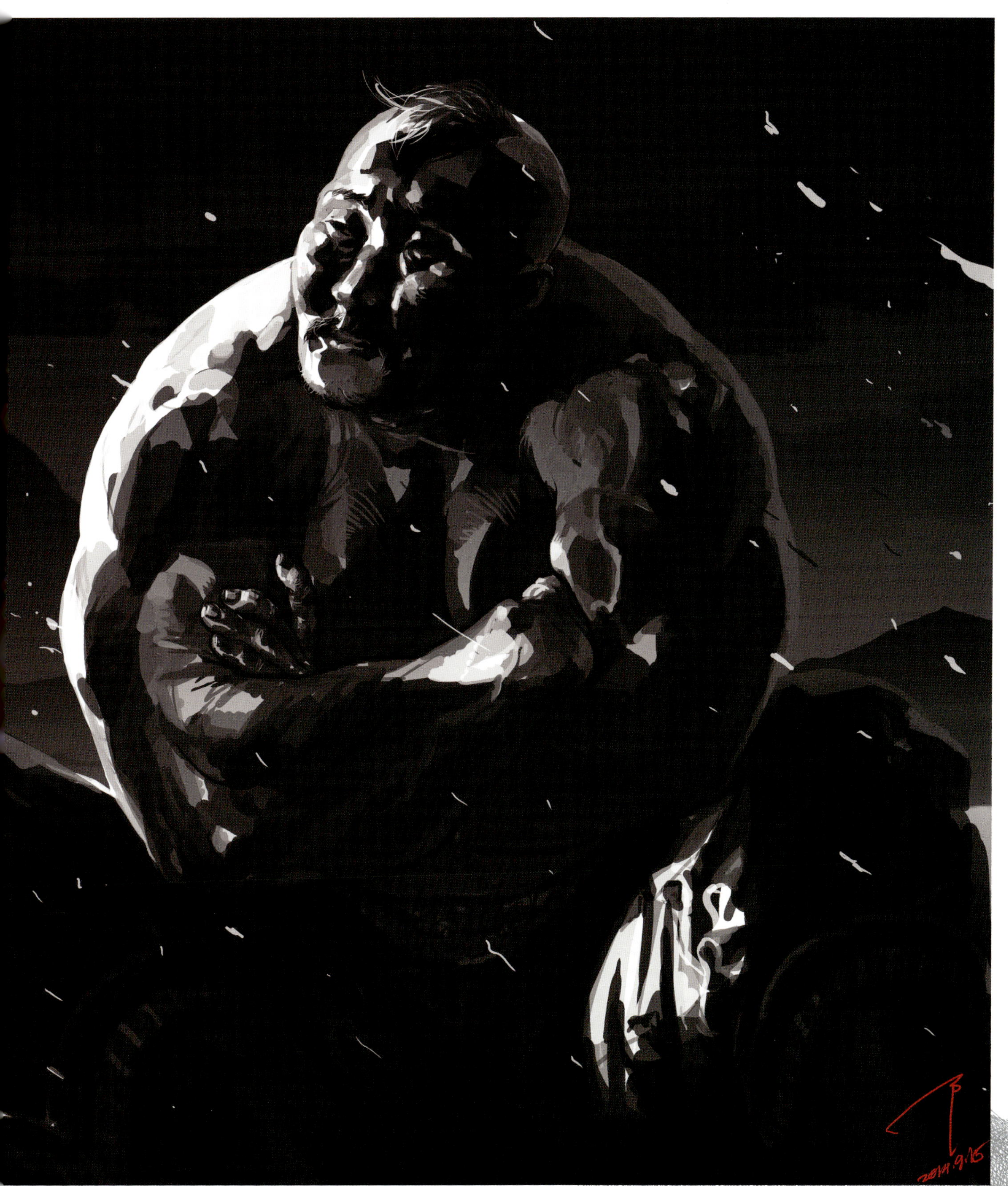

HARD MELODY

It's the year 2000, I'm 18.

I'm starting to publish longer comics in Shaonian Manhua teen magazine. Before that, I was the kind of kid who couldn't sit still but could spend an entire day sitting on a stool drawing. I had moved five times, changed schools twice, and had been kicked out three times. I had also met a lovely young woman who I had loved in secret for seven years.

The first time I called her was on the evening of my eighteenth birthday. When she rejected me, I did two hundred push-ups and, for the first time, downed a whole bottle of hot Chinese rice wine. I like to see things through to the end.

Comparing myself to other people my age, it seemed that my time in this world was passing much slower. After that eighteenth birthday alone, drenched in alcohol and sweat, I began to use my moments of freedom to explore the world. I put my brush down, stopped fighting, and went out to meet other people. Sometimes I managed to generate interest. Growing up in a traditional communist military family, I have never known the luxury of pocket money and video game consoles. Even on special occasions like Chinese New Year or birthdays, I wasn't allowed to get excited. The only thing I could do was conform to the attitude of the people in the room during the day. Family reunions. I never had a consumer's way of enjoying life the way other young people of my generation knew.

With my brushes and my guitar under my arm, I went out into the world. It was strange to me, and not understanding its logic, I opted for silence. But my gaze was all the more inquisitive as this silence left immense space for inner thoughts. I was thinking too much, and all these thoughts deep inside needed to be expressed even more.

It seems that our destinies have the same finality because there comes a day when we have to go, and no one can determine whether the current sweeping our destinies will take us to hell or to heaven.

Life is like stars that glow from their formation until they leave a trail of light in the sky as they go out.

And if you were one of those stars, even for a moment, why couldn't you light up those complicated nights?

Eighteen years… Twenty-some comic books of different lengths.

During my high school years, I wasted time using brushes to draw my own world. Then, in 2002, I discovered new, random perspectives from the pages of a book. After that, I took interest in my ancestors' journeys. My stories are inspired by my ancestors. Every stain and stroke of my paintings have been imbued with their presence. Something from them is present in my work. Over the past few years, I have produced a lot of comic books and one poem keeps coming back to me, and that is my Man Jiang Hong.

Its first line reads:

Build yourself or disappear!

RIGHT: Pencil drawing for the cover of *Hard Melody*, 2014.

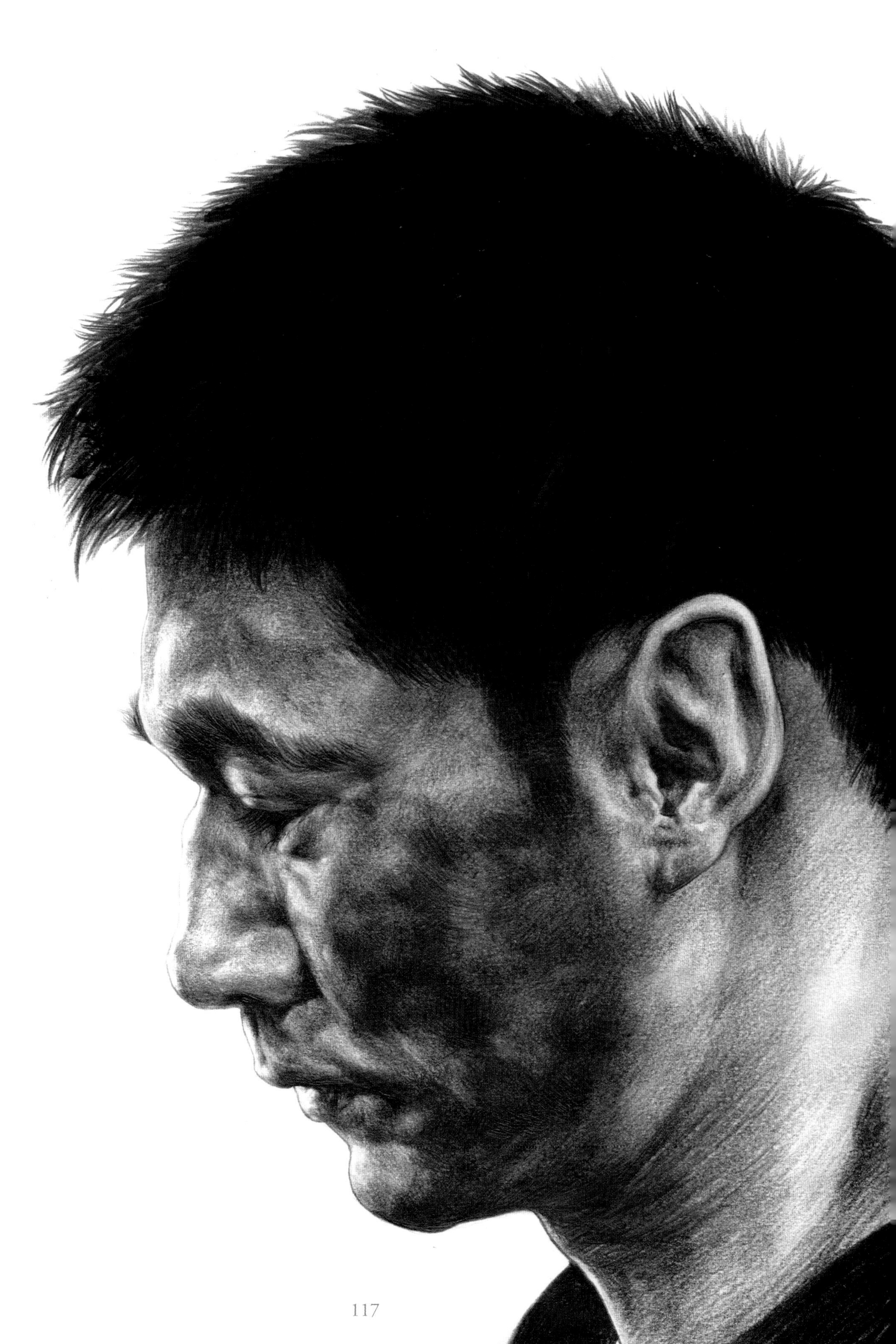

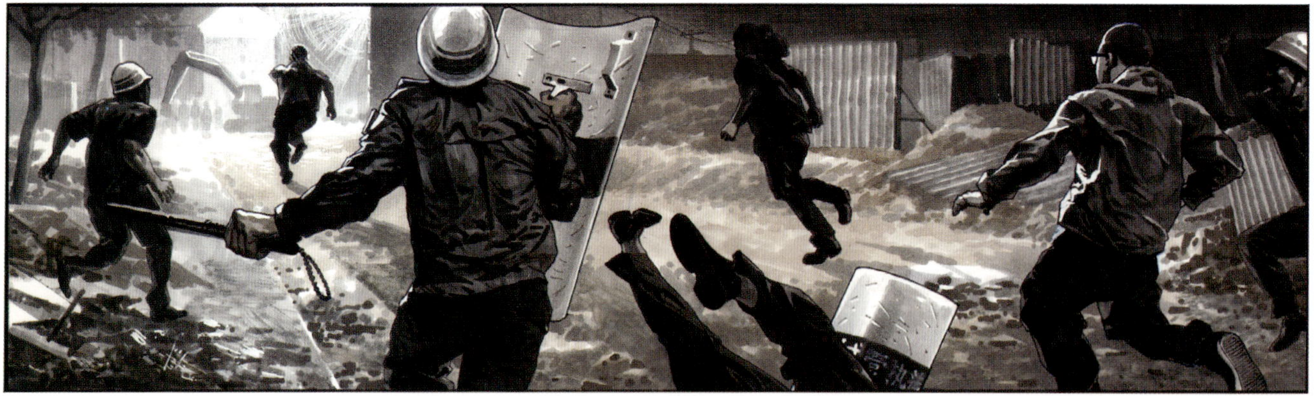

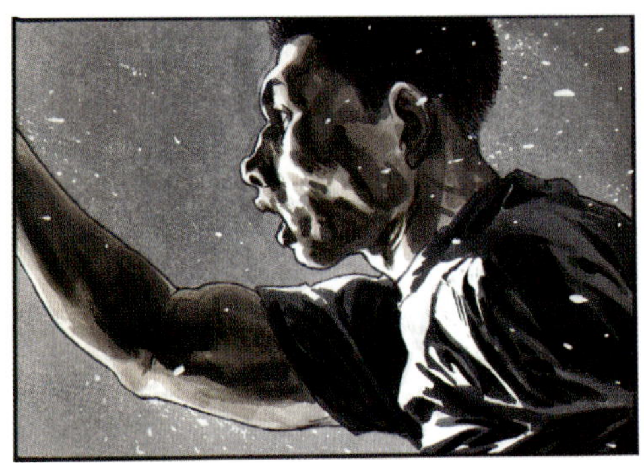

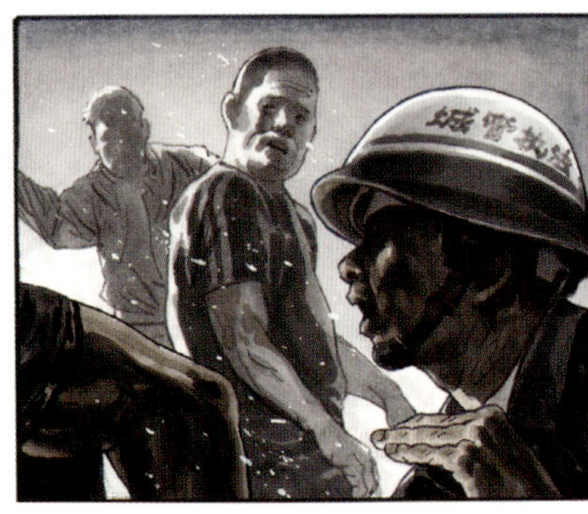

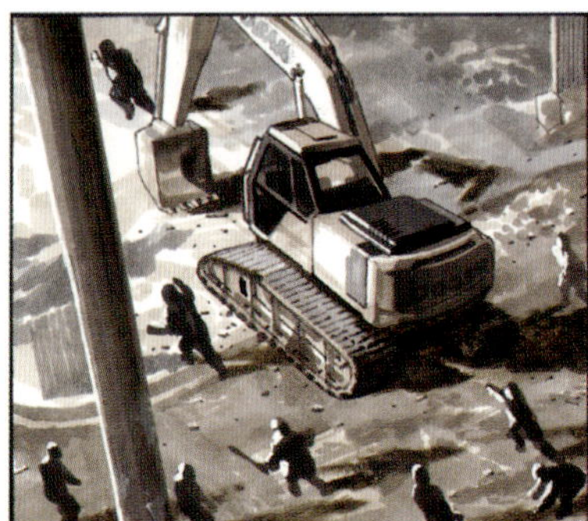

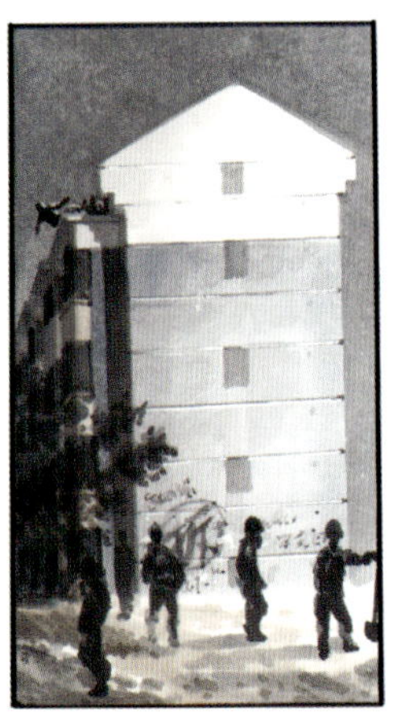

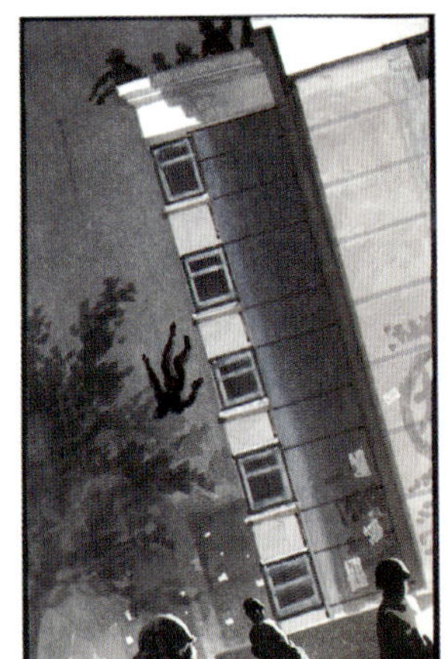

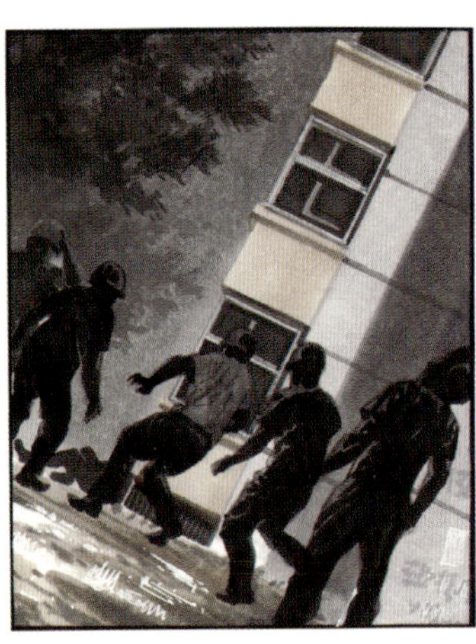

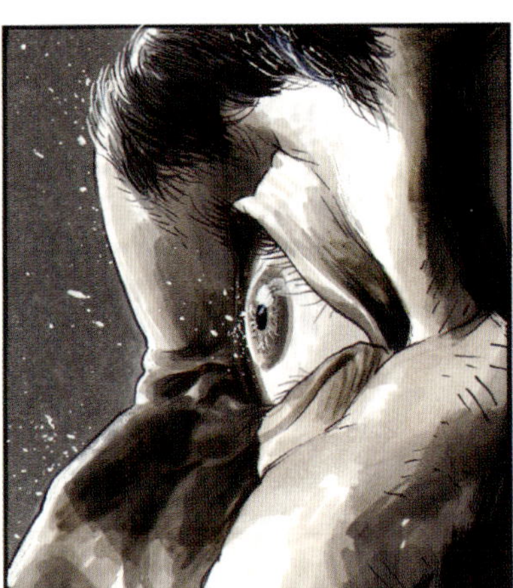

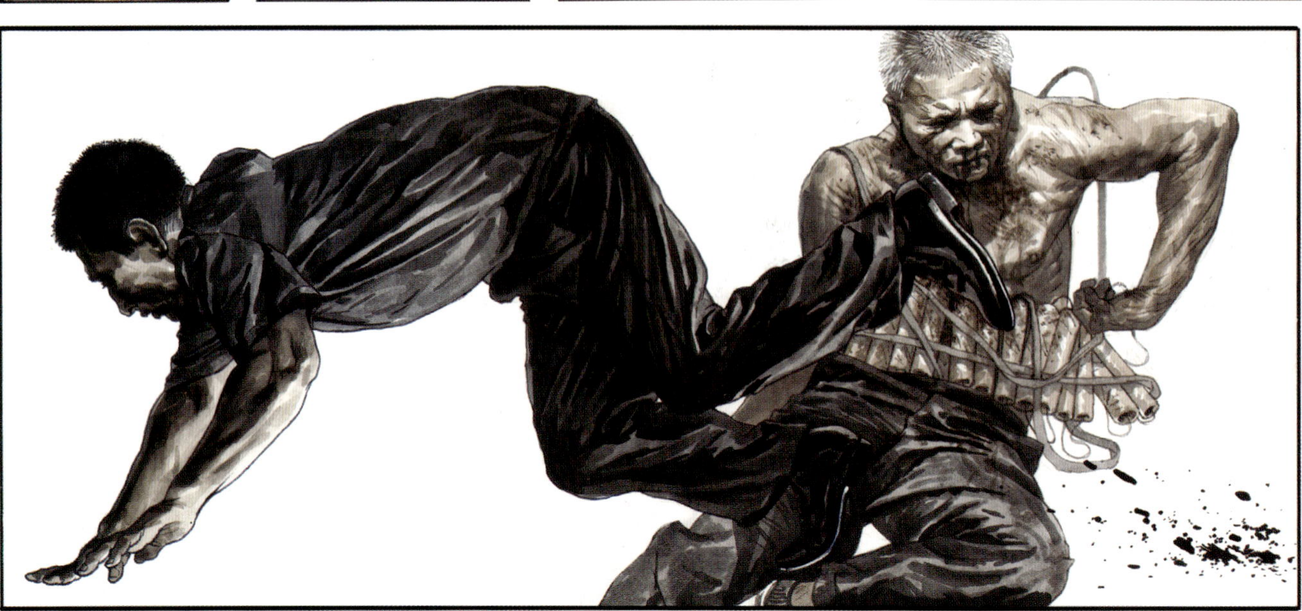

Pages from *Hard Melody*, colorized, 2014.

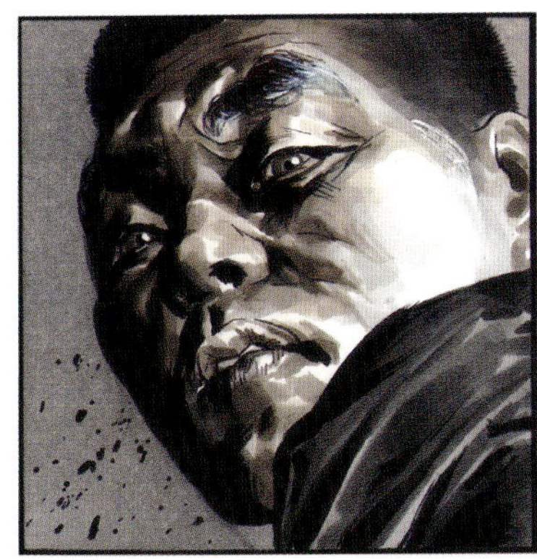
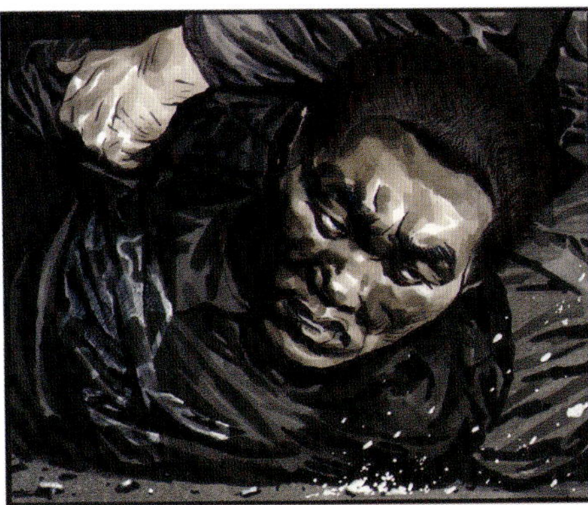
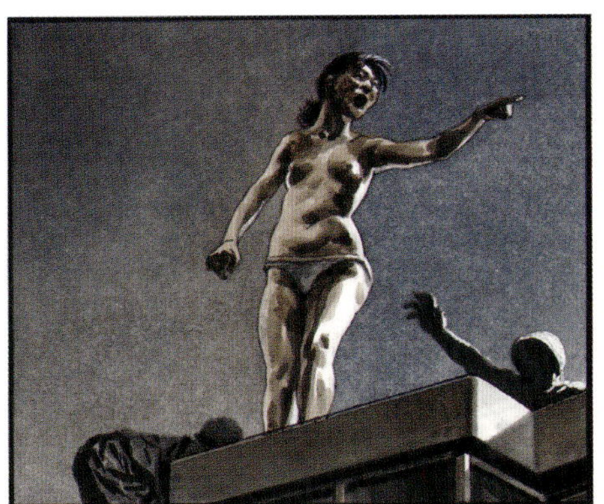
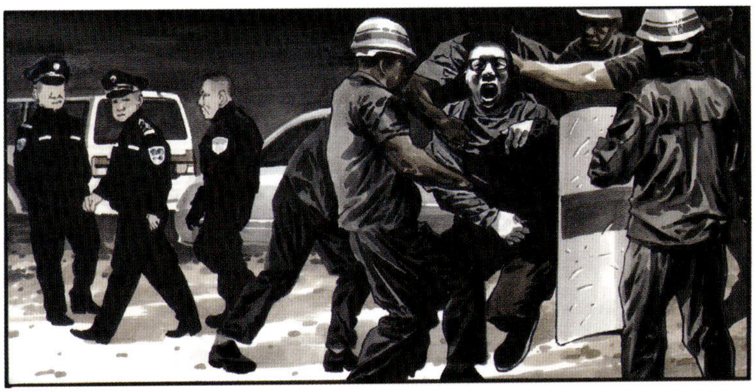
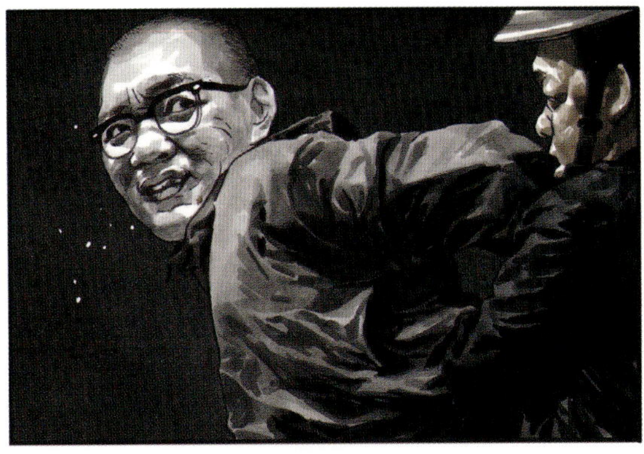
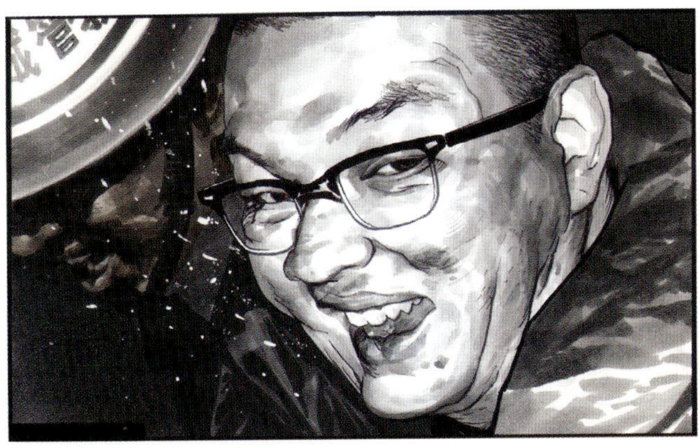
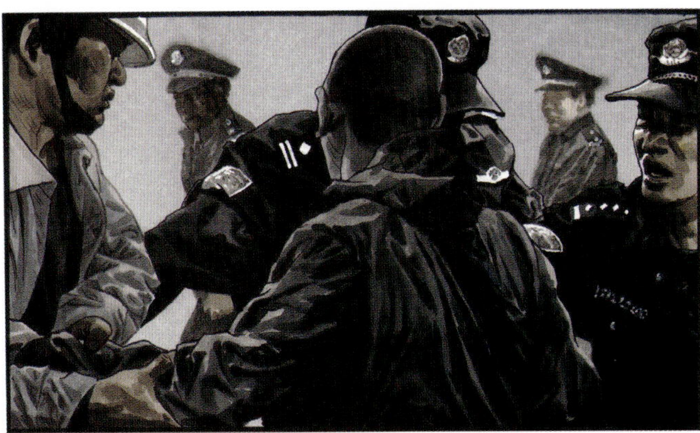
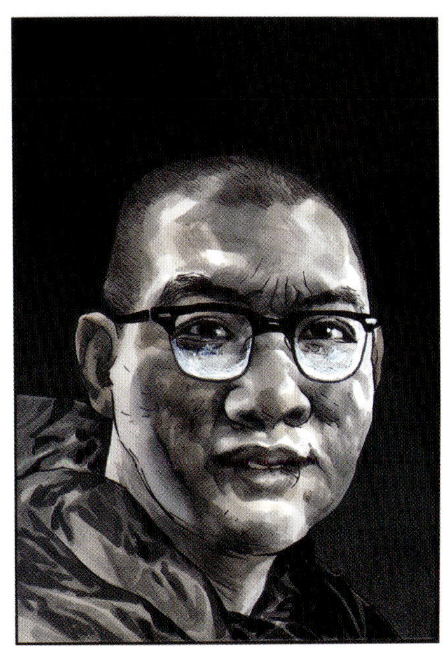
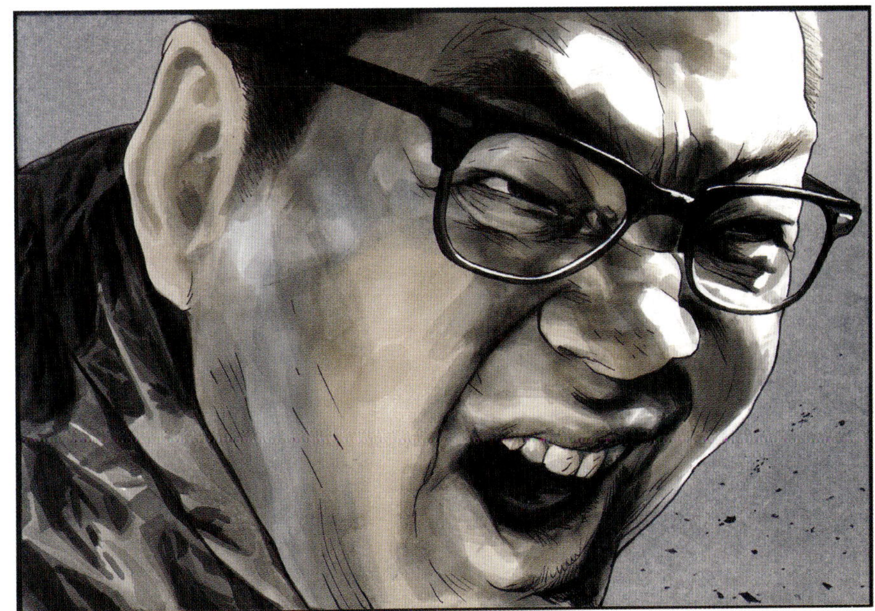

MAN JIANG HONG

Man Jiang Hong is the title of a lyrical poem that emerged at the end of the Tang Dynasty. By following its fixed form of rhythm and tonality, a poet is led to transpose this base verse with improvised lyrics and songs. In other words, on a musical scale, it's the ancient Chinese version of beats, loops, and blues. Subsequently, this form of spoken music became very popular under the Song Dynasty and was also called Yanbo Yu. With the fall of the Song Dynasty, the people grew bloodless and had no time for melancholy. It is a rare form that people continue to create.

My wrath bristles through my helmet, the rain stops as I stand by the rail;

I look up towards the sky and let loose a passionate roar.

At the age of thirty, my deeds are nothing but dust, my journey has taken me over eight thousand miles

So do not sit by idly, for young men will grow old in regret.

The Humiliation of Jingkang still lingers,

When will the pain of the Emperor's subjects ever end?

Let us ride our chariots through the Helan Pass,

There we shall feast on barbarian flesh and drink the blood of the Xiongnu.

Let us begin anew to recover our old empire, before paying tribute to the Emperor.

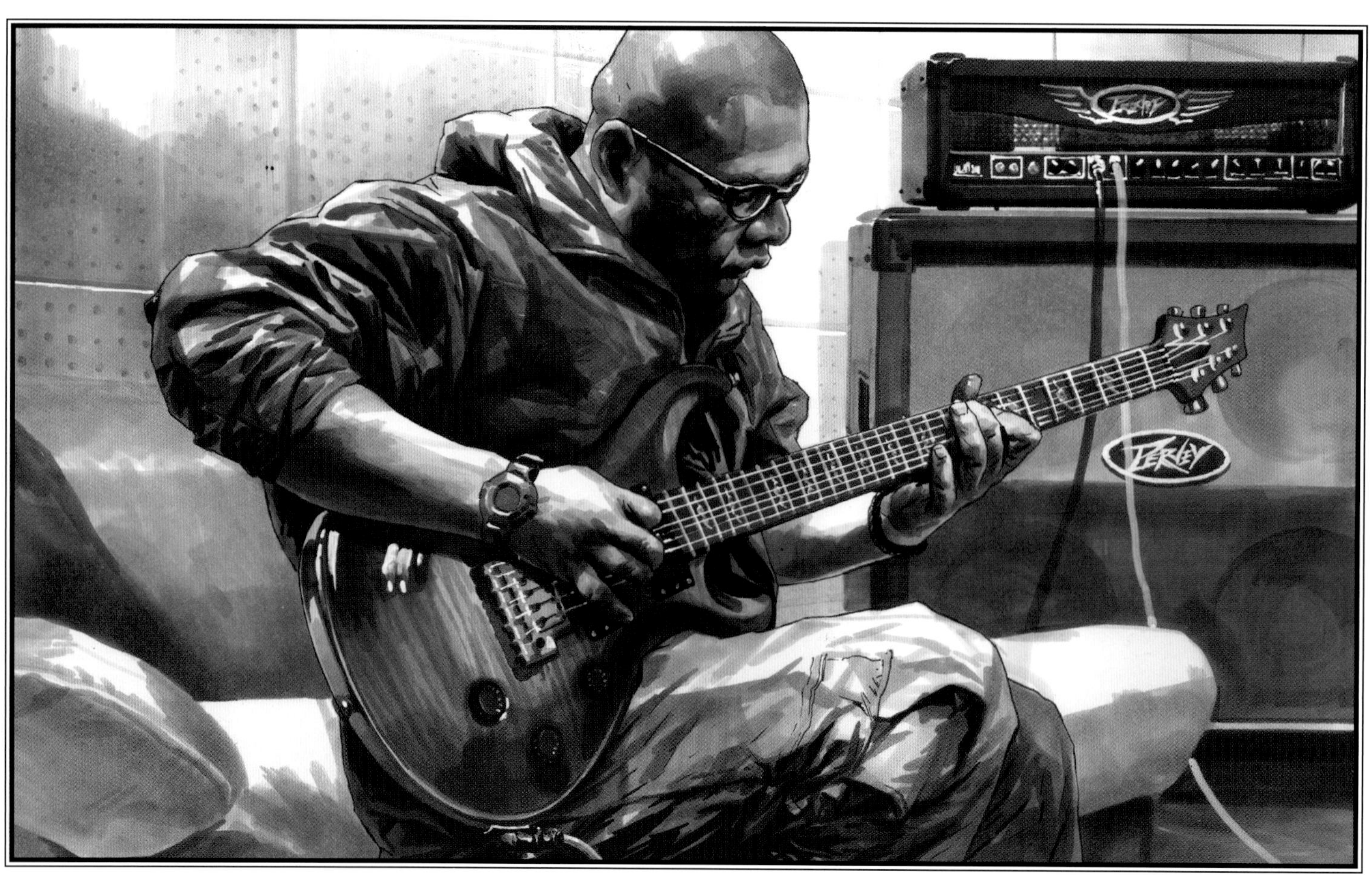

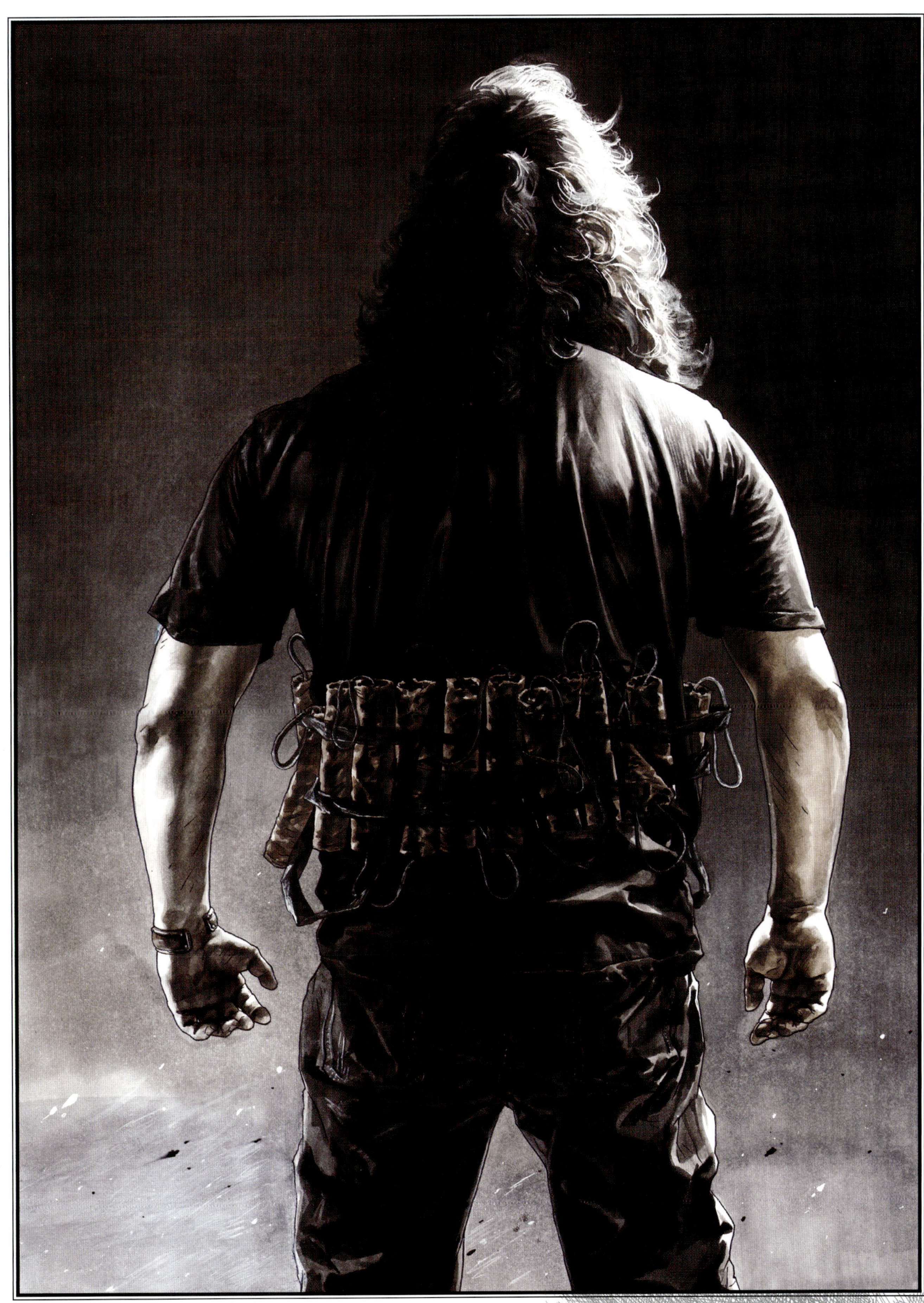

Image from the book *Hard Melody*, colorized, 2014.

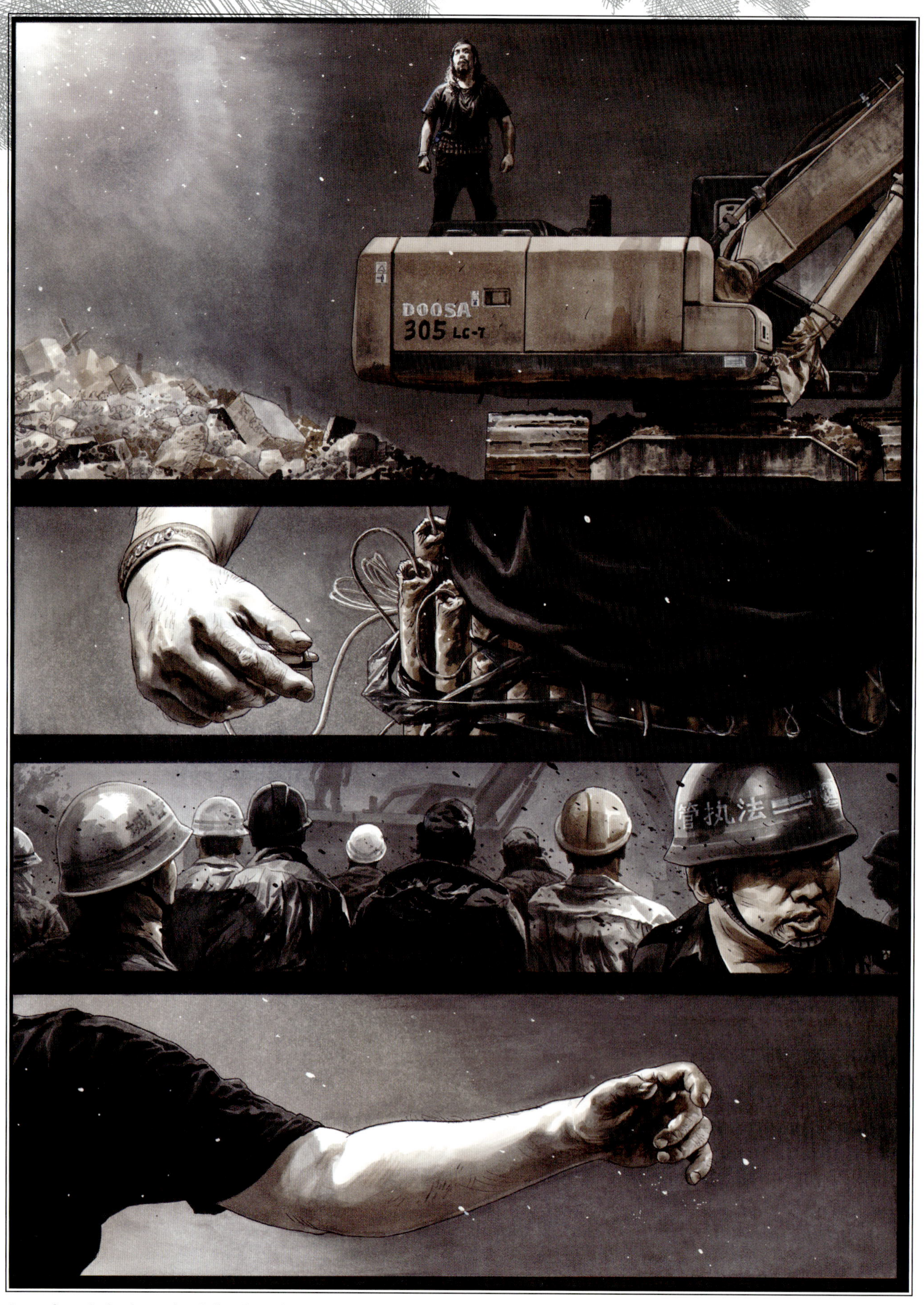

Image from the book *Hard Melody*, colorized, 2014.

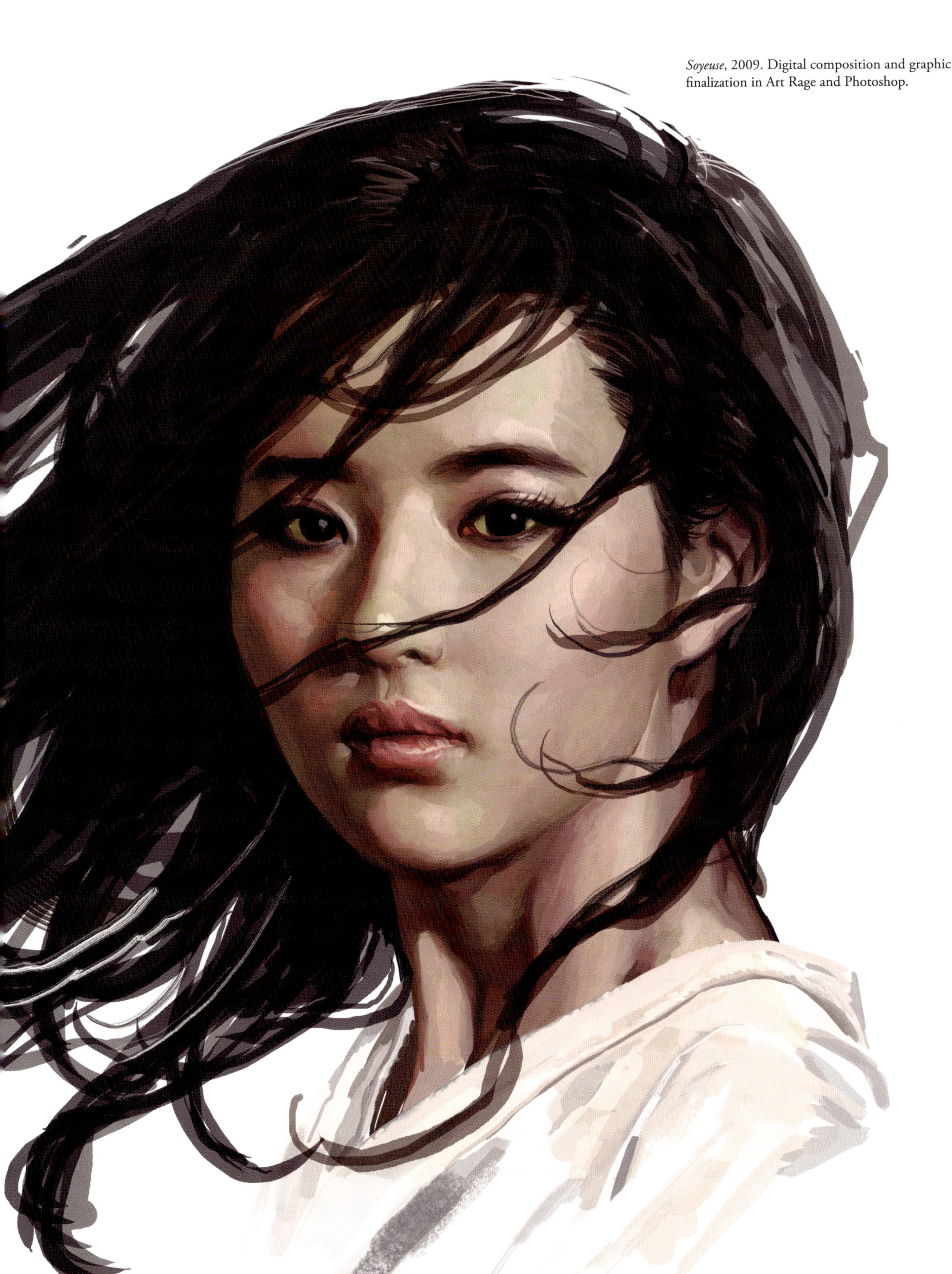

Soyeuse, 2009. Digital composition and graphic finalization in Art Rage and Photoshop.

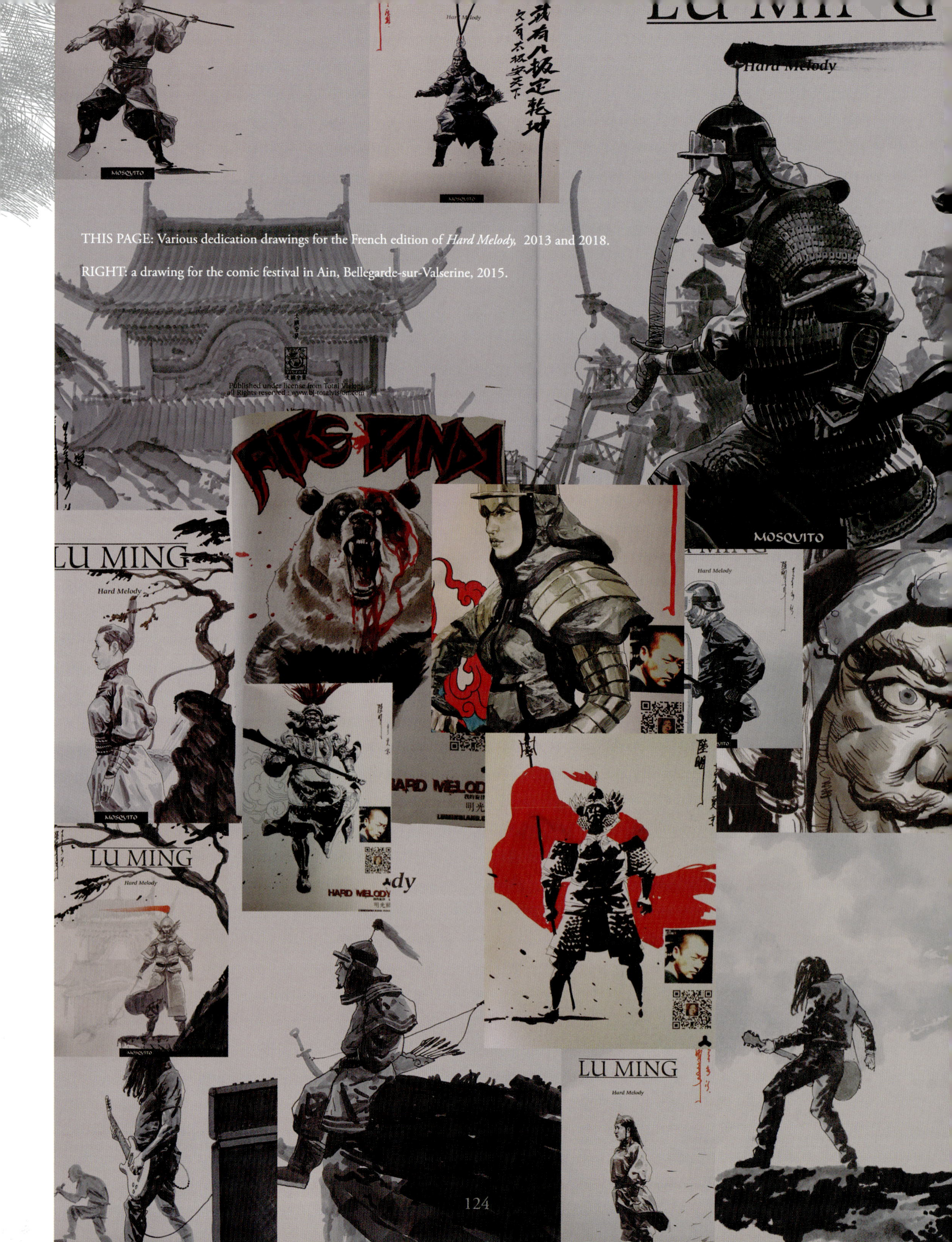

THIS PAGE: Various dedication drawings for the French edition of *Hard Melody,* 2013 and 2018.

RIGHT: a drawing for the comic festival in Ain, Bellegarde-sur-Valserine, 2015.

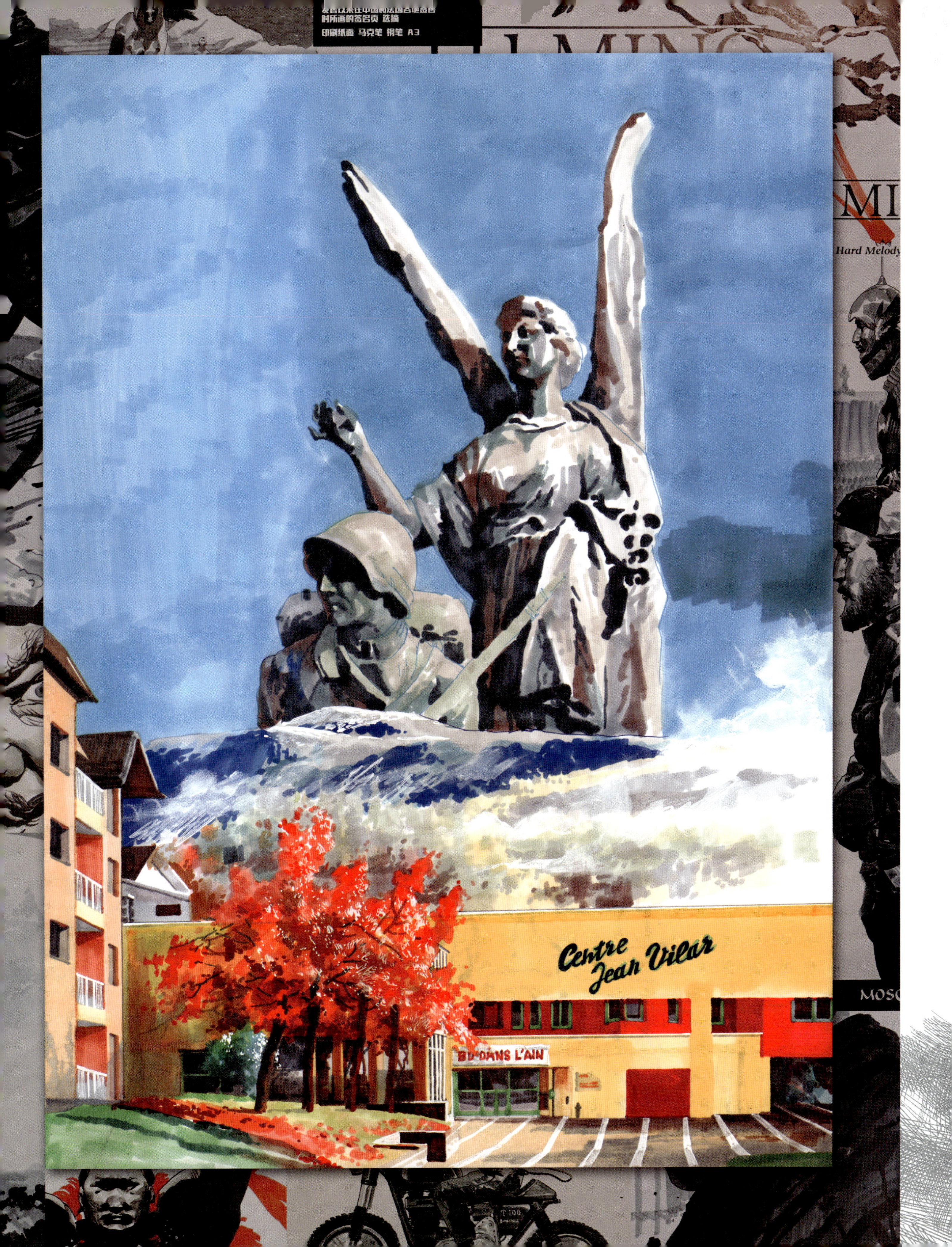
Centre Jean Vilar
BD DANS L'AIN
Hard Melody
MI
MOSC

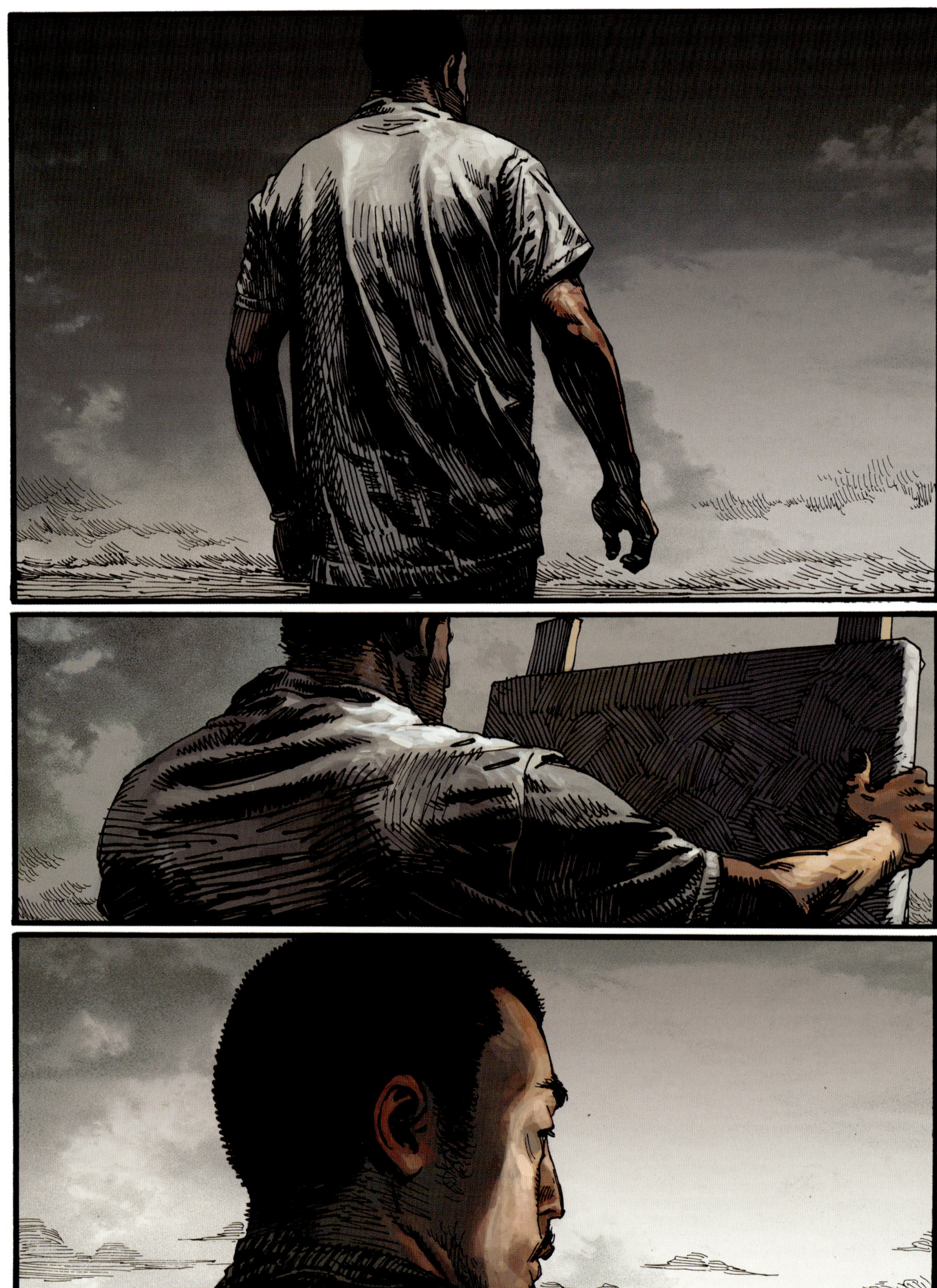

Amour, page 12 and 13, 2004. Pen and ink. Digital composition finalized in Photoshop.

EPILOGUE

I, who was never very good at expressing my feelings in words, ended up saying what was in my heart through drawing. All of those subtle things that language fails to articulate in its triviality are transmitted quite well through Art. It is this mode of expression that I have been pursuing, and I have steered my boat with passion and sincerity. With each of my creations, I have tried to be original and to not be influenced. I have learned a lot from these experiences and from the encounters I have had along the way. I thank the readers who have accompanied me — we have a similar vision of the world. And although I have often gone it alone, stopping to listen to those with kind words, gazing up at the multitude of stars in the sky, it has all contributed to my feeling of absolute happiness.

I am not alone!

Thanks to all of you! Thank you for accompanying me on this journey.

Let's meet in the next book!

Lu Ming
Beijing, Winter 2018.

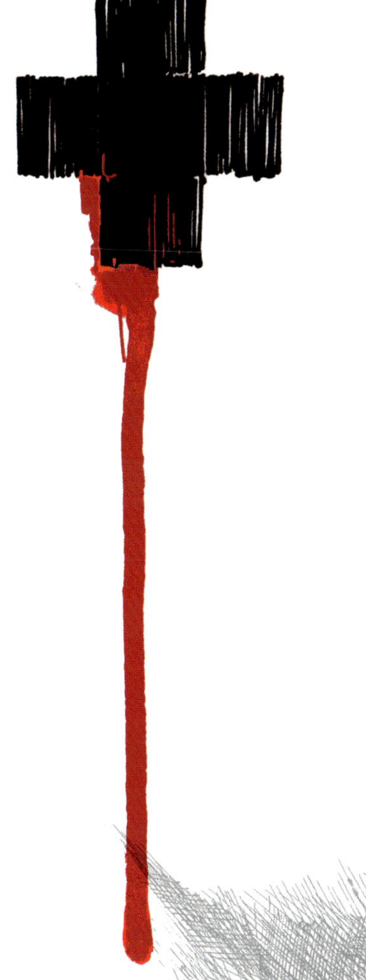

Lu Ming

Painter
Illustrator
Comic book Author
Cinematic Art Director
Animated Film Director
Advertising Graphic Designer
Guitarist & drummer in a heavy-metal band
Practicing Kung-Fu

Lu Ming never forbids himself the pure enjoyment
of a piece of graphic virtuosity.

And he's right.

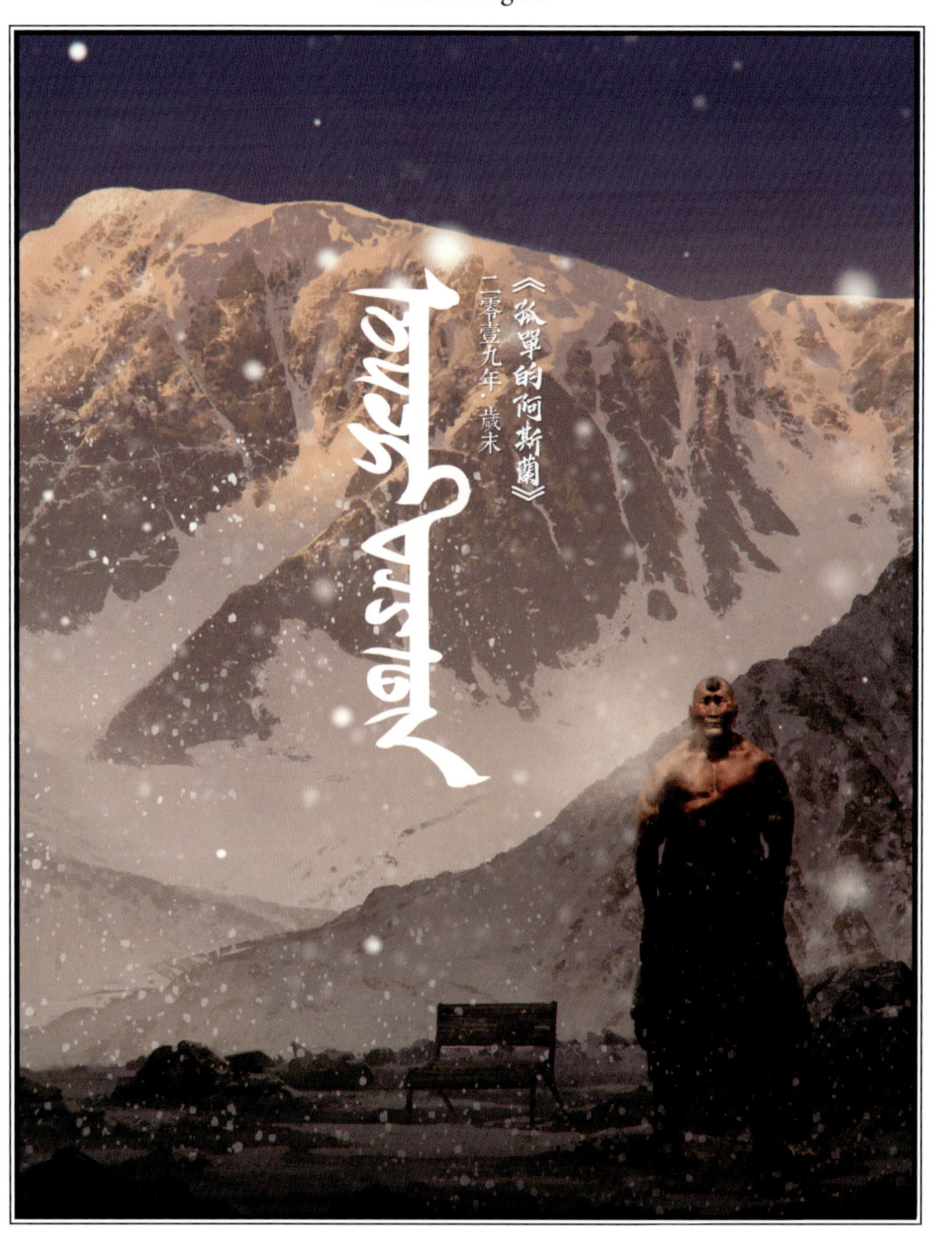

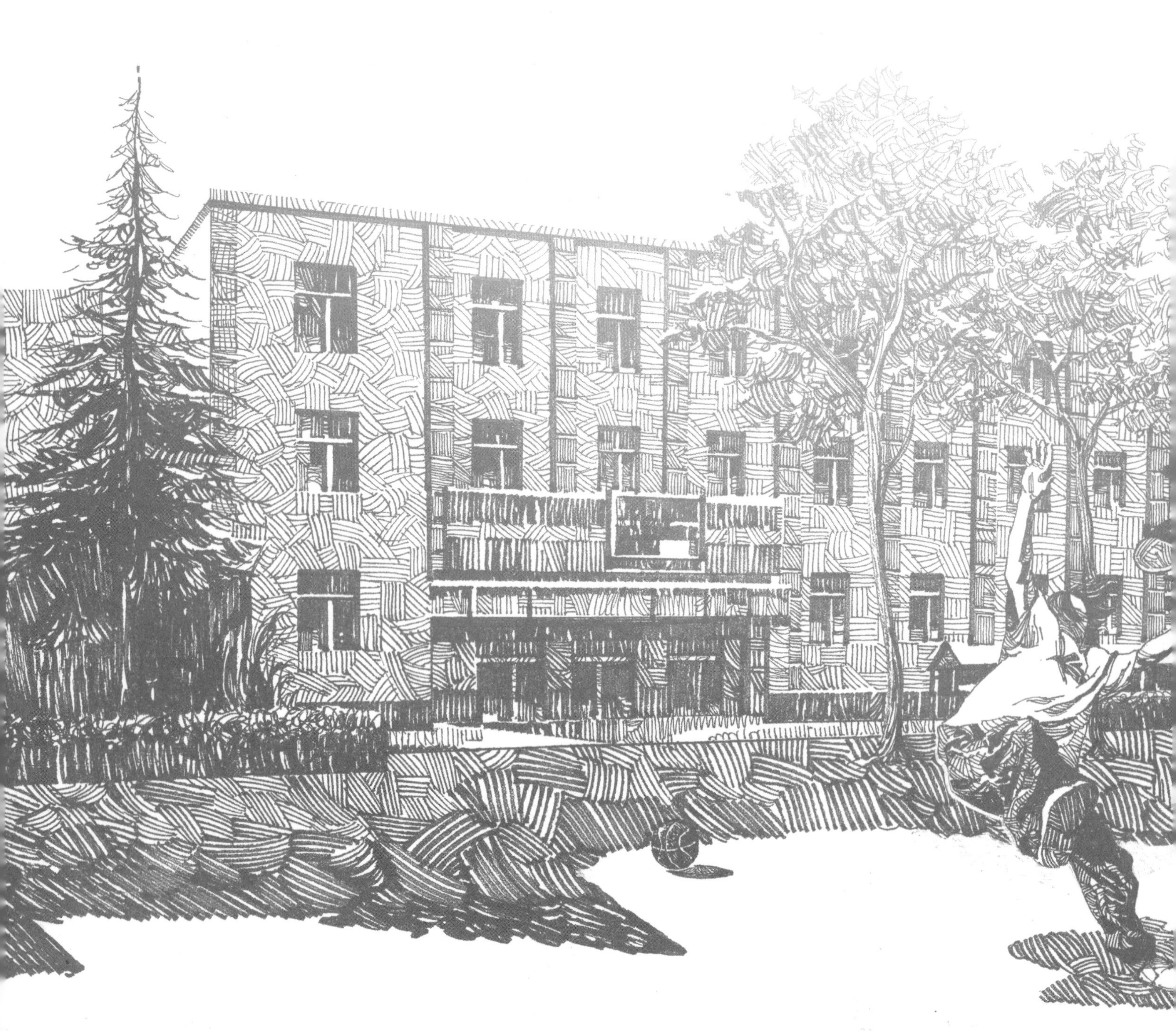